English Dictionaries for
Foreign Learners: A History

To my wife, Cabu

English Dictionaries for Foreign Learners: A History

A. P. COWIE

CLARENDON PRESS · OXFORD
1999

OXFORD
UNIVERSITY PRESS

Great Clarendon Street, Oxford OX2 6DP
Oxford University Press is a department of the University of Oxford.
It furthers the University's objective of excellence in research, scholarship,
and education by publishing worldwide in

Oxford New York

Athens Auckland Bangkok Bogotá Buenos Aires Calcutta
Cape Town Chennai Dar es Salaam Delhi Florence Hong Kong Istanbul
Karachi Kuala Lumpur Madrid Melbourne Mexico City Mumbai
Nairobi Paris São Paulo Singapore Taipei Tokyo Toronto Warsaw

and associated companies in Berlin Ibadan

Oxford is a registered trade mark of Oxford University Press
in the UK and in certain other countries

Published in the United States
by Oxford University Press Inc., New York

© A. P. Cowie 1999

British Library Cataloguing in Publication Data
Data available

Library of Congress Cataloging in Publication Data
Cowie, Anthony Paul.
English dictionaries for foreign learners: a history / A. P. Cowie.
    p.   cm.
Includes bibliographical references and index.
1. English language—Lexicography.   2. English language—Study and
teaching—Foreign speakers—History.   3. English language—Textbooks
for foreign speakers—History.   I. Title.
PE1611.C58   1999
423'.028   dc21   99–21395
ISBN 0–19–823506–2

10 9 8 7 6 5 4 3 2 1

Typeset by Peter Kahrel, Lancaster
Printed in Great Britain
on acid-free paper by
Biddles Ltd., Guildford and King's Lynn

Publisher's Acknowledgement

This book was originally commissioned for publication in the former series *Oxford Studies in Lexicography and Lexicology* under the series editorship of Richard W. Bailey, Noel Osselton, and Gabriele Stein, whose role in the conception and development of this book the publisher most gratefully acknowledges.

Acknowledgements

A large number of friends and colleagues have given me help and encouragement during the preparation of this book. My first debt is to Professor Randolph Quirk (Lord Quirk) and Professor Gabriele Stein, with whom the idea originated of a book on the history of the learner's dictionary. A debt of gratitude is also due to Gabi Stein, and to Professor Noel Osselton, for their detailed and invaluable comments on the entire text at an early stage. I have greatly appreciated, too, the information provided by Mrs Phyllis Willis, the daughter of A. S. Hornby, about her father's life and career. David Neale and Jonathan Crowther helpfully gave information about his career in the 1950s, for which I thank them. Particularly valuable have been gifts of, or information about, material published in Japan. Professor Shimizu generously provided me with copies of Professor Saito's works on grammar and phraseology, and Peter Collier and Simon Nugent, both former OUP editors, with books from A. S. Hornby's original Tokyo library. Richard Smith has been particularly helpful in allowing me to draw on his recent research into the life and career of Harold Palmer. Grateful thanks are due to Peter Howarth, Thierry Fontenelle, Christina Ruse, and Carla Marello for commenting in detail on earlier drafts of various chapters. I would like to thank Sarah Dobson too, for expert guidance, and for seeing the book through to publication. Finally, no acknowledgement would be complete without some mention of my wife Cabu, whose moral and practical support at every stage of the book's progress has been constant and indispensable. The book is dedicated to her in warm gratitude.

A. P. Cowie

Contents

List of Figures

List of Tables

Abbreviations

AILA	Association Internationale de Linguistique Appliquée
ALD	(*Oxford*) *Advanced Learner's Dictionary*
AP	adjective-pattern
BAAL	British Association for Applied Linguistics
BBI	M. Benson, E. Benson, and R. Ilson, *BBI Combinatory Dictionary of English*
BEJD	A. S. Hornby and R. Ishikawa, *A Beginners' English–Japanese Dictionary*
CIDE	*Cambridge International Dictionary of English*
COBUILD	Collins–Birmingham University International Language Database
Cobuild	*Collins COBUILD English Language Dictionary*
COD	*Concise Oxford Dictionary*
CPD	J. Windsor Lewis, *A Concise Pronouncing Dictionary*
CV	controlled vocabulary
ELEC	English Language Exploratory Committee
ELF	English as a foreign language
ELT	English language teaching
ELT	*English Language Teaching*
ELTJ	*English Language Teaching Journal*
EPD	D. Jones, *English Pronouncing Dictionary*
Euralex	European Association for Lexicography
fml	formal
GEW	H. E. Palmer, *A Grammar of English Words*
GSL	M. P. West, *The General Service List of English Words*
infml	informal
IPA	International Phonetic Alphabet
IRET	Institute for Research in English Teaching
ISED	*Idiomatic and Syntactic English Dictionary*
KCEJD	*Kaitakusha's Contemporary English–Japanese Dictionary*
KDEM	Kurzweil Data Entry Machine
KWIC	Key Word in Context
L1	first language
L2	second language
LDB	lexical database

LDEI	T. H. Long and D. Summers, *Longman Dictionary of English Idioms*
LDOCE	*Longman Dictionary of Contemporary English*
LF	lexical function
LOB	Lancaster–Oslo–Bergen (Corpus)
MLD	monolingual learners' dictionary
MRD	machine-readable dictionary
NMED	M. P. West and J. G. Endicott, *The New Method English Dictionary*
NP	noun-pattern
obs	obsolete
OCR	optical character reading machine
ODCIE 1	A. P. Cowie and R. Mackin, *Oxford Dictionary of Current Idiomatic English*, vol. i
ODCIE 2	A. P. Cowie, R. Mackin, and I. R. McCaig, *Oxford Dictionary of Current Idiomatic English*, vol. ii
OED	*Oxford English Dictionary*
OENO	A. S. Hornby and H. Svenkerud, *Oxford Engelsk–Norsk Ordbok*
OSDCE	A. S. Hornby and C. Ruse, *Oxford Student's Dictionary of Current English*
OSDHS	A. S. Hornby and J. Reif, *Oxford Student's Dictionary for Hebrew Speakers*
RP	Received Pronunciation
SEC	C. D. Kozłowska and H. Dzierżanowska, *Selected English Collocations*
TWE	H. E. Palmer and A. S. Hornby, *Thousand-Word English*
VP	verb-pattern

Chronological List of Dictionaries Analysed

West, M. P., and Endicott, J. G., *The New Method English Dictionary*, 1935.

Palmer, H. E., *A Grammar of English Words*, 1938.

Hornby, A. S., and Ishikawa, R., *A Beginners' English–Japanese Dictionary*, 1940.

Hornby, A. S., Gatenby, E. V., and Wakefield, H., *Idiomatic and Syntactic English Dictionary*, 1942.

Hornby, A. S., Gatenby, E. V., and Wakefield, H., *A Learner's Dictionary of Current English* (First edition), 1948.

Hornby, A. S., Gatenby, E. V., and Wakefield, H., *The Advanced Learner's Dictionary of Current English* (Second edition), 1963.

Hornby, A. S., with Cowie, A. P., and Windsor Lewis, J., *Oxford Advanced Learner's Dictionary of Current English* (Third edition), 1974.

Cowie, A. P., and Mackin, R., *Oxford Dictionary of Current Idiomatic English*, Volume 1. *Verbs with Prepositions and Particles* (First edition), 1975.

Procter, P. (ed.), *Longman Dictionary of Contemporary English* (First edition), 1978.

Long, T. H., and Summers, D., *Longman Dictionary of English Idioms*, 1979.

Cowie, A. P., Mackin, R., and McCaig, I. R., *Oxford Dictionary of Current Idiomatic English*, Volume 2. *Sentence, Clause and Phrase Idioms*, 1983.

Benson, M., Benson, E., and Ilson, R., *The BBI Combinatory Dictionary of English: A Guide to Word Combinations* (First edition), 1986.

Sinclair, J. M., Hanks, P., Fox, G., Moon, R., and Stock, P. (eds.), *Collins Cobuild English Language Dictionary* (First edition), 1987.

Summers, D., and Rundell, M. (eds.), *Longman Dictionary of Contemporary English* (Second edition), 1987.

Kozłowska, C., and Dzierżanowska, H., *Selected English Collocations* (Second edition), 1988.

Cowie, A. P. (ed.), *Oxford Advanced Learner's Dictionary of Current English* (Fourth edition), 1989.

Introduction

This book traces the history of monolingual English dictionaries for foreign learners from their origins in the vocabulary-control movement of the 1920s and 1930s to the appearance of the large-scale, computerized compilations of the late 1980s. Monolingual learners' dictionaries (MLDs)—also called English as a Foreign Language (or EFL) dictionaries—are now worldwide in their diffusion, and represent a coming-together of intellectual, technological, and commercial forces scarcely equalled in present-day lexicography. The advanced-level works which we shall chiefly focus on, and which dominate the current market, cater to a constantly rising demand for English, a global appetite which explains the intensity of competition among the major publishers involved, and has helped to promote the development, since the early 1980s, of large-scale text corpora and sophisticated processing tools geared to dictionary production (Sinclair 1987*d*, 1991; Ooi 1998; Rundell 1998).

If demand for learners' dictionaries, and the way in which they have evolved over the past twenty years in particular, have been increasingly *user-driven*—determined, that is, by what users require, or are thought to require—this was not the case at the beginning. In the 1930s and 1940s, potential users of the EFL dictionary could hardly be expected to articulate their needs in the absence of existing models, or of any informed understanding of the role of dictionaries in language learning. By contrast, its potential producers were sure of the need for the 'practical dictionary' and satisfied that it should be monolingual. These certainties were *research-driven*—they sprang from experience of linguistic analysis and from a particular approach to language pedagogy. Learner's dictionaries were needed because linguistic information of a certain specificity and depth—information that was essential to the advanced learner especially—had been brought to light, and only special dictionaries could capture its fullness and complexity. These early works were also, with one curious and interesting exception, monolingual. This preference reflected the close links which existed at the times between dictionary design and language teaching methodology, with stress being laid—certainly by some experts—on the avoidance of the mother tongue in the teaching of new meanings.[1] Such notions had an important bearing on the

---

[1] Even when introducing a new bilingual dictionary to a group of teachers, as we shall see, A. S. Hornby did not recommend the use of the mother tongue (i.e. Japanese) for the presentation of new meanings (Hornby 1938).

early development of the learner's dictionary and it will be part of the aim of this book to examine them closely.

The book has both a chronological and a thematic structure. Three of its six chapters (1, 3, and 5) deal in historical sequence with all of the major—and some of the minor—monolingual EFL dictionaries published over a period of 60 years, beginning with the pioneering works of Michael West, Harold E. Palmer, and A. S. Hornby and concluding with the 'third generation' general-purpose dictionaries of the late 1980s. Those largely analytical chapters alternate with three thematic chapters dealing with phraseology, computers and corpus linguistics, and research into dictionary users and uses. Phraseology (treated in Chapter 2) first began to interest applied linguists before learners' dictionaries were first thought of, and has come into prominence again since the early 1980s, as a result of the development of large-scale text corpora. In our treatment, we shall deal with issues of theory and description but describe a number of phraseological dictionaries as well. The involvement of computers in a wider sense (treated in Chapter 4) has affected the course of learner lexicography in recent years more than any other single influence. A further development of crucial importance, again in the period since 1980, has been the growth of research into the users and uses of dictionaries (described in Chapter 6). User-centred investigations have deepened our understanding of the purposes for which language learners, at various levels of proficiency, refer to their dictionaries—for example, whether they use them predominantly for reading or writing—and of the poor standards of reference skill which they often display.

I have deliberately stopped short of discussing the four most recently published dictionaries, one of which—the *Cambridge International Dictionary of English* (*CIDE*) (1995)—is entirely new and marks the entry into the field of a fourth major publisher. I have sought to be as detached in this volume as it is possible to be when much of one's professional life has been taken up by dictionary-making, and I have found detachment easier to achieve by confining myself to works published at least a decade ago. This is not to say—and this is a central theme of the book—that research conducted and dictionaries compiled sixty years ago do not continue to be of profound relevance to EFL lexicography in the 1990s.

The earliest monolingual learners' dictionaries were largely the achievement of three expatriate Englishmen—Harold Palmer, Michael West, and A. S. Hornby —who were the founding fathers of applied linguistics in this century and whose research experience was, in great measure, gained in Japan or (in the case of West) India. It was as part of a global intellectual movement, but within particular cultural and educational settings, that their dictionaries were produced. I have provided biographical sketches of Palmer, West, and Hornby here, not only because their personalities and professional careers are interesting in themselves, but because these brief personal histories throw much light on the intellectual climate in which their dictionaries were conceived and brought to fruition.

Harold E. Palmer (1877–1949)

Harold Edward Palmer was without doubt the leader of the wider movement to which I have referred. Mercurial, extrovert, and innovative, it was his extraordinary energy which drove forward the projects he set up in Tokyo, just as it was his acknowledged expertise across a range of disciplines which helped to establish his Institute as a research centre of international standing.[2]

There was little in the circumstances of his early life, except perhaps the energy and enterprise of his father Edward, to suggest that Harold would eventually achieve such eminence both as a linguist and as an authority on language teaching. Born into a lower-middle-class family in London on 6 March 1877, his secondary schooling was incomplete and he never went to university. He attended primary schools in London and at Hythe, in Kent, where the family moved in 1883, while his elementary education beyond the age of 10 was extended at home, perhaps mainly or solely by his parents. However, from 1890 to 1892, Edward's success as a shopkeeper, and as a newspaper editor and proprietor, enabled him to send Harold to a small private school (Prospect House), where the principal and other teachers were Oxford graduates (Smith 1998*b*: 16). A school report dated Easter 1892, when Harold was 15, shows that he was first in several subjects, including French, English Language, and History (Anderson 1969: 135), though it is unlikely that, at that stage, he showed much interest in language studies (Bongers 1947). In that same year, Palmer's formal education ceased. His later expertise in such fields as phonetics—an expertise which would enable him to teach at university level— would be achieved not through tuition but through private study.[3]

After helping his father for some years with printing work and, later, acting as a reporter, columnist, and editor for his newspaper, Palmer 'felt that he must break away from work that was leading nowhere' and 'had the urge to go abroad' (Anderson 1969: 136). He moved, in February 1902, to Verviers in Belgium, where it is likely that he found work at the École Internationale de Langues Vivantes, a small school claiming to employ the Berlitz method (Smith 1998*b*: 30; cf. Bongers 1947, Anderson 1969). It was in Verviers that Palmer first began to develop a strong interest in languages, and, specifically, to admire the Berlitz method. The Berlitz experience also awoke in him an awareness of the notion of a 'minimal vocabulary', one whose value depended essentially upon the 'structural' words it contained (Bongers 1947). The choice of 'content' words,

---

[2] According to his daughter Dorothée, Palmer's outstanding characteristic was 'creative versatility' (Anderson 1969: 143). According to his friend and colleague H. Vere Redman, Palmer 'was possessed of a dynamic personality devoured by enthusiasm and entirely bereft of cynicism' (Redman 1966).

[3] In September 1892, Harold was sent to Boulogne on a six-month exchange visit. Here, his knowledge of French was probably improved, though by informal means rather than formal tuition (Smith 1998*b*: 18).

provided they served the learners' needs and interests, was less important. Though many years were to pass before this distinction was embodied in any principles of vocabulary selection—or any work of reference—Palmer was already becoming aware that while most structural words presented learning difficulties, content words, because linked to communicative needs, were relatively easy to acquire.

In 1903, Palmer opened his own school of languages, after which followed twelve years of experimentation. Already noticeable was his essentially pragmatic approach to teaching methodology: Palmer adopted, adapted, and rejected according to the findings of research and experience (Anderson 1969: 136). In 1911–12, he compiled a list—consisting chiefly of structural words—which experience had shown gave the most trouble to learners.

In 1915, Palmer was invited by Professor Daniel Jones, with whom he had been corresponding since 1907, to give a course of lectures on methods of language teaching at University College London (Redman 1967). A year later he was appointed to the regular staff of the Phonetics Department. His experience of lecturing on methodology formed the basis of his first major publication, *The Scientific Study and Teaching of Languages* (1917). It was at this stage also that his serious interest in lexicology began. According to his daughter, he appears to have 'exhibited some well-thought-out word-lists prepared independently of, and probably without knowledge of, any work that was being done by others in this field' (Anderson 1969: 140). It was then also that he first addressed the problems of category definition that, in the late 1920s, were to become his chief concern as he confronted the problems of vocabulary control.

Also produced during the London period was *A Grammar of Spoken English* (1924). This was a scholarly work but was seen by Palmer essentially as a practical guide to the learning of English. Its treatment of sentence patterns in a series of tables anticipated by over a decade the presentation of 'verb-patterns' in the earliest learners' dictionaries. As Hornby later wrote, Palmer's 'work on English grammar was marked by a fresh approach. He believed that grammar should be a catalogue of existent phenomena . . . rather than a collection of problems explainable by logic' (Hornby 1950).

In 1921, Harold E. Palmer was invited to visit Japan to examine and report on the teaching of English in secondary schools (Hornby 1950). On his arrival the following year, he was appointed Linguistic Adviser to the Japanese Ministry of Education. The person chiefly responsible for bringing Palmer to Japan was Dr Masataro Sawayanagi, a former university vice-chancellor and, by the early 1920s, the leading figure in education in Japan (Imura 1997: 29–30; Smith 1998a). Alarmed at the poor standards of English in Japanese schools, Sawayanagi visited London in 1921, and discussed his concerns with a Japanese academic, Masao Kinoshita, with whom Palmer had worked on a Japanese beginners' vocabulary in 1916 (Palmer 1936a). Kinoshita felt that Palmer was the person to breathe fresh life into English teaching in Japan (Sawayanagi 1924: 4). It was thanks to another visitor to London, the Japanese businessman and philanthropist Kojiro Matsukata, who offered to pay Palmer's salary, that he was actually brought to Japan, though not before Sawayanagi had satisfied himself that Palmer was 'fair-minded', i.e. that he would carefully examine prevailing teaching methods and their effects before devising and applying new procedures of his own (Sawayanagi 1924: 5).

When Palmer was first appointed as Linguistic Adviser, it was widely felt by teachers committed to the reform of language teaching methods in Japan that Palmer should be invited to head this movement, and that an association should be formed which would meet the immediate need to compile, print, and distribute various types of English language course, and in so doing encourage existing reform efforts and provide an impetus to 'research and experimental work' (Palmer *et al.* 1923: 2). With those aims in mind it was decided to make a direct approach to Palmer. Emphasis was diplomatically laid on the need to bring together those 'with knowledge of Japan and the Japanese' and 'the expert and scholarly experience of Mr Palmer' (ibid.). The result was the setting up, in May 1923, of the Institute for Research in English Teaching (IRET), with the approval of the Department of Education, and financial support from Matsukata and Sawayanagi (who was Palmer's chief intermediary and advocate with ministry officials). Palmer himself was appointed director.

The aims of IRET were nothing less than the encouragement of 'reform' methods of English teaching, research and experiment in linguistics, and the training of teachers. Palmer was also appointed editor of the Institute's *Bulletin*, which was issued at low cost and with articles designed to appeal to teachers everywhere (Hornby 1966). The Institute's ideas and research findings were also disseminated through an annual convention, which brought together teachers from all over Japan, and by Kaitakusha, a publishing house set up by Naoe Naganuma with the express purpose of publishing research reports and teaching materials (Kunio Naganuma 1978).

Palmer and the Institute exerted a considerable influence on English teaching in Japan, an influence which has survived to this day, despite competition, in the immediate post-war years, from linguistically trained American experts (Hornby 1966). However, since the Japanese government was never fully involved in its activities, the reforms envisaged by Palmer and IRET were not implemented on a national scale (Redman 1967). On the other hand, the Institute fulfilled another role which none of its associates, with the possible exception of Palmer himself, had foreseen. Largely as a result of Palmer's own standing, it became a centre for research into the problems of teaching English which was of significance worldwide. This was demonstrated and reinforced by Palmer's world tour of 1931–2, his leading role in the Carnegie Conference of 1934 and 1935, and his authoritative published work on grammar and lexicology.

By the mid-1930s, Palmer was beginning to feel that there was much to be said for 'getting out in order to pursue his task in a more congenial atmosphere' (Anderson 1969: 157). In 1936, he returned to the UK, where he became English Language Teaching adviser to Longman and published *A Grammar of English Words* (1938*a*), which, despite its title, was a highly innovative foreign learners' dictionary, and—as part of a collaboration with Michael West—the *New Method Grammar*. Unlike Hornby, whose involvement in overseas lecturing after the Tokyo years was to continue in parallel with work on dictionaries and teaching materials, Palmer appears to have done little subsequent teaching and academic research, though this may be because the British Council's ELT programmes were not as firmly established (the Council was founded in 1934) as when Hornby left Japan in 1942. In any event, Palmer devoted his years in retirement to writing further books, mostly for foreign learners of English.[4]

During 1944, Harold Palmer was invited by the British Council to give a series of lectures in South America. Though he was in poor health, his doctors and family felt that a tour of this kind would do him good. Ronald Mackin, then Director of Studies at the Instituto Cultural, in Montevideo, later told Palmer's daughter that her father had lectured brilliantly even though he had been prevented by illness from completing the tour. Five years later, on 16 November 1949, Harold Palmer collapsed and died in his study.

Michael Philip West (1888–1973)

The educational background and early career of Michael Philip West were in marked contrast to those of Harold Palmer. Educated at a public school and at Christ Church, Oxford, West went straight from graduation, in 1912, to a career post in the Indian Education Service.[5] His most fruitful and influential years were spent in Bengal, where he eventually became Principal Inspector of Schools in Chittagong and Calcutta, Principal of the Teacher's Training College in Dacca and Honorary Reader in Education at Dacca University (Howatt 1984).

The most important succession of events in West's career, however, unfolded ten years after his first appointment. In 1923, the Imperial Education Conference had called for 'scientific investigation of the facts of bilingualism with reference to the intellectual, emotional, and moral development of the child, and the importance of the questions of practical educational method arising out of the investigation of such facts'. West's response to this appeal was an experimental project, written up in the report *Bilingualism* (*with special reference to Bengal*)

---

[4] I am grateful to Richard Smith for helpful discussion of this point.

[5] According to Tickoo (1988: 294), West studied psychology at Oxford, a training which inclined him towards experimentation and, incidentally, seems to have made him suspicious of phonetics.

(1926). Here, West challenged the educational policy, known as 'filtering', by which a small number of very able students were fed through the system to end up with degrees and civil service jobs, but by which the great majority dropped out, at successive stages, with no useful benefit derived from their incomplete course of instruction (Tickoo 1988: 295). The wastage was made worse by the time devoted to developing spoken skills, which took too long to provide any measurable benefit for those leaving the system. Reading skills, on the other hand, could be acquired more rapidly and more pleasurably, and did not depend on the constant presence of a teacher. Viewed within a wider developmental context, West's approach held out the prospect of opening up to all Bengalis, and not just a privileged few, reading materials on practical subjects that were simply not available in the mother tongue. This meant the development of improved materials based on principles of strict vocabulary control. There were two ways, West recognized, in which the existing reading texts could be improved. The first was to *simplify* the vocabulary by removing rare or dated words and substituting more common modern equivalents. The second principle which he applied entailed *distributing* the new words in such a way that they were not presented too closely together for the reader to be able to absorb and practise them thoroughly. In the new readers that West adapted or wrote (they were published in Bengal from 1927 onwards) the overall number of new words dropped, while the total number of words of running text rose steeply. In consequence, the average rate at which new words were introduced went, in the case of his *New Method Primers*, from a mean of 1 in 7.4 to no less than 1 in 44.7 (Howatt 1984: 248–9).

Though much had been achieved by the late 1920s in vocabulary limitation (by Palmer and the American Thorndike, as well as by West), by the mid-1930s it was time to encourage collaboration, and to attempt to resolve procedural issues. It was on the initiative of West, provoked by the challenge of Ogden's 'Basic English', that the Carnegie Corporation organized in New York, in 1934, the first conference to be devoted to vocabulary limitation. The conference resulted in a close collaboration between him, Palmer, and Lawrence Faucett. The 'General Service List' that formed part of the *Interim Report on Vocabulary Selection*—which emerged from the reconvened conference in London, in 1935—eventually became West's project and, after frequency statistics had been added by Irving Lorge for the forms and meanings recorded, this was published separately as *The General Service List of English Words* (*GSL*) (1953). For many years after its publication, *GSL* continued to serve EFL teachers and textbook writers in their search for the commonest uses of common words (Tickoo 1988).

During the 1930s, West became one of the best known and most prolific authors in the field of English as a Foreign Language. There were various multipart courses, whose titles (e.g. *New Method Conversation Course*), reflected West's continuing commitment to the principles developed earlier. The close understanding already reached with Harold Palmer led to a working collaboration in the course of which Palmer wrote a *New Method Grammar* (1938*b*) and a number of *New Method Readers*.

West's career was marked by controversy. Enlightened though his proposals for a reader-centred approach undoubtedly were, they did not find much favour in official circles in India. Indeed, in his later writings he found fault with aspects of his own earlier work (Tickoo 1988: 299). In the 1950s and 1960s, he remained active, contributing regularly to *English Language Teaching* and other journals. He also wrote a short manual, *Teaching English in Difficult Circumstances* (1960), which included as an appendix his minimum adequate vocabulary. He retired to Painswick in the Cotswolds, where he died in March 1973.

A. S. Hornby (1898–1978)

Albert Sydney Hornby (in later years always known to his friends and colleagues as 'Ash') was born in August 1898 in Chester. After war service in the Royal Navy, he entered University College London, where in 1922 he took a degree in English Language and Literature (Howatt 1984). The following year, Hornby was invited by the Appointments Board at UCL to meet a young Japanese visiting London at the time and was recruited by him to teach English at the Oita Higher Commercial School on the island of Kyushu (Hornby and Ruse 1974). With a fondness for long-distance travel which he seems to have acquired in the Navy, Hornby and his wife journeyed to the Far East via the Trans-Siberian Railway. They arrived in Japan in 1924 and in the same year Hornby's name appeared for the first time in the *IRET Bulletin* as a newly registered member.[6] Though he had been recruited to teach English Literature, Hornby was quickly attracted to the teaching of language—a recognition, like his early membership of IRET, that the pressing need in Japanese schools was language teaching, not literature teaching. It was the same sense of priorities that led him to support Palmer's movement for the reform of English language teaching in Japan (Imura 1997: 209). As Hornby himself put it, 'I found myself facing classes . . . and I found that they were reading English literature. . . . I decided that I must give much more attention to language teaching and leave the teaching of literature to their Japanese professors' (Hornby and Ruse 1974).

Hornby quickly became fascinated by questions of language and began to de/velop an understanding of linguistics, initially through reading. But he also started a correspondence with Harold Palmer, and 'through my correspondence with him I became more and more interested in linguistics, especially linguistic

---

[6] The entry, under the heading 'New members registered (up to Nov. 6, 1924)', reads 'Hornby, Mr. A. S., Oita Higher Commercial School, Oita' (*IRET Bulletin*, new series, no. 8, Oct.–Nov. 1924, p. 13).

methodology' (Hornby and Ruse 1974). Palmer was sufficiently impressed by his young colleague to invite him, in the Spring of 1931, to assist in the compilation of a list of collocations (a project which had been initiated in 1927 and which will be described in greater detail in Chapter 2).[7] In December of the same year, Hornby published in the *IRET Bulletin* his first article on a grammatical theme: 'Some grammatical implications of doubt and negation' and, a year later, a second on the determiners 'some' and 'any'. After a period of home leave, and at Palmer's instigation, he was brought to Tokyo in 1934 (Kunio Naganuma 1978). A notice in the *Bulletin* announcing the 11th Annual Conference refers to a lecture by 'Prof. Hornby of the Tokyo University of Literature and Science'. Later on, Hornby was to hold two posts simultaneously, one at the Tokyo School of Foreign Languages (now Tokyo University of Foreign Studies), the other at the Tokyo Higher Normal School, a leading teacher-training institution (Hornby and Ruse 1974; Ogawa 1978).

In 1936, Palmer handed over to Hornby the editorship of the *IRET Bulletin* before leaving Japan permanently. At the Annual Convention later that year, Professor Rinchirou Ishikawa, of the Tokyo University of Literature and Science, was appointed Director of IRET, with Hornby as 'technical adviser'. However, as is clear from a later interview with his OUP publisher, Christina Ruse, Hornby was de facto director of the research team (Hornby and Ruse 1974).

Besides Palmer, Hornby had close personal and professional ties with Vere Redman, a lecturer in English at Tokyo University of Commerce with whom Palmer had collaborated and for whom Hornby's daughter Phyllis was to work in later years, and, in the late 1930s, his fellow dictionary compilers, Edward Gatenby and Harold Wakefield.[8] A popular annual meeting-point for teachers and missionaries at the time was the summer colony (or 'hill station') at Karuizawa, some 90 miles north-west of Tokyo. The colony provided Palmer and Hornby with an ideal setting for informal discussion of professional matters (Anderson 1969).

In later years, Hornby, who was exceptionally modest about his achievements, as well as personally shy, but who had a gift for friendship, formed close ties with his OUP editors, Eric Parnwell, David Neale, and Peter Collier. Later still there was Christina Ruse, who collaborated with him on the *Oxford Student's Dictionary of Current English* (1978). Hornby had had a love of classical music from his student days in London, and would entertain his colleagues at Glyndebourne, where he was a member (Brown 1978).

Unlike Palmer and Gatenby—Hornby's collaborator on *ISED*—both of whom

---

[7] The first reference to Hornby as 'our research colleague' appeared in the issue of the *Bulletin* for Apr. 1931, p. 1, where he is referred to as still living in Oita.

[8] Gatenby taught at Sandai, in the north. Wakefield was recruited by Hornby, during his 1933 furlough, as his successor at Oita (Phyllis Willis, personal communication).

spoke Japanese to a high standard and showed a deep and informed interest in the local culture, Hornby made no serious attempt to learn the language.[9] Though he inspired great respect, and indeed affection, in his Japanese pupils and colleagues, Gatenby was described as having the greater interest in things Japanese and a better command of the language.

Hornby always portrayed himself as 'a simple teacher'. It is a description, however, which is belied by the academic professionalism which pervaded Hornby's activities throughout the previous two decades, and subsequently: his linguistic scholarship; his firm and enthusiastic commitment to applied research; and his pioneering editorship of *English Language Teaching*, one result of which was to bring to a readership of practising teachers the developing alliance between ELT professionals and Firthian linguists.

Shortly after Pearl Harbor, in December 1941, foreign nationals were repatriated by the Japanese, in the first instance to the United States. As their mother had died in 1940, Phyllis Hornby and her sister were part of this early exodus, being taken care of by an American missionary family. In the meantime, Hornby himself had been interned—being confined in a Catholic monastery run by Germans (Imura 1997: 236). He was well treated, and his publisher and friend Naoe Naganuma did what he could to make conditions tolerable. Eventually Hornby was repatriated aboard the same ship as the diplomatic staff. It seems that much of his library remained in Tokyo, and was destroyed when his house was hit in an American bombing raid. However, Harold Palmer was later able to replace many of the books and papers which Hornby had lost (Hornby and Ruse 1974). It is thanks to the OUP editors and managers to whom these were eventually given that I have been able to trace the sources of several of the words and phrases included in the *Idiomatic and Syntactic English Dictionary* of 1942.

On his return to England in 1941, Hornby was recruited by the British Council and spent the rest of the war in Persia (as it then was), teaching at the University of Teheran and at the Anglo-Persian Institute (Hornby 1966). It was in Persia that he met his second wife, Marian de la Motte. In 1945, he returned to England and was appointed to the headquarters of the British Council in London as Linguistic Adviser. For the most part this meant administrative work and, sensing that 'whatever knowledge I might possess was not being used in the right way', Hornby sought permission from the British Council to start up a periodical which, like the *IRET Bulletin*, would be devoted to problems of English language teaching (Hornby 1966). *English Language Teaching*, issued at a low cost to make it accessible to the teachers of the Third World with whom Hornby's sympathies chiefly lay, and with articles designed to appeal to teachers everywhere, was duly

[9] I am grateful for this information to Mrs Willis, who was herself encouraged to learn Japanese by a German Jesuit, Father Roggendorf.

launched under Hornby's editorship in October 1946.[10] *English Language Teaching* (or *English Language Teaching Journal*, as it later became) eventually acquired a reputation for combining expert practical advice with contributions from linguists written in a style accessible to non-experts. According to his daughter Phyllis, who returned home from work in Japan in 1948, Hornby was also at this time making a major contribution to the BBC series 'English by Radio', though in her view he never received due credit for his leading role.[11]

In 1950, Hornby resigned the editorship of *English Language Teaching* to devote himself full-time to writing. His publisher, Eric Parnwell, had suggested that he might like to work in the country, producing smaller, lower-level dictionaries based on *ALD* but also preparing a number of language courses, including *Oxford Progressive English for Adult Learners*, a three-volume course published from 1954 onwards. For variety, Hornby would occasionally undertake a long lecture tour overseas for the British Council (Hornby and Ruse 1974). During the earlier part of this period Hornby and his wife were living at Shermanbury, in Surrey, but by early 1961 they had moved to Appledore, in Kent.

In 1954, Hornby published *A Guide to Patterns and Usage in English*, a practical grammar whose approach to analysis and tabular style of presentation reflected the methods employed in *ALD*. The patterns were also a central feature of his *Oxford Progressive English* (1954–6) and of his practical course-book for teachers, *The Teaching of Structural Words and Sentence Patterns* (1959–62).

An episode which reflected the continuing influence in Japan of Hornby and Palmer during the immediately post-war period—one in which American political influence in the region was dominant—was the conference which Hornby was invited to attend, as the representative of the British Council, in September 1956. This so-called 'specialists' conference' of the English Language Exploratory Committee (ELEC) was originally intended to elicit the views of American and British experts on how to improve English Teaching in Japan, even though the American experts Fries and Twaddell would arrive in the country for the first time only a few days before the conference opened. Wisely, the Americans spoke on topics with which they were more familiar, namely ways in which advances in structural linguistics and the Oral Approach would benefit the teaching of English in Japan (Henrichsen 1989).[12] According to Donald H. McLean, the on-site representative of Rockefeller at the conference, Fries and Twaddell were much more impressive than Hornby, who was 'overshadowed completely. In the process the British and Palmer have, I feel, been reasonably well eliminated as ghosts, which greatly simplifies matters and clears the road for progress'

[10] Initially, Hornby made use of some articles from the *IRET Bulletin*. The *Bulletin* was not widely known outside Japan and Hornby felt it a pity that so much useful material should not be made available to a wider readership.

[11] According to Mrs Willis, the programme was often referred to at the time as 'Hornby by Radio'.

[12] I am grateful to Richard Smith for bringing this study to my attention.

(McLean to Rockefeller, cited in Henrichsen 1989: 143). McLean's joy was premature, however, as later events were to prove. There was, for instance, a strong tendency among more conservative teachers either 'to stick to the old grammar-translation method or to be loyal to and defend Palmer's oral method against the oral approach' (Yambe, cited in Henrichsen 1989: 143). Nor was Hornby's performance unimpressive to all of those who witnessed it. His emphasis, characteristically, was on the importance of *experience* in language teaching: 'he pointed out that any teacher of English with a number of years of experience was aware of the special difficulties of Japanese learners' (Ogawa 1978: 9). As for the influence of structural linguistics, it is true that 'pattern practice' became the focus of attention of English teachers in Japan, but in the view of Ogawa, 'this is merely a different version of the exercise known as "substitution drill", advocated by Palmer and Hornby thirty years earlier' (ibid.).

Hornby's influence on English language teaching has been enduring and profound, not simply because of his contributions to language teaching methodology and his work on learners' dictionaries but also through the A. S. Hornby Educational Trust, which he set up in 1961 (Brown 1978). This was a far-sighted and generous initiative whereby a substantial part of Hornby's income from royalties was set aside to improve the teaching and learning of English as a Foreign Language, chiefly by providing grants to enable teachers of English from overseas to come to Britain for advanced professional training. Hornby's aim was that the Trust's money should be used for education and 'go back to the countries from which it comes' (Collier, Neale, and Quirk 1978: 3). The generosity was part of a wider humanity. Hornby was never a remote, dry-as-dust academic, but a man of broad sympathies and practical instincts who believed that the knowledge of the expert should be put to the service of the ordinary learner and teacher.

Hornby's pre-eminence in the field of learner lexicography and language teaching methodology was recognized, towards the end of his life, by the award of several honours. He was appointed OBE and made a Fellow of University College London and a Master of Arts of the University of Oxford. Shortly before his death in 1978, the volume *In Honour of A. S. Hornby*, edited by Peter Strevens and with contributions by many of his friends and former colleagues, was presented to him to mark his eightieth birthday.

Conclusion

As we turn, in Chapter 1, to consider in much greater detail the lexical research of the 1920s and 1930s and the dictionaries which eventually grew from it, we shall see that in both fields Palmer, West, and Hornby played a dominant role, and that, though in dictionary-making their achievements were distinctive and original, their work touched and overlapped at several points.

Harold Palmer produced a pioneering encoding dictionary—*A Grammar of English Words*—to which his own structured word-lists had paved the way but which drew on a word-list originally prepared by Hornby. Michael West, as we have seen, took from his research into vocabulary limitation the simplified defining vocabulary of the very first EFL dictionary—the *New Method English Dictionary* —but enjoyed a fruitful collaboration with Palmer. A. S. Hornby, who played a leading part in a scheme of phraseological research which ran parallel to collaborative work on word-lists, was the originator of the 1,000-word vocabulary which provided much of the macrostructure of *A Grammar of English Words*. In return, the Palmer dictionary, with its verb-pattern scheme, its labelling—for the first time in any dictionary—of the countable-uncountable distinction, and its original approach to indicating variation in examples, left its mark on Hornby's *Idiomatic and Syntactic English Dictionary* (later to be the *Advanced Learner's Dictionary*) and helped to shape its strongly 'productive' character.

1. The Genesis of the Learner's Dictionary

1.1. Introduction

At various times during its sixty-year history the learner's dictionary has been strengthened and enriched by programmes of lexical research with an applied linguistic focus. This chapter traces the multiple connections between research carried out from the late 1920s onwards—chiefly in the Far East—and four pioneering English dictionaries compiled specifically for foreign learners a decade or so later. Significantly, the three sole or principal authors of those dictionaries—Michael West, Harold E. Palmer, and A. S. Hornby—were all centrally involved in major research activity, but the projects mounted by the Tokyo Institute for Research in English Teaching (IRET), of which, as we have seen, Palmer was director from 1923 till 1936, and where Hornby succeeded him as head of research, addressed so many issues of crucial importance to language teaching and dictionary development, that they will have pride of place in this critical survey.

The chapter is divided into three broad sections. In the first two, I shall survey two major fields of research and review some of the key publications which flowed from them, laying particular stress on those findings which had the greatest influence on dictionary-making. These areas are the vocabulary control movement (1.2) and pedagogical grammar (1.3). In the third major section (1.4), I survey the period, from the mid-1930s onwards, when the attention of the major participants was turning increasingly from research to the practical application of its findings, and attempt a critical analysis of the four dictionaries for the learner which then appeared. In order of publication, these were: *The New Method English Dictionary* (West and Endicott 1935), *A Grammar of English Words* (Palmer 1938*a*), *A Beginners' English–Japanese Dictionary* (Hornby and Ishikawa 1940), and the *Idiomatic and Syntactic English Dictionary* (Hornby *et al.* 1942).

1.2. The Vocabulary Control Movement

The vocabulary control movement, which focused the intellectual energies of the leading figures in this survey during the late 1920s and early to mid-1930s, played a vital part in the genesis of the monolingual learner's dictionary. In fact, it would be no exaggeration to say that research into vocabulary control, with associated work on phraseology and grammar, gave birth to it, though—

paradoxically—Palmer does not seem to have become wholly aware until 1936 that only a *dictionary* could draw together fully and satisfactorily the manifold complexities which, by that time, the research had brought to light.[1]

In 1927, the research department of IRET was asked to 'compile a controlled English vocabulary suitable for schools of middle grade' (Palmer 1936*a*: 16). Palmer, who had been interested in vocabulary limitation since the period, over twenty years earlier, when he had been director of his own language school in Belgium, recognized that the fundamental problem he faced was one of categorization. How was he to define the various kinds of lexical units—inflected forms, derivatives, compounds, idioms, and so on—that were to make up the limited vocabulary? At the time, there was far less agreement than today on how such categories should be delimited and named, which helps to explain Palmer's almost obsessive interest in such matters (reflected in the titles of two articles published in 1929: 'What shall we call a word?' and 'What is an idiom?'). But his concern was wholly justified, since unless the problem was resolved of 'what is to be reckoned as *one word*, *something less than one word* and *something more than one word*' (1936*a*: 16), the composition and structure of any word-list would be meaningless.

Palmer became convinced that a controlled vocabulary was a more complex affair than a simple alphabetical inventory of word-forms, based on frequency of occurrence. From 1930 onwards, he, A. S. Hornby, and Michael West, acting singly or cooperatively at different stages, and from theoretical foundations that were quite different from those of their American rivals, succeeded in producing what were in effect a number of structured lexicons. Their vocabularies, that is to say, were not simply alphabetical sequences of word-forms—*fasten, fastened, fastener*, and so on (Palmer 1930*b*; Hornby 1947*a*)—but listings of structured entries, where each entry consisted of a root and a cluster of inflectionally and derivationally related forms, thus: FASTEN, *fasten, fastens, fastened, fastening; fastener*.[2] From that point, the path clearly led forward to a practical dictionary for the foreign learner, except that, as we shall see, there were interesting differences in the directions eventually taken by the three colleagues.

1.2.1. Vocabulary Control: Limiting the Burden on Memory

The vocabulary control movement arose from a simple pedagogical need—to reduce the effort required to learn a foreign language by identifying those

---

[1] Writing in that year, and referring to the 'General Service List' which had been prepared by West, himself, and others attending the Carnegie Conference of 1934–5, Palmer predicted the compilation of 'Dictionaries and a Thesaurus based on the vocabulary' (1936*a*: 23). As it happened, though, his own first dictionary would have an altogether different basis.

[2] Palmer went to some lengths to invent special terms (e.g. 'primary monologeme' for inflected form, 'secondary monologeme' for derivative), but they did not catch on, and he often fell back on more familiar equivalents (Palmer 1930*a*).

(relatively few) words which carried the main burden of communication in most everyday encounters (Bongers 1947). Indications from studies made early in the century, including Palmer's own, were that this necessary minimum was perhaps as little as 1,000 words, and that they would account for the great bulk of any text composed in 'everyday English'.[3] It should be noted that one of the requirements of such a reduced vocabulary, for Palmer as for others, was that naturalness should be achieved within its limits. It should be borne in mind, too, that the notion of restricting the vocabulary presented to beginners in a language, with later expansion in careful stages, had been understood by teachers for centuries (Palmer 1936*a*). The entirely new element was that such vocabularies could now be drawn up systematically and in collaboration with others working in the field.

Identifying such a central core of words could bring particular advantages to specific learner groups as well as conferring the general benefits already described. If, as investigations in Dutch and British schools had shown, secondary pupils could learn three thousand—or even one thousand—words of this kind, they would 'have acquired something of fundamental and permanent value', even if they made no further progress in the language (Palmer and Hornby 1937: 10).

1.2.2. The Objective Quantitative Approach

Research into vocabulary control in the 1920s and 1930s was characterized by two widely differing approaches. The first to emerge was associated with a group of American linguists, among whom the leading figure was Edward L. Thorndike of Columbia University. The so-called 'objective quantitative' method was to count words in a body of written texts amounting, in the case of Thorndike's highly influential list *The Teacher's Word Book* (1921), to four million. Thorndike took note not only of the overall 'frequency credit', or frequency of occurrence, of a given word, but also of its 'range credit', i.e. of the number of different texts in which it appeared, which in this case could be as many as forty-one. Though Thorndike was not only concerned, in this project, with counting words as spelling-forms—except in special cases, separate entries were not made in the *Word Book* for the regular plurals of nouns, or adverbs formed by adding -*ly*— the objective approach had weaknesses arising from the types of material selected. Though the counts were capable of determining the first thousand words with small likelihood of error, beyond that limit wide differences could appear

---

[3] According to Michael West, a carefully selected 1,000-word vocabulary, 'which a child can learn in three years, is capable of telling in easy and effective style a 50,000 word novel' (1929: 118–19). Palmer claimed that it was possible to compose texts 'of literary and cultural value' within such limits (1930*c*: 1).

according to the sources used. A selection made up of children's classics, readers, popular newspapers, and so on, as in Thorndike's case, would yield different results from a body of scientific or technical material (Palmer and Hornby 1937).[4] Moreover, Thorndike's studies especially were based on a reading rather than a speaking vocabulary, and would need modification if they were to be useful for language production ('encoding') as well as reception ('decoding') (Faucett *et al.* 1936).

1.2.3. The Subjective Approach

Palmer's approach was strikingly different, and was called by several observers 'subjective', because of a firm belief that the personal judgement of the investigator and the experience of teachers were essential factors in vocabulary control, and that a compilation which took account of such factors would prove more satisfactory than any based on objective findings alone (Bongers 1947: 45; Battenburg 1994: 136). Central to that personal involvement, as we have seen, was a concern with fundamental questions of definition and with the search for appropriate terms for various linguistic units. It is not for nothing that Palmer, Hornby, West, and others who thought like them, came to be known as 'the lexicologists'. Yet their research was not carried out in total isolation from the 'word-counters', and indeed the Carnegie Conference of 1934–5 encouraged collaboration between followers of the two major movements (Faucett *et al.* 1936). Though few other major projects involved cooperation between theoretical rivals, word-lists were as a general rule the product of 'organized effort and collaboration rigorously tested over and over again' (Palmer and Hornby 1937: 8).

We have seen how Palmer was firmly opposed to the counting of word-forms ('spelling-forms') without regard to differences of function or meaning, and during his 1931 world tour—which included the United States—he urged on his American colleagues the need for 'precise definitions as a prerequisite for any statistical work' (Bongers 1947: 81). He had observed that in many word-counts homonyms (e.g. *can*, noun and *can*, modal verb) were conflated, while the relationship between roots and their derivatives (*happy*, say, in relation to *happiness* and *unhappy*) were ignored. He was aware, too, of the failure to take account of words in their various senses or, as he would say, of their 'semantic varieties' (Palmer 1938*a*), a perception which he shared with Michael West (Tickoo 1988).

The critical and analytical work which flowed from the IRET decision of 1927 culminated in two major reports, published in 1930 and 1931. The *First Interim Report on Vocabulary Selection* contained 3,000 'word-units'. For its successor,

---

[4] The range of material on which Thorndike drew included ten chapters of *Black Beauty*, two history textbooks, thirty school readers, and 'newspapers, private and business correspondence', and amounted in all to four million running words (Fries and Traver 1960: 21).

the vocabulary was divided into five layers, corresponding to the five middle-school years (Palmer 1931*a*; Hornby 1937*b*). The 'word-units' were like the entries of a typical dictionary in that each was based on a root (or simple word) but also contained principal sense-divisions, inflected forms, and derivatives. It was clear that what was emerging, even then, was a Saussurean view of the 'word', defined in terms of its place in a spectrum of relations, semantic, morphological and syntactic.[5] However, it was not until 1934 that Palmer began to address the lexicographical implications of such research, and specifically to ask how, in a dictionary 'meant to cater for the foreign learner', semantic values, collocations, and examples might be structured and arranged (1936*b*: 7).[6]

Beyond the need for rigorous definition of categories, which was paramount, there was another priority. Palmer was no newcomer to vocabulary selection and grading, as we have seen. In Belgium, before World War I, he had worked on a number of small vocabularies, including (in 1907) a learner's vocabulary in Esperanto embodied in a textbook for French learners, and (in 1911) a 500-word English vocabulary (Palmer 1936*a*). In those projects, Palmer placed constant emphasis on 'structural' (i.e. 'grammatical') rather than 'content' (i.e. 'open-class') words, since the former made the greater contribution to sentence build-ing, while the latter could be picked up as the need for them arose. This simple division was further refined in *Principles of Language-Study* (1921), where Palmer drew a distinction within the 'content' category between 'words of special utility (such as names of plants, animals, parts of the body . . . and such-like semi-technical words)' and 'words which may occur in any context and which are common to any subject' (Palmer 1921: 128). Significantly, he regretted the ten-dency to give preference in vocabularies to the former, whose representation in word-lists could vary quite markedly according to the specialist field of the texts under scrutiny (cf. West 1935). The distinction between special-purpose and general-purpose content words, incidentally, harks back to that drawn earlier by Henry Sweet (1899) between 'encyclopaedic' and 'lexical' words, and points for-ward to the emphasis placed on 'heavy-duty' lexical words (and structural words) in Palmer's own *Grammar of English Words* (1938) and Hornby, Gatenby, and Wakefield's *Idiomatic and Syntactic English Dictionary* (1942).[7]

---

[5] Palmer and Hornby were both influenced by de Saussure (Hornby 1946). During his world tour of 1931, Palmer attended the Congress of Linguists in Geneva, where he met Sèchehaye, joint editor of de Saussure's *Cours de linguistique générale* (1916). In 1933, on the tenth anniversary of the setting-up of IRET, it was Sèchehaye who composed the tribute to Palmer for a special commemorative volume (IRET 1934).

[6] He did this in a remarkable exploratory document, *An Essay in Lexicology* (1934*c*), in which a model was proposed, with examples, for the internal organization of entries in a learner's dictionary (see 1.4.2, below).

[7] As his daughter was later to recall, Palmer was out of sympathy with those aiming at selections of words 'which carried the greatest weight of meaning; he was after words with the maximum of actual and potential usability' (Anderson 1969: 141).

1.2.3.1. Palmer and Hornby: *Thousand-Word English*

The pattern laid down for one word-list often provided the blueprint, sometimes with comparatively minor variations, for later schemes. One project linking the *Second Interim Report on Vocabulary Selection* of 1931 and Thorndike's earlier *Teacher's Word Book* is particularly interesting because it was the first of its kind in which A. S. Hornby collaborated with Palmer on an equal footing. In 1933 Hornby came to Palmer with a preliminary 1,000-word list, 'for the purpose of re-writing stories of more ambitious content' (Palmer 1936*a*: 21). This was afterwards compared to various 'objective' lists to ensure that no word of common occurrence had been overlooked. According to Bongers (1947), Palmer and Hornby also drew on the research of Michael West. In a final 'testing' phase they took texts and attempted to rewrite them within the limits of the list. Rewritings of further texts served to make them aware of the absolute claims of previously unconsidered words and the usefulness or otherwise of words placed on a reserve list during earlier testings. Such meticulousness in relation to the needs it was intended to serve resulted in the list—published in 1937 as *Thousand-Word English*—being hailed as the most useful and practicable of its kind for writing or adapting reading materials.

The methodology employed in *TWE* is also highly interesting from a linguistic standpoint. The list embodies a microstructure more or less common to earlier IRET projects, i.e. a 'word' is roughly equivalent to a root, and heads an entry containing its inflected forms, common derivatives, and semantic varieties. (It also distinguishes, if only by labelling, between the word classes to which the headword belongs.) Second, the approach drew on 'quantitative' as well as 'qualitative' sources, and stressed the principle that no vocabulary of a given radius could be composed without reference to a much larger one from which the more important words are selected. The thousand words of this vocabulary were chosen from among those of the *Second Interim Report*—three times as large—and this in turn was partially based on the 10,000 words of Thorndike's *Teacher's Word Book*. Interestingly, too, Palmer and Hornby took care when selecting a given word that other words related in terms of antonymy, instrument, and associated activity, etc., were also chosen (cf. *thick* and *thin*; *tooth* and *bite*; *key* and *lock*). In so doing they provided for the needs of the 'association' method of vocabulary teaching—of which more is said below. A final point illustrates the honesty of the approach as well as highlighting a problem which continues to dog all compilers, and all users, of controlled vocabularies. A vocabulary can be kept artificially small by stretching the form and meaning of any component word to such an extent that anyone 'knowing the word in its isolated and simplest form and with its most usual meanings will no longer recognize or understand it' (Palmer and Hornby 1937: 14). One could argue, for instance, that the noun *flight*, as in *during the flight to London*, is straightforwardly related to the verb *fly* and could be included in the same entry in a word-list. Not so *flight* as in *a flight of steps*, which calls for separate listing. With such pitfalls in mind, and in over sixty cases, *Thousand-Word English* sets out as two or more entries items that could have been smuggled in as one (thus: *break, breakfast; cloth, clothes; mind* (verb), *mind* (noun), etc.).

1.2.3.2. *Thousand-Word English* and *A Grammar of English Words*

From the lexicographical point of view, the most interesting application of *Thousand-Word English* is its use by Harold Palmer as a partial basis for *A Grammar of English Words* (*GEW*) (1938a). Though there is no direct reference in *GEW* to the word-list itself, Palmer's Introduction recognizes that A. S. Hornby 'collaborated to a considerable extent in its general design' (1938a: xii), a possible reference to the period after work on the list (1933–5), when Palmer's thoughts may already have been turning to compilation of a dictionary. It is true that, when writing of his specimen entries in *An Essay in Lexicology*, Palmer affirmed that they were not 'a series of extracts from any dictionary in preparation or contemplation' (1934c: 1). However, when the notion of compiling *GEW* eventually came to him, he must have realized how well suited the entry models presented in the *Essay* were to the design of the dictionary.

TWE and *GEW* of course contain the same number of words—in the sense already defined—and as a comparison of their macrostructures reveals, these often turn out to be the same items. As can be seen from the two sequences

Table 1.1. *A comparison of two sequences of headwords in* TWE *and* GEW

TWE	GEW	TWE	GEW
HAIR, *n.*	hair, *n.*	MIND, *v.*	mind, *n.*
HALF, *n.* halves, *pl.n.*	half, halves, *n. and det.*	MIND, *n.*	mind, *v.*
HALL, *n.*	—	MINUTE, *n.*	minute, *n.*
HAND, *n.*	hand, *n.*	MIS-, *prefix.*	—
HANG, *n.* [*sic*]	hang, *v.*	MISS, *prefix before name.*	Miss, *n. Prefix-title.*
HAPPEN, *v.*	happen, *v.*	—	miss, *v.*
HAPPY, *adj.*	happy, *adj.*	MISTAKE, *n.*	mistake, *n. . . . . v.*
HARBOUR, *n.*	—	MISTRESS, *n.*	mistress, *n.*
HARD, *adj.*	hard, *adj. . . . adv.*	MIX, *v.*	mix, *v.*
HARDLY, *adv.*	hardly, *adv.*	MOMENT, *n.*	moment, *n.*
HARM, *n.*	harm, *n. . . . v.*	MONDAY, *n.*	—
HAT, *n.*	—	MONEY, *n.*	money, *n.*
HATE, *v.*	hate, *v. . . . n.*	MONTH, *n.*	month, *n.*
HAVE, *v.*	have, *v.*	MOON, *n.*	—
HE, *pers. pron. subj.*	he-him, *pers. pron.*	MORE, *det. adv.*	more, *det. . . . adv.*

(from letters H and M, respectively) of paired entries in Table 1.1, the headwords in *TWE* and *GEW* are very often the same, the only discrepancies here being the absence, from *GEW*, of five nouns of specific reference (*hall, harbour, hat, Monday*, and *moon*), and the exclusion from *TWE* of *miss* (verb). (The *mis-* prefix, present as a headword in *TWE*, is part of the entry for *miss* (verb) in *GEW*.)

There are also close similarities between the microstructures of the two works. Of the 33 derivatives, prefixes, and sense divisions in the *TWE* samples, 31 also appear in *GEW*, and as can be seen from the following, definitions in polysemous entries often appear in the same order and in a similar form:

(1) MIND [maind], *v.*
    (1. take care of)
    (2. = pay attention to)
    (3. = have objection) (*TWE*)

mind [maind] . . ., *v.*
1. = take care or charge of.
2. = pay attention to, notice
3. = object to. (*GEW*)

This is not to say there are not considerable differences, but these tend to take the form of additions to a given stock, most particularly in the areas of compounding, phraseology, and exemplification. This is well borne out by a comparison of the entries for *morning* in the two works:

(2) MORNING ['mɔːniŋ], *n.*
    this, last, to-morrow morning, *adv.*
    on Monday morning, *adv.* (*TWE*)

morning ['mɔːniŋ], mornings
['mɔːniŋz], *n.*
the morning is the first part of
    the day.
this [to-morrow, yesterday]
    morning.
on Sunday, *etc.*, morning.
on the morning of the 18th, *etc.*
¶ **in the morning**
He works in the morning and
    plays in the afternoon.
be morning.
When he awoke it was morning.
Comps. morning coat, morning
    dress, morning star
Phr. **Good morning.** (*GEW*)

Various aspects of the microstructure of *GEW* will be analysed later when the early dictionaries of West, Palmer, and Hornby are examined in greater depth, and also in the thematic chapter devoted to phraseology (Chapter 2). For the moment, we can simply applaud Palmer's striking originality of purpose—recalling the priorities of his earliest teaching days—in devoting a dictionary to those words which, because of their multiple meanings, syntax, phraseology, and patterns of derivation, are found 'to constitute the bulk of learning-effort on the part of the student of English as a foreign language' (Palmer 1938a: iii).

1.2.4. The Contribution of Michael West

1.2.4.1. West, and the Minimum Adequate Vocabulary

Michael West was separated geographically, but also in academic background and to some extent in educational philosophy, from his Tokyo colleagues. Palmer and Hornby had a solid (if largely self-acquired) grounding in phonetics and grammar, and their approach to vocabulary analysis and limitation was essentially linguistic (Palmer 1931b, 1932a). West, by contrast, had received a university training in psychology and education, and had come to accept the need for vocabulary control as a means of producing simplified readers, which in turn subserved his overriding objective for English teaching in British Bengal: prioritizing the development of reading as an answer to the educational needs of a bilingual society.

West's scheme for a full reading development programme is of special interest to lexicographers because the first of its three stages was one in which each new word was introduced carefully up to a limit of about 1,500 words, close to the figure of 1,490 that was eventually decided on for the definition vocabulary of the *New Method English Dictionary*.[8] Though publication of this dictionary was some way off, and its defining vocabulary was to be exhaustively tested and refined before publication, it seems that West had already lighted on the principle that, if learners were to develop a reading vocabulary, they would first need an explanatory sub-lexicon.

1.2.4.2. West and the *General Service List*

In the mid-1930s, Michael West became involved, together with other leading figures of the vocabulary control movement, in a project that would stand as a major landmark in its history. This was the Carnegie Conference, which met on the initiative of West and under the auspices of the Carnegie Corporation, first in New York in October 1934, and afterwards in London in June 1935 (Palmer 1936a). Its primary purpose was to examine 'the part played by word lists in the teaching of English as a foreign language' (Faucett *et al.* 1936: 1) but it also aimed to bring together experts representing various theoretical positions (thus the 'word-counters' as well as the 'lexicologists'), to invite them to draw up a word-list and to encourage a collaborative approach to future research. Interestingly, in the light of this call for collaboration, Edward L. Thorndike seems to

---

[8] As Battenburg has remarked, 'the *NMED* must be viewed in light of West's work with the reading method and vocabulary control. It was designed primarily to assist language learners with reading' (Battenburg 1994: 138).

have played a rather minor role in the programme of work undertaken by the Conference. The vital task of laying down the theoretical basis of the analysis, including the identification of criteria to be used in the preparation of limited vocabularies, was entrusted to Lawrence Faucett, Harold Palmer, and Michael West, while in the framing of the word-list itself, Thorndike and Edward Sapir acted as consultants (Palmer 1936a). The itemizing of the 'General Service List', which was to form the major component of the *Interim Report* of the Conference—and was to be published in 1953 separately, and in a modified form, as probably the most authoritative, and certainly the best-known, of all the word-lists—was entrusted to Palmer and West.

Since Palmer and West had already collaborated, and were in sympathy with each other's principles and methods (McArthur 1978), it is hardly surprising that the *General Service List* (*GSL*) should resemble, in several respects, the word-lists produced under the auspices of IRET, including *TWE*. Once again we find an alphabetical listing of simple words (or roots), each introducing an entry containing its principal derivatives and a set of numbered sense-divisions, as in the following (simplified) example:

(3) **EXTEND**

extend, v.	(1) (*stretch out, be stretched out*)
	The garden extends as far as the river
	(2) (*continue, enlarge, protract, lengthen*)
	Extend one's visit
	Extend a business
extent, n.	To the full extent of the garden
extension, n.	An extension of the hospital
extensive, adj.	Extensive repairs, enquiries
extensively, adv. (*GSL*)	

There are, however, certain major differences, as shown here, between *GSL* and the earlier lists. The first is that headwords and their derivatives are supported by illustrative examples, many of which are familiar, ready-made word-combinations (i.e. collocations). At **EXTEND**, for instance, one finds *Extend one's visit*, *Extend a business*, and *Extensive repairs, enquiries*. The List is further enriched by the inclusion of many idioms and phrasal verbs (provided by A. S. Hornby and his wife) such as *break to pieces, break one's heart, break down, break off, break up*.[9]

1.2.4.3. West's *Definition Vocabulary* and *The New Method English Dictionary*

During the period leading up to the Carnegie Conference, Michael West had

---

[9] As Palmer recalled, shortly afterwards, 'the result of their efforts was the object of special commendation by the Conference at the meeting in London' (Palmer 1936a: 23).

been compiling, in collaboration with J. G. Endicott, a foreign learners' dictionary eventually to appear as *The New Method English Dictionary* (*NMED*) (1935).
The work had—as an entirely original feature—definitions based on a 'minimum
adequate definition vocabulary', and in the same year as the dictionary itself
appeared, West published *Definition Vocabulary*, a research report describing
how the vocabulary had been selected, checked and revised. The project entailed
compiling a preliminary version of the dictionary, in which a vocabulary of
1,799 words—eventually to be reduced to 1,490—was used to define 23,898
vocabulary items (West 1935: 34–41).

In *Definition Vocabulary*, West identified and attempted to solve many of the
difficulties that would later (in the 1970s and 1980s) confront lexicographers
designing limited defining vocabularies for advanced-level learners' dictionaries.
The discussion is in fact remarkable for the range of theoretical issues raised.
West put his finger unerringly on the characteristic weaknesses of definitions in
the mother-tongue dictionary—the fondness for defining the known (say, *pencil*)
in terms of the unknown ('instrument'? 'tapering'?), and the tendency to fall
back on 'scatter-gun' techniques, whereby 'one fires off a number of near or
approximate synonyms in the hope that one or other will hit the mark and be
understood', as in: '**sinuate** = tortuous, wavy, winding' (1935: 8).

West also faced up squarely to the problems of dictionary *size* posed by a
limited defining vocabulary. He saw, first, that in defining within a small
wordstock, especially for foreign users, we are often compelled to expand the
definitions and possibly provide more examples. He recognized, too, that in
some cases we may be forced to use double definitions (as in the definition of
gherkin, in which first *pickles* has to be defined, and then—as part of the definition of *pickles*—*vinegar*).[10] Such requirements will tend to increase the length of
the dictionary beyond acceptable limits of size or cost. Careful thought must
therefore be given to selecting not only the items for defining but also the items
to be defined.

One class of items that cannot with confidence be removed from the list of
dictionary headwords consists of the defining vocabulary itself, since the lexicographer cannot be sure that these are already known by the dictionary users.
(It was partly with this problem in mind that Gabriele Stein later proposed (in
1990) a 'bridging' bilingual dictionary to teach the definition vocabulary used in
the appropriate advanced monolingual dictionary.)

As regards the criteria for limiting the defining vocabulary, a question of
critical importance is the extent to which one can assume some degree of inference on the part of the user. West lists the commonest prefixes and suffixes

---

[10] Double definitions could of course be avoided, as West was aware, by treating any defining word
from outside the limited vocabulary as a cross-reference to its own place in the dictionary. This device
was later to be a standard feature of the *Longman Dictionary of Contemporary English* (first edition 1978).

(thus, *dis-*, *in-*, *-able*, *-en*) in the defining vocabulary, and in the definitions he allows these to be attached to various words—provided their meanings are regular. So the deadjectival suffix *-en* can be added to *hard*, *soft*, *rough*, etc., on the assumption that the user will infer the meanings of *harden*, *soften*, and *roughen* (West 1935: 16). By such means great economies can be achieved. At the same time, West, like Palmer and Hornby in their work on *TWE*, was aware of the danger of introducing into definitions derivatives or compounds whose meanings were not straightforwardly relatable to those of their elements (cf. Cowie 1990). However, he was not entirely successful in spotting those lexicalized complex or compound words which could not be used in definitions as if transparent, and which did need to be treated in main entries. Consider *happening* (not simply 'something that happens') or *harbour-master* (more than 'the master of a harbour') which, according to West's recommendations, could be removed from the entry-list of a learner's dictionary (1935: 17).

As I have already shown, West's systematic approach to testing and refining the defining vocabulary of the *NMED* involved taking a word-list and then attempting to write a preliminary version of the dictionary within it, in the process modifying the vocabulary first selected. The word-list was in fact one that West had already used for producing simplified readers.[11] While it is not necessary to describe here the various processes of enlargement, reduction, and comparison through which the vocabulary was passed, one final theoretical point should be made. In the course of drafting, West realized that to provide a satisfactory definition in a large number of cases it was necessary to 'force in' 61 additional words. These are included, specially marked, in the list of words that formed the bedrock of the defining vocabulary. It is particularly interesting to note that at least seventeen of these items—*behaviour*, *belief*, *engine*, *furniture*, *insect*, *instrument*, *metal*, *noun*, *ornament*, *quality*, *relation*, *science*, *skill*, *solid*, *surface*, *thread*, *vegetable*—are superordinate ('genus') terms of some generality considered essential for defining many specific objects, substances, animals and plants. It is worth noting, too, that all of these key items are included in the defining vocabulary of *ALD 5* (1995), while all except *ornament* feature in that of *LDOCE 3* (1995).

1.3. Pedagogical Grammar and the Learner's Dictionary

Harold Palmer's analytical interest in modal verbs, determinatives (i.e. determiners), and countable and uncountable nouns can be traced back to the period

---

[11] *New Method Readers*, 1–5. The fact that several of West's projects draw on common sources and methods is reflected in such titles as *New Method Conversation Course*—and of course *The New Method English Dictionary*.

in Belgium when he first became aware of the vital importance of structural (or function) words in the learning of English. As well as recognizing that the '100 English words of most frequent occurrence' (1936*a*: 14) were almost exclusively function words, Palmer was aware that they were the essential elements of sentence construction, and by 1917, he was working on an English structural vocabulary 'to be used in a sort of sentence building machine' (1936*a*: 15). Already, as we can see, he was drawing practical inspiration from his linguistic insights. One outcome of the growing interest in syntax was a two-volume text-book, *Systematic Exercises in Sentence Building* (1925), in which patterns of the simple sentence were presented in the form of substitution tables. These were intended to support systematic exercises in sentence building, and looked forward to the period in the early 1930s when Palmer would first develop a scheme of 'construction-patterns' that could be used in a learner's dictionary.

1.3.1. The 'Noun Complex' and the 'Anomalous Finites'

Before that important stage was reached, Palmer attempted to get to grips with a number of other key issues in grammatical description. Interestingly, his studies of the 'noun complex'—what today would be called the noun phrase—and the 'anomalous finites' made constant reference to the function of those types in larger constructions.

Palmer's article 'The noun complex' dates from 1926, but it is strikingly modern, both in its terminology and its analytical approach. The article is concerned with the subclassification of nouns, and straight away Palmer lays down the cardinal principle that to arrive at such a subclassification, the analyst must take account of 'determinative' usage, since determinatives show 'to what extent the noun is definite or indefinite, and what sort of definiteness or indefiniteness is to be understood' (1926*a*: 1). Though the term 'determinative' has long since been replaced by 'determiner', Palmer is referring here to the broad category under which articles, partitives (i.e. *some, any, no*), and demonstratives can all be subsumed. He draws attention, too, though under another name, to the category of 'zero determiner', represented by such examples as *We need to buy sugar and coffee,* and to the now familiar distinction between 'countable' and 'uncountable' nouns.[12] The same emphasis on rigorous formal analysis, incidentally, is evident from a later article, 'When is an adjective not an adjective?' (Palmer 1935). Here, by providing a definition of 'qualificative' adjectives (specifically *slow* and *soft*) in terms of their inflected forms, derivatives (e.g. *slowness, softness*), and syntactic functions, Palmer is able to point up the key differences

---

[12] The terms were first introduced by Jespersen in his *Modern English Grammar* (1914: 114–15). They were adopted by Palmer, whose *Grammar of English Words* (1938*a*) was the first learners' dictionary to indicate the distinction.

between qualificatives (i.e. adjectives as normally understood) and determinatives.

Of the various categories which Palmer set out to define, the so-called 'anomalous finites' were certainly given a high priority, since Palmer devoted to them two detailed analytical papers (1926*b*, 1934*b*), the former being accompanied by a set of questions designed to test understanding of the system, and even an examination paper for teachers.

In speaking of the anomalous finites, Palmer had in mind the eleven finite forms of what are now commonly called the 'primary' verbs, i.e. 'be', 'have', and 'do', and the thirteen forms of the modal and semi-modal auxiliaries, thus: *shall/should, will/would, can/could, may/might, must, ought, need, dare*, and *used* (*to*). Palmer's definition of this set of forms, it is true, had certain shortcomings. He attached too much weight, for instance, to the fact that they do not occur in the so-called 'compound present' and 'compound past' (cf. *I do go, I did go* and **I do be, *I did be*). In fact, this is an invalid test, since the forms *I do go, I did go*—unless they are emphatic, with nuclear stress on *do/did*—are not acceptable in Standard English either. However, by an indirect route, Palmer offers several helpful criteria, since by referring to syntactic *problems* which require reference to the anomalous finites, he simultaneously provides the means to define them. As he points out, the forms can be used:

(4) (a) to form negative sentences: He might go. ⇒ He mightn't go.
    (b) to form interrogative sentences: He might go. ⇒ Might he go?
    (c) to form the emphatic affirmative: He might go. ⇒ He 'might go!
    (d) to prevent repetition by allowing   A: He might go. B: Yes, he
         ellipsis of main verbs, complements,   might.
         etc.:
    (e) to form disjunctive (i.e. 'tag') ques-   He might go. ⇒ He might go,
         tions: mightn't he?

These criteria, of course, are now invoked in many standard treatments of the modal auxiliaries and primary verbs (Quirk *et al.* 1985: 121–8; Greenbaum and Quirk 1990: 34–6).

1.3.2. Palmer's Construction-Pattern Schemes

Harold Palmer first attempted a systematic treatment of construction-patterns, complete with structural formulae and example sentences, in 1932. His objectives at the time were chiefly practical. He wished to provide middle-grade pupils with a handy guide to verb syntax, and to this end had the patterns printed on sheets so that they could be pasted into students' exercise-books. All the same, *Some Notes on Construction-Patterns* (1932*b*) marked an important step towards the fully-fledged verb-pattern scheme of *A Grammar of English Words* (1938*a*).

The scheme pointed the way forward in three important respects: it focused on sentence structure, and specifically on complementation patterns of the verb; it arranged the patterns into numbered groupings (called Divisions) of more-or-less related types; and it revealed an experimental interest in labelling. The following extract, Division 6, which illustrates all these features, is additionally interesting in that the four patterns represented were also to appear—in the same order—in the 1938 scheme (see Table 1.2).

TABLE 1.2. *Simple sentences containing a simple finite (SSSF patterns)*

DIVISION 6

Pattern 6a	N_1 x (always) x F x Extent We walked three miles. It lasted two hours.
Pattern 6b	N_1 x (always) x F of *take* x N_2 x Extent It always takes me three hours. That took him ten days.
Pattern 6c	N_1 x (always) x F of *weigh* x Weight It weighs a pound. It always weighs too much.
Pattern 6d	N_1 x (always) x F of *cost* x (N_2) x Price It costs me five shillings. It cost a lot of money.

In some respects, the 1932 scheme would not have met the needs of dictionary users, especially students at an advanced level of proficiency. First, it was concerned only with *simple* sentence patterns: none of the structures represented contained a subordinate clause. Second, the scheme contained not only declarative patterns, but their imperative and interrogative transformations as well. Entire Divisions were devoted to those derived structures, so that Division 9, for example, was made up of imperative patterns corresponding to the declaratives of Division 3. On grounds of economy alone, it would have been impossible to accommodate full sets of common transformations in a scheme intended for a dictionary, and in fact imperatives and interrogatives are introduced only as occasional examples in the Verb-Pattern scheme of Hornby's *Idiomatic and Syntactic English Dictionary* and not at all in the corresponding scheme of Palmer's *A Grammar of English Words*.

A further stage in the progression towards the verb-pattern scheme of Palmer's dictionary was *Specimens of English Construction Patterns* (1934a). This was a highly sophisticated scheme and evidence—if further evidence were needed—of Palmer's originality and prescience. At the same time, it was extremely complex and not at all easy to interpret. Drawing on the analogy of the railway network, Palmer produced a synoptic chart (see Figure 1.1) that was generative

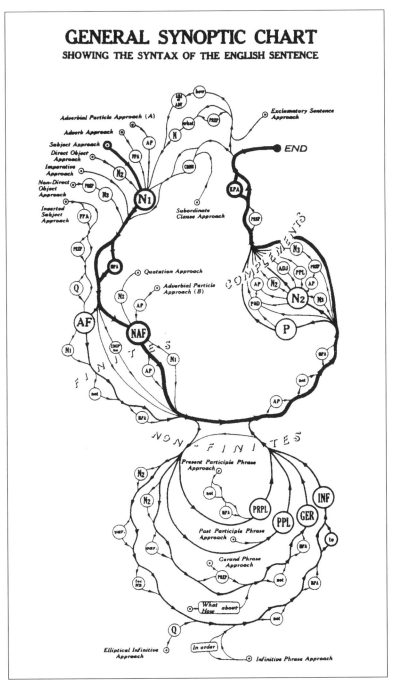

FIG. 1.1. General Synoptic Chart from *Specimens of English Construction Patterns* (Palmer 1934*a*)

TABLE 1.3. *Construction-pattern 4131.1: simple examples (tabulated)*

	N1 (Subject)	(MPA) (Mid-position Adverbs)	NAF (Finites of Non-anomalous verbs)	(EPA) (End-position Adverbs)
1	Birds		fly.	
2	A bird		flies.	
3	I		understand.	
4	He	(always)	walks	(quickly).

in the sense that it aimed to account for a theoretically infinite number of distinct sentence patterns. By beginning at any one of the 'approaches' (top left-hand corner) and finishing at the point marked 'end' (top right), the reader could trace out any of a number of 'routes', each of which represented a specific sentence construction. Each route, with its stopping points, or nodes, corresponding to structural elements such as N_1 (subject) or N_2 (direct object), could be written out as a formula, with examples arranged in a table, though inevitably the report provided only a small sample (fifteen) of a potentially limitless number of tables. In the (simplified) table for an intransitive pattern (see Table 1.3), structural elements are displayed at the top. This was a highly ingenious model, but it could not serve as a verb-pattern scheme for a learner's dictionary, even at advanced level. First, the highly productive mechanism of the synoptic chart recognized the difference between finite and non-finite sentence constructions, making the scheme far too complex for a student dictionary. Second, optional elements such as the adverbs in the above table were also included in the model. These added to its productive capacity too, but introduced an unnecessary complication for students, who needed a scheme that focused on *obligatory* elements (such as objects and complements), not optional ones.

The system of 27 verb-patterns eventually adopted for inclusion in *GEW*—the one by which Palmer is best known, but which was not published separately beforehand—was more modest and better suited to potential dictionary users. In contrast with *English Construction Patterns*, it was chiefly concerned with the syntax of simple, finite sentence constructions and with the complementation patterns of their verbs (i.e. with phrases functioning as objects, complements, and so on). It was concerned with subordinate clauses only insofar as they functioned as post-verbal elements too. It thus represented a sensible narrowing down of the descriptive aims of the earlier scheme.

Though the issue was not fully discussed at the time, it was important that, as far as possible, verb-pattern schemes should reflect underlying (or functional) rather than superficial (or constituent-class) similarities and differences, and in fact, in a number of patterns in Palmer's scheme, the post-verbal elements consisted of one or more (suitably labelled) objects, or an object and a complement.

Direct objects, in fact, were given the appropriate functional label in all patterns in which the object was realized by a *noun phrase*—as it was in VP 4 and VP 7:

(5) VP 4 Verb x Direct Object *Somebody shouted my name.*
VP 7 Verb x Direct Object x Adjective *I paint the door green.*

Subject complements, too, were identified as such in the relevant pattern codes, but on condition that they too were realized by a phrase—a noun phrase or an adjective phrase—as in these examples:

(6) VP 2 Verb x Subject Complement *He is chairman. She was very happy.*

The limitation which Palmer seems to impose on the kinds of constituent which can occur as clause elements will be returned to later. For the moment we can consider the structural parallel which exists between certain pairs of patterns in his VP scheme containing objects and/or complements. There is, for example, the parallel between sentences containing a direct object alone and those containing an indirect object in addition. Compare:

(7) VP 4 Verb x Direct Object *I bought a book.*
VP 11 Verb x Indirect Object x Direct Object *I bought John a book.*

There is also a clear structural and semantic relationship between VP 2, as illustrated above, and VPs 9 and 7:

(8) VP 9 Verb x Direct Object x Object Complement *They elected him chairman.*
VP 7 Verb x Direct Object x Adjective *They made her very happy.*

As can be seen from the numbers of the patterns, however, Palmer's ordering hardly reflects these relationships. Note too that in one case (VP 7), the category label 'adjective' is used instead of 'object complement'—a choice that obscures the further parallels between VPs 7 and 9 (where the difference is one of realization alone, viz. adjective phrase vs. noun phrase).

True, there is systematic arrangement elsewhere in the Palmer scheme. One feature that is interesting from the standpoint of later developments is Palmer's handling of the various indirect-object structures. The pattern featuring an indirect object (VP 11) is in fact divided into two groups, 1 and 2, illustrated by *I give you something* and *I buy you something*, respectively. The basis of the division is the possibility or otherwise of converting a VP 11 sentence into VP 10 with *to* (as in the first case) or VP 10 with *for* (as in the second). Compare:

(9)   *Group* 1. Convertible into *V.P.* 10 with *to*
        I **give** [bring, lend, owe, sell, tell, *etc.*] **you** [him, *etc.*] **something** [*etc.*].
        Cf. Give me one *and* Give one to me.

> *Group* 2. Convertible into *V.P.* 10 with *for*
> I **buy** [get, find, leave, make, offer, *etc.*] **you** [him, *etc.*] **something** [*etc.*].
> *Cf.* Buy me one *and* buy one for me.

This approach was later followed by Hornby, with minor modifications, in *ISED* (*ALD 1*) and in the second and third editions of *ALD*, and is a simple and un-mistakably clear method of presenting a familiar transformational relationship.[13]

This account of Palmer's VP scheme has so far been limited to simple sentence patterns (i.e. those in which *phrases* function as objects and complements). If we now turn to the complex patterns (i.e. those with a finite or non-finite subordinate clause as all or part of their complementation), we find first that all these structures are helpfully set aside as a block (starting with VP 14), but also that Palmer arranges the individual structures systematically, so that at VPs 15 to 18, for instance, we have first a contrast between a *to*-infinitive (15) and a *how to*-infinitive (16), and then a parallel between that pair and another similar pair (17, 18), except that 17 and 18 contain a direct object:

(10)   VP 15 VERB x "TO" x INFINITIVE *I want to go.*
       VP 16 VERB x "HOW TO" x INFINITIVE *I ask how to do it.*
       VP 17 VERB x DIRECT OBJECT x "TO" x INFINITIVE *I ask him to do it.*
       VP 18 VERB x DIRECT OBJECT x "HOW TO" x INFINITIVE *I show him how to do it.*

Such an orderly arrangement was no doubt found helpful by students at the time. However, some of the patterns reflect only superficial category differences and similarities. We are not shown whether, in *I want to go*, the final infinitive functions as the direct object of *want*, and it is certain that a description such as 'verb x direct object x "to" x infinitive' does not reflect the functional differences underlying the superficial similarities in examples such as:

(11)   I want him to do it. I ask him to do it. I force him to do it.

1.3.3. Hornby's 1938 Verb-Pattern Scheme

The scheme of verb-patterns designed by Hornby for the *Idiomatic and Syntactic English Dictionary* was announced to the annual IRET Convention in 1938, published in the same year in the *Bulletin*, and later incorporated with only minor modifications in the dictionary itself (Hornby 1938: 20–8; 36).[14] The new system departed from Palmer's in two important respects. First, by organizing

---

[13] In *ALD 3* (1974) the patterns with *to* and *for* are VP 13A and VP 13B, respectively. The corresponding indirect-object patterns are VP 12A and VP 12B.

[14] Specimen entries for *mind* (noun) and *mind* (verb), with more examples than would eventually appear in *ISED* itself, were published in the June 1939 issue of the *IRET Bulletin* (Hornby 1939a: 156–7).

the patterns into two major blocks (transitive verbs first, intransitive verbs afterwards), Hornby made the overall arrangement more systematic (Cowie 1989*b*). Second, he went some way towards tackling the problem illustrated above in relation to Palmer's VP 17—that of assigning to one pattern sentences that were functionally distinct. In one of the few recorded instances of a theoretical disagreement between them, Hornby (1939*a*: 147–57) successfully challenged the grounds on which Palmer (1938*c*: 7–10) had asserted that *to go* in *I want to go* was not a direct object. In a reply which combined descriptive precision and pedagogical good sense, Hornby pointed out (1939*a*: 151) that 'the infinitive can in very numerous cases be replaced by an abstract noun which may be a direct object' (citing in support *They expect success* vs. *They expect to succeed*). The pedagogical good sense amounted to making clear that while it was helpful to lay out the structure of a sentence in terms of its phrase and clause constituents, it was also wise 'not to offend too much against the traditional scheme of transitive and intransitive verbs' (1939*a*: 152). Hornby did not, as it happened, confirm the transitivity of *want* or *promise* before a *to*-infinitive by applying the label 'direct object' to the latter (as Jespersen, for instance, had done, in two grammars to which Hornby referred—*Essentials of English Grammar* and *Analytic Syntax*). However, he was careful to show that cases such as *It happened to occur* and *I came to realize this* contained intransitive verbs by assigning them to a separate verb-pattern (Pattern 25). Indicating those underlying differences, if not always with the help of a clarifying label, was a significant step forward, and helped to shape developments in subsequent editions of *ALD* and in later rival publications (Hornby 1939*b*; Cowie 1992*b*).

1.4. The Pioneering English Learners' Dictionaries—Theory into Practice

1.4.1. Michael West and James Endicott's *A New Method English Dictionary*

The first monolingual learner's dictionary to appear was *A New Method English Dictionary*, compiled by Michael West and James Endicott. Containing, as we have seen, 23,898 items defined within West's controlled vocabulary of 1,490 words, this was a work intended to meet the decoding needs of the intermediate foreign student. As such it reflected West's belief in the overriding importance of developing the reading skill. The low priority assigned to encoding was evident from the uneven treatment of inflection, the absence of syntactic information, and a pronunciation scheme which was idiosyncratic and difficult to apply. By contrast, successful decoding was promoted by West's rigorously selected and tested defining vocabulary, the cornerstone of the whole work.

Turning first to the handling of inflection in *NMED*, we find that the treatment of the irregular forms of nouns, adjectives, and verbs is rudimentary in the extreme. The irregular past tense and past participle forms, for instance, do not appear in all cases where they are called for. The forms *flew* and *flown* appear in the entry for **fly**, but *had* is absent from the entry for **have**. There is no indication, either, at the points of entry, or in the preface, of the problems of pluralization associated with nouns ending in *-y* (cf. *toy, pony, turkey*) or in *-o* (cf. *tomato, banjo*). Some highly irregular plurals are included, but not others. For instance, *women* is given at **woman**, but not *men* at **man**. Finally, there is a complete absence of the syntactic information later provided in the *Grammar of English Words* and the *Idiomatic and Syntactic English Dictionary*. There are no verb-pattern codes and no markers of the difference between countable and uncountable nouns.[15]

As regards the pronunciation system, this too was unlikely to meet the encoding needs of the foreign student, even though it was said to be 'a very simple system, easily learned and unmistakably clear' (West and Endicott 1935: vii). The ingenious method adopted by West and Endicott was to replace each of the IPA symbols used for the vowels with a number (doubled when the vowel was long). The diphthongs were represented by replacing the two elements of the relevant IPA symbol (e.g. the /e/ and /i/ of /ei/) by the numbers corresponding to those elements in the simple vowel chart—in this case 21. Few consonant symbols were provided, it being assumed that most consonants would be unproblematic for learners. (Indeed, for the most part, consonants were not included in pronunciation codes in the dictionary itself.) The guide to the vowel symbols provided in the dictionary is shown in Table 1.4.

Arguably, the system is simple and clear as presented in the Guide, but there are a number of factors which make the transcriptions as they appear in entries hard to interpret. Whereas in a majority of cases—those in which the pronunciation of consonants is not problematical—consonants are not represented, in a number of entries they are. Consider, for example, **discountenance** (1–47–1–9–s), **discourage** (1–8–1j), and **discretion** (1–2shn). In these cases the final consonant—in the last entry, the final consonant cluster—is thought likely to cause difficulty. However, such codes are far from easy to decipher, as users must come to terms with the absence of some consonants and the presence of others, and they must strive to understand why final 's' is separated from the preceding vowel symbol in the first code while final 'shn' is joined to it in the third. All in all, pronunciation in *NMED* is one of its least successful features.

If *NMED* is essentially an intermediate-level dictionary for *readers*, how does its organization facilitate access to headwords and sub-headwords? As far as the arrangement of derivatives, including zero-derivatives, is concerned, the principle

---

[15] In the major revision of *NMED* which appeared under the title *An International Reader's Dictionary* in 1965, *has* and *had* appear at **have**, but not *men* at **man**. The most radical change is the introduction of IPA transcriptions.

applied more often than not is to include all derivatives of a particular simple word in the entry for that word, provided there is a recognizable orthographic link and some—if now possibly distant—semantic connection. (This 'word-family' arrangement, it will be remembered, was a standard feature of *Thousand-Word English* and the *General Service List* of 1936.) There are two flaws in the arrangement as applied to *NMED*, one to do with linguistic analysis, the other with difficulty of access. As regards the first, one sometimes finds that a simple orthographic connection between headword and derivatives is allowed to override a more fundamental semantic one. In the following entry, for instance, the meanings of the derivatives *referee* and *referendum* cannot easily be related to the senses of the headword given at (1) and (2), and arguably the derivatives should appear as separate entries:

(12) **ref′er** . . . (1) point to as a cause; (2) pass on a matter to some other person; *Let us refer the matter to Mr. X* = ask Mr. X to settle it; *He referred me to X* = told me to ask—; *To refer to a book* = look in a book for a certain fact; . . . **refer′ee** . . . judge, e.g. in a game; **reference** . . . act of referring; thing referred to (see above); . . . **refer′endum** . . . asking all the people of a country to give an opinion on a law or question of government.

As regards accessibility, we need to recall that the clustering of derivatives within

TABLE 1.4. *Guide to vowel symbols in the* New Method English Dictionary

Short	Long	Phonetic symbols	
Hit	Heed	i	iː
1	11		
Head	—	e	—
2			
Hat	—	æ	—
3			
—	Hard	—	ɑː
	44		
Hot	Hall	ɔ	ɔː
5	55		
Obey	—	o	—
6			
Hood	Hoot	u	uː
7	77		
Hut	—	ʌ	—
8			
About, Sofa	Herd	ə	əː
9 9	99		

entries, as in a number of word-lists would, if transferred to a dictionary, serve the needs of the writer (Cowie 1983*b*). When writing, we often need to be reminded of forms related morphologically to the headword either to avoid direct repetition or to achieve cohesion. When decoding, on the other hand, the orthographic form may be the only information about a word that the user possesses. Alphabetical order, as the quickest means of access to related spellings, requires that, in a reader's dictionary, derivatives are entered as headwords (Dubois 1981).

1.4.2. H. E. Palmer's *A Grammar of English Words*

A grammar, as the term is normally understood, provides a description of constituent classes (nouns, pronouns, adjectives, etc.) and the syntactic functions they fulfil (subjects, objects, complements, etc.), dealing with particular instances only insofar as they throw light on the characteristics of general categories. By contrast, Harold E. Palmer's highly original *Grammar of English Words* (1938*a*) was concerned with the particular item, not the general class, his purpose being to describe, in an alphabetical arrangement, 'the grammatical peculiarities pertaining to individual words' (1938*a*: iii). Of course, Palmer was not concerned with *all* words known to have grammatical features peculiar to themselves. His attention was confined to those thousand or so words whose associated grammatical problems were most numerous and complex, and which formed the most serious stumbling-blocks for foreign students of English.

As so often before in his research into vocabulary control, Palmer was focusing on a core vocabulary which presented difficulties not so much of meaning but of construction, word-formation, and collocation. The value of such a vocabulary was out of all proportion to its size, because, once mastered, it would ensure flexibility and acceptable standards in the *productive* use of English. Palmer makes several direct references to the encoding function of *GEW* in his Introduction—as for instance when he refers to its 'value in correction of compositions' (1938*a*: v), but it is in any case clear from many aspects of its structure and content that *GEW* is intended to serve as a writer's rather than a reader's dictionary. This degree of specialization to function has seldom been aimed at in a learner's dictionary, let alone achieved.

As we have seen, Palmer had, in his *Essay in Lexicology* (1934*c*), made various proposals concerning the design features of a 'learner's dictionary' (the term is Palmer's own). Several of these features would reappear in *GEW*: the division of the entry into numbered 'semantic varieties' ('semantic values' in the *Essay*) and the positioning of collocations either at the end of those numbered divisions or, occasionally, in place of a sense division of the headword. Verb-patterns (referred to in the *Essay in Lexicology* as 'construction formulae') were also an essential part of the design.

Verb-patterns were intended to contribute to sentence building, and in deciding how they were to be recorded in *GEW*, Palmer hit upon a method that was later to be applied, with minor or major variations, in the first four editions of *ALD* and in various rival compilations. The method was to set out the verb-patterns, with supporting examples, in a systematic arrangement outside the main text (here in an Appendix), to give each pattern a code, and then to insert the codes, as appropriate, in the verb entries themselves. In this way the dictionary user was provided with a key to detailed information about specific verbs which took up little space in the entries themselves (Cowie 1983*a*, 1984, 1987*a*). Ideally, the arrangement of the patterns in the Appendix (or Introduction) should be systematic, so that the learner, through a perception of order, might better be able to master the whole series. (We saw earlier how Palmer and Hornby agreed on the need for a systematic arrangement, but disagreed over the kind of system to adopt.)

We have already discussed Palmer's verb-pattern scheme from a linguistic standpoint. Here we shall be concerned with the arrangement and presentation of the patterns in the special Appendix, and in the entries, and with their accessibility, intelligibility, and practical usefulness to the learner. In the Appendix, Palmer provided for each of the 27 patterns a structural description and for most of them a list of examples as well. He devised a simple but effective means of linking description and examples, which was to highlight in bold print those items in the examples which realized structural elements of the pattern, which were themselves printed in capitals in a formula set just above. The effectiveness of this device can be seen from two examples provided for Pattern 7, where **beat** and **break** realize VERB, **it** and **the door** realize DIRECT OBJECT, and **flat** and **open** realize ADJECTIVE:

(13)   VERB PATTERN 7
                    VERB X DIRECT OBJECT X ADJECTIVE
         I **beat** [bend, crush, keep, pack, *etc.*] **it** [them, *etc.*] **flat**, *etc.*
         I **break** [burst, cut, push, pull] **the door** [window, box, *etc.*]
                              open.

Perhaps the relationship between general and specific is not as sharply conveyed there as in the tabular layouts later introduced by Hornby, but it is certainly clear, and it has the further advantage of setting out, as in those two examples, lists of alternative verbs, nouns, pronouns, etc., enclosed between square brackets. This bracketing is found in the dictionary itself, so that an example can become a miniature substitution-table or in Palmer's words 'a model for sentence building' (1938*a*: xi). It will be noted, incidentally, that the alternative verbs are more or less compatible with their object nouns or pronouns, and that *etc.* represents an extendable list. (For the notion of 'skeleton example', of which the patterns at (13) are one type, see 2.4.2, below.)

As for the positioning of references to the verb-pattern scheme in dictionary entries, the appropriate code, or codes, are usually positioned after the definition, as in this example:

(14) **mind** . . .
>   2. = pay attention to, notice.
>   *See V.P.* 1, 4 & 26
>   Mind!
>   Mind the step!
>   Now please mind what I say.

This entry also illustrates an early and successful attempt to marry up the appropriate patterns in a given case and their illustrative examples (cf. Cowie 1978*b*, 1989*b*). The method is to illustrate all the patterns by means of separate examples, arranged in the same order as the pattern codes. However, the positioning of VPs in *GEW* is far from consistent. In the entries for *hand* (verb) and *hang* (sense 1), VPs appear alongside examples, though not alongside every example that requires one. In general, one feels that the treatment of verb-patterns in entries in *GEW* is still at a provisional or experimental stage.

As for definitions in *GEW*, a limited defining vocabulary of the kind which features so strongly in West's *New Method English Dictionary* has no place here. This is partly because the chief purpose of *GEW* is not to clarify meanings but to explain and illustrate structure and usage. The meanings of the great bulk of the words listed in *GEW* must surely, moreover, have been known to its users. It is with that probability in mind that we should view Palmer's decision not to use definitions to clarify meaning in monosemous entries (e.g. *language, large, lend*).

There was, however semantic support of another kind in many entries, chiefly in the form of synonyms and antonyms. We shall see below with reference to *ISED* that the paradigmatic relations of dictionary entries were, until the 1970s, largely neglected in EFL dictionaries. This however is not true of *GEW*, where one is struck by the inclusion, alongside the headword, of antonyms ('SCARCE. Contrasted with PLENTIFUL'), polar opposites ('NORTH. Contrasted with SOUTH') and complementary terms ('SHUT. Contrasted with OPEN') (cf. Lyons 1977; Cruse 1986). Such information appears at the head of complex as well as simple entries and is clearly intended to extend understanding (by reference to another entry) as well as give immediate support to the writer.

Synonyms included within the entry structure are placed alongside the definition, as here: 'minute . . . 2. = a very short space of time. Cf. MOMENT.' Their function may be to draw the user's attention to areas in the polysemy of one word where the other word is, or is not, precisely equivalent. (Cf. '*It was all over in a few minutes/moments*' and '*The train was ten minutes/*moments late.*')

1.4.3. A. S. Hornby and R. Ishikawa's *A Beginner's English–Japanese Dictionary*

A. S. Hornby's name is so closely associated with the *Idiomatic and Syntactic English Dictionary* (later to receive worldwide acclaim as the *Advanced Learner's Dictionary*) that his shared authorship of an elementary-level bilingual dictionary, *A Beginners' English–Japanese Dictionary (BEJD)*, is usually overlooked, as is the fact that it was compiled and completed while work on the major monolingual work was still in progress. Appearing when it did—it went to press in 1938 and was published two years later—*BEJD* gives rise to a number of questions concerning its purpose and structure. First, why a beginners' *bilingual* dictionary? Second, what functions was it designed to serve? And, third, was the bilingual dictionary linked in content and structure to the still incomplete monolingual work?

As we have already seen, Palmer and Hornby were firmly committed to the pedagogical principle that, as far as possible, English should be learnt through the medium of English. For this reason, IRET procedures for teaching word-meanings laid special emphasis on ostensive and contextual methods and on definitions in simple English (Palmer 1927; and cf. Hornby 1947*b*). Translation was to be resorted to 'where the other three procedures are difficult, impossible or wasteful of time'—in other words it was a procedure of last resort (Hornby 1938: 22). Yet as Hornby recognized, some learners lacked regular contact with a teacher and so could not benefit from procedures which required his or her presence. For such learners, at least, he might have gone on to argue, the bilingual dictionary was a desirable—indeed essential—learning tool. However Hornby refused to concede that translation could be the *initial* means of access to new words and meanings. He thus arrived at a curious justification for *BEJD* —and one which flies in the face of much classroom experience, then and since —that it would serve 'as a reference-book, a reminder of what has already been learnt, but for the moment forgotten' (1938: 22).

A later generation of researchers has been less coy in justifying, and indeed promoting, the use of bilingual dictionaries as a source of new meanings. As many have shown, foreign learners turn chiefly to their dictionaries to clarify a point of meaning. For a wide range of medium- and low-frequency words (including many monosemous technical and scientific terms) an equivalent in the mother tongue often provides a quick and satisfactory explanation, a point which Hornby himself recognized in the introduction to *ISED* (1942). Moreover, while learners at all levels of proficiency refer to bilingual dictionaries as a source of meanings, *beginners* tend to depend exclusively on this type for semantic guidance (Bareggi 1989). Focusing as he did on lower-proficiency students and possibly too on their needs as readers of the L2, Hornby would certainly have been right to adopt a bilingual solution, though to have promoted *BEJD* for such purposes would have meant for him a fundamental change of theoretical stance.

Perhaps the true value of *BEJD* has very little to do with meanings. In the first place, and as Hornby points out, *BEJD* inherits the Palmer–Hornby preoccupation with structural and heavy-duty words. One finds, for instance, that entries for words such as *about* and *above* provide more examples than even the corresponding entries in *ISED*, while the entry for *able* contains an explanatory section

acid	5	act

The boy soon became accustomed to hard work and poor food. 少年はつらい仕事にもまづい食物にも直ぐ慣れた.

ac-id [ǽsid]【形】酸い, 酸性の.【名】❶《不算》酸. Don't use too much acid. 酸を餘り使ふな.
❷ 酸類. There are many different acids. 酸には異つたものが澤山ある.

¹a-cross [əkrɔ́s]【前】❶ 横切つて, 交叉して. There is a bridge across the river. 川に橋がかゝつてゐる. Run across the road while there's no traffic. 往來の止つてゐる間に, 走つて道を渡れ. He wrote his name across the back of the cheque. 彼は小切手の裏に自分の名を書いた. The kind girl helped the blind man across the street. 親切な少女は盲人を助けて道を横切らせた. Draw a line, and then draw another line across it. 線を一本引け, それからもう一本これと交る線を引け. ¶ across country, 眞直に, 横斷して.
❷ 向ふ側に (=on the other side of). My house is across the road. 私の家は道の向側にある. There is a forest across the river. 川向ふに森がある. ¶ come [run] across (a thing, 又は a person), 偶然に出會ふ, 偶然見つける. I came across an old friend while I was in Kobe. 神戸に居る間に偶然古い友達に廻り合つた. I came across some curious old books in a Kanda bookstore. 神田の或る本屋で珍らしい古い本を見つけた.

²a-cross【副】色々の動詞の後に附けて「横切つて, 越えて」の意を表す (一々日本語に譯さず). Come across to this side of the room. 部屋のこつち側へ來い. Bring it across to me. それを私の所へ持つて來い. The soldiers made

their way across to the opposite side of the valley. 兵士達は谷の向ふ側へと進んで行つた. Can you find your way across from Ueno to Aoyama? 君は上野から青山へ (自分で道を探して) 行けるか. I'll go across to his office and see him. 彼の事務所へ行つて會つてみよう. You must come across and see me some time. 君はいつか私の所へやつて來給へ (やつて來なくてはいけないよ).

³a-cross【副】❶ (十字に) 組んで, 交叉して. He was standing with his arms across. 彼は腕を組んで立つてゐた.
❷ 横切つて, 越えて. The river is a mile across. 川幅は一哩ある.
❸ 斜に, 傾いて.

¹act [ækt]【名】❶ 行爲, 行ひ, 動作. It is an act of kindness to help a blind man across a busy street. 盲人を助けて人通りの繁しい道を横切らせてやるのは親切な行爲だ.
❷ (戲曲の) 幕. Hamlet I. iii. (act one, scene three と讀む), ハムレット第一幕第三場.

²act【自・他】❶ 行ふ, 行動する. The time for thinking is past; we must act at once. 考へる時は過ぎた, もう我々は直ぐ實行しなくてはならぬ. He acts as a guide. 彼は案内を勤める. ¶ act on [upon] advice, 勸めに從つて行動する. ¶ ...act for, ...の代理をする.
❷ 振舞ふ. You have acted foolishly. 君は馬鹿なことをしたものだ (愚かに振舞つた). act wisely, 賢明に振舞ふ. ¶ act the fool, 馬鹿の風をする.
❸ (芝居等で或る役を) 演ずる. act a part in a play, 芝居の一役をやる. Who is acting (the part of) Hamlet? ハムレット (の役) は誰がやつてゐるか.

Fɪɢ. 1.2. Excerpt from *A Beginners' English–Japanese Dictionary* (Hornby and Ishikawa 1940) on the modal auxiliaries. It seems then that *BEJD* is in part an—admittedly modest—resource for the *writer*. This view is supported by the links with Palmer's *GEW*, to which Hornby acknowledges *BEJD*'s indebtedness, and whose productive functions it partly shares (Hornby 1938: 23).

However, the major link is probably with *ISED* itself. Hornby, as we have just seen, included a good deal of information on grammar in *BEJD* and a number of standard grammatical terms (translated into Japanese). The value of this guidance was to make it 'possible for [pupils] to understand and use verb-patterns . . . in the later years of their course' (1938: 23). To which he might have added: 'and in *ISED* also'. In other words, he probably saw the minor work as contributing to a fuller understanding and more effective use of the major one. This view of a smaller bilingual dictionary as a 'bridge' is echoed by Gabriele Stein's recent suggestion that a bilingual work, with ample explanatory material in the L1, needs to be designed to ease the transition to the monolingual learner's dictionary (Stein 1990).

It seems probable, then, that *BEJD* was partly intended to ease the transition to *ISED*. What is clear beyond doubt is that Hornby drew on the structure and content of the latter in compiling the former. By the end of 1938 he had already completed *BEJD*, and by about the same time the Verb-Pattern scheme which was later to be incorporated in *ISED* was also in place (1938: 23). It seems likely that prior to that stage Hornby, with his collaborators Gatenby and Wakefield, had gathered together entry material destined for the monolingual title, and that at least some of this material was used for its smaller predecessor. This supposition is well borne out by a close comparison of entries in the two dictionaries.

BEJD, a dictionary of 2,000 entries, drew in fact upon two sources for its content and structure. It took its word-list from the *Interim Report on Vocabulary Selection* (1936), which incorporated a 'General Service List' of 2,000 words, and certain details of its microstructure and many of its examples from the emerging *ISED*.[16] The proficiency level at which it is aimed is confirmed by the degree of support given in Japanese to the prospective user. In *BEJD*, as the extract shows, we find part-of-speech labels in Japanese, Japanese equivalents in place of the definitions, and Japanese translations positioned alongside each English example.

As regards the connection with the General Service List, a comparison between the main entries **a,an** to **²act** in the dictionary with the corresponding run in the List shows that of 29 entries in *BEJD*, 23 are also present, as entries or

---

[16] It was thus not a 'bilingualized' or 'false bilingual' work, which by definition is based on the macrostructure of an existing dictionary. Hornby's later two-language dictionary for the Japanese market, *Kaitakusha's Contemporary English–Japanese Dictionary* (*KCEJD*) (1981), which is based on *ALD 3* (1974), is bilingualized in the strict sense. The type is discussed in greater detail later (in Chapter 6) within the context of research into dictionary users and uses.

sub-entries, in the List, while of 28 entries and sub-entries in the List, 23 are also found in the dictionary.[17] As for the links with *ISED*, we note that over the same run of 29 *BEJD* entries, no less than 40 out of the 110 examples are identical with those in *ISED* as finally published (except for an occasional preference in *ISED* for such contracted forms as *won't, don't*), while a further group of 21 are undoubtedly related to examples later to appear in the monolingual dictionary. The following set of examples shows the close correspondences that are often found:

(15) *BEJD*   *ISED*
    A square has four sides.   How many sides has a square?
    A Mr. Smith called to see you.   A Mr. Smith has called to see you.
    Don't leave waste paper about.   Don't leave empty bottles and waste
                                             paper about.
    I have an account with the   I have an account with the Midland
    Yokohama Specie Bank.   Bank.

It is also worth noting that parenthetical glosses in English—a characteristic feature of *ISED*—also appear in *BEJD*, many being identical to those which eventually appeared in the major work:

(16) *BEJD/ISED*
    able . . . Is the baby able to walk yet? . . . (= can the baby walk yet?)
    Shall you be able to come (= Will it be possible for you to come) to-
    morrow?

1.4.4. The *Idiomatic and Syntactic English Dictionary*

The idea of a monolingual general-purpose dictionary designed especially for Japanese advanced learners of English first arose from discussions between Harold Palmer and Naoe Naganuma of the Kaitakusha Company (Kunio Naganuma 1978: 11). Its design specification included the distinction between countable and uncountable nouns, the presentation of as many collocations as possible and the introduction of a system of construction-patterns. In other words, the design priorities for *ISED* were points of grammar and phraseology that had figured prominently in the applied research undertaken by Palmer and Hornby.

By including the words 'idiomatic and syntactic' in the title of the first general-purpose dictionary to be compiled for advanced learners, A. S. Hornby was placing the work firmly within a line of descent running from the earliest IRET research, through several major research reports, to the small-scale spe-

---

[17] The macro- and microstructures of the two works differ: in *BEJD*, derivatives are listed as main entries; in the 'General Service List', they are nested.

cialized predecessors of *ISED* itself. He was at the same time affirming its commitment to the productive or encoding function. This would not be enough, though, for the high school, pre-university students for whom the dictionary was chiefly intended. For them, *ISED* would need to be a decoding dictionary as well, and it is greatly to Hornby's credit that he was able, while fulfilling the students' productive needs, to go a long way towards meeting their receptive needs as well. For a reading vocabulary broad enough, and diversified enough, for its intended users, Hornby turned to, and adapted, the vocabulary of the *Concise Oxford Dictionary*, the third edition of which had appeared in 1934.

The 'idiomatic' element is of such great importance in *ISED*, as in *GEW*, that a special chapter in this volume has been devoted to the theme of phraseology in the learner's dictionary, with attention given both to the treatment of word-combinations in *ISED* and *GEW* and to specialized dictionaries of idioms and collocations. In the present chapter, other key features of *ISED* will be critically surveyed, including pronunciation, the verb-pattern scheme, the language and structure of definitions, and the treatment of synonyms and antonyms.

1.4.4.1. Pronunciation

Though the emphasis which both Palmer and Hornby laid on the teaching of the spoken language is not fully reflected in the illustrative examples chosen for their dictionaries, they were careful to include phonetic transcriptions not only in *GEW* and *ISED* but also in the jointly compiled *Thousand-Word English*, where in entries for simple words such as *happy*, each of the listed derivatives is given a transcription, with stress marks as appropriate:

(17) HAPPY ['hæpi], *adj.*
      happily ['hæpili], *adv.*
      happiness ['hæpinis], *n.*
      unhappy [ʌn'hæpi], *adj.*
      unhappily [ʌn'hæpili], *adv.*
      unhappiness [ʌn'hæpinis], *n.*

Hornby also gave a detailed treatment of pronunciation in *ISED*, though as a rule, full phonetic transcriptions were confined to headwords and derivatives. The choice of model was RP—referred to by Hornby as 'Southern English', or 'what Professor Daniel Jones calls "Received Pronunciation"'(Hornby *et al.* 1942: xxvii). The use of IPA symbols was harmonized with Daniel Jones's *English Pronouncing Dictionary*, probably in its fifth edition of 1940, in which (as in all subsequent versions until the fourteenth of 1977) the following vowel pairs, which are in fact contrastive in terms of quality, were distinguished orthographically in terms of length alone: /i, i:/, /ɔ, ɔ:/, /u, u:/.

Though this was a preference he would later revise, Hornby adopted a non-IPA approach to marking stress (Windsor Lewis 1978: 183). Primary and secondary stresses were shown by placing acute and grave accents, respectively, above the relevant vowels:

(18) kɔ̀rispɔ́ndəns
     rèvəljúːʃən

Except for a key displaying and illustrating the vowel, diphthong, and consonant symbols, the guidance offered to the user in the Introduction was limited to brief notes on stress and variant forms. This was not necessarily a weakness. As Gimson would later argue: 'the foreign learner will expect his information on pronunciation to be given clearly at the point of entry and . . . not to rely on general rules stated in the Introduction' (1981: 251). Gimson went on to say that in general users were not interested in variants, either within one accent or between accents. Nevertheless, Hornby allows for variation both within the dictionary itself and in the Introduction, where he shows how parentheses may be used in transcriptions to indicate variant pronunciations, and especially the contrasts found in rapid and deliberate speech. In the case of /pous(t)póun/, for example, we are shown that the word can be pronounced with /t/ or, as in rapid speech, without /t/. Transcriptions included in the dictionary itself, with variants representing rapid speech, include /póus(t)mən/, with elided /t/, and /póus(ts)kript/, with elided /ts/.

Variation such as is found between two speakers is shown by giving two transcriptions at the point of entry. In the entries for words such as **pour** and **four**, for instance we find /-ɔə, -ɔː/, while in the entries for **poor, moor**, there is parallel variation (i.e. between /-uə/, and /-ɔː/).

ALD 1 provides a good deal of information about the pronunciation of derivatives. This is partly a result of treating many complex words as main entries. Thus, **immensity, immersion**, and **imitation** (derived from **immense, immerse**, and **imitate**, respectively) are all transcribed because they appear as main entries. But the help provided for the user goes further. If derivatives are entered as run-ons, whether defined or not, they too are transcribed, unless they are -*ly* adverbs presenting no pronunciation difficulties. Thus **imbecility**, run on at **imbecile**, is transcribed, but not **immensely**, run on at **immense**. The same descriptive fullness does not extend to compounds, which are given a transcription when they are main entries (as in the case of **post**(=)**card** /póus(t)kɑːd/), but not when they appear as part of an entry. As we shall see, *ALD 2* was to go far towards making good this deficiency.

1.4.4.2. The Verb-Pattern Scheme

The verb-pattern scheme in *ISED* is set out, with accompanying notes and examples, as part of the front matter. (Grammatical information generally, under the heading 'Notes on syntax', dominates the front matter of *ISED*.) In a style which recalls *GEW*, each pattern is identified by means of a number code, and one or more codes are included, as required, in verb entries. Alongside the similarities, though, there are important differences of content and layout. To Hornby must go the credit for first presenting patterns and illustrative examples in a series of tables. If we compare his presentation of the pattern 'Verb x Object x Adjective' with Palmer's handling (cf. 1.4.2, above) of the corresponding pattern in *GEW* (also VP 7), we can see immediately the advantages of a tabular arrangement (see Table 1.5).

The chief advantage is that the vertical divisions within the table are made to correspond to the major structural elements of the pattern. Here, the eye running down the columns easily confirms what 'Object' suggests—that here we have a set of noun phrases, in which the definite articles, where they occur, are also helpfully aligned. True, we have lost the expanded examples—the substitution tables in miniature—of the *GEW* scheme, but this is made up for by a general increase in the number of examples displayed.

Correspondences between structural elements and columns are not always as well motivated as in the VP 7 table, and throughout we find a coupling-up of subject and verb in a single column. This stratagem, as here in Table 1.5, allows the inversion of subject and verb characteristic of interrogative sentences, and the deletion of the subject associated with imperatives, to be included with plain indicatives without distortion of the tables. (Consider examples 1, 3, 4, and 8 in Table 1.5.)

Two further innovations deserve comment. The first is that, in a treatment that is generally more elaborate than Palmer's, Hornby provides detailed explanatory notes, pointing out, for instance, the various factors which determine the choice of one variant of a pattern (say, *Don't throw stones at the dog*) rather than another (*Don't throw at the dog anything that might hurt him*), or cases where the verbs used in one pattern may also function in another. Hornby also pro-

TABLE 1.5. *Verb-Pattern 7*

	Subject x verb	Object	Adjective
1	*Don't get*	*your clothes*	*dirty.*
2	*The sun keeps*	*us*	*warm.*
3	*Get*	*yourself*	*ready.*
4	*Don't make*	*yourself*	*uneasy.*
5	*I found*	*the box*	*empty.*
6	*We painted*	*the door*	*green.*
7	*They set*	*the prisoners*	*free.*
8	*Can you push*	*the door*	*open?*
9	*The cold weather turned*	*the leaves*	*red.*
10	*He wished*	*himself*	*dead.*

vides—for most of the transitive patterns that allow the passive transformation—examples illustrating its appropriate form. This guidance, which is provided in notes, is especially helpful in cases where the passive requires the introduction of initial *it* (as in Pattern 11):

(19) He saw that the plan was useless. ⇒ It was seen that the plan was useless.

This is valuable information for the advanced student (or teacher), even though individual transitive verb entries are not coded to indicate the possibility or otherwise of a passive transformation (cf. Cowie 1987*a*).[18]

As regards the inclusion and positioning of verb-pattern codes in entries, *ISED* marks a clear advance on *GEW* as regards both brevity of reference (cf. the instruction '*See V.P.* 4', in *GEW*, with the simple code 'P4', in *ISED*) and consistency of placement. With the major exception of phrasal verbs in the entries for some 'heavy-duty' verbs (e.g. *run*), verb-pattern codes are now regularly positioned, in complex entries, immediately after the numeral introducing the sub-sense and before the definition, as here:

(20) **fasten** . . . ❶ (P1, 10, 18) make fast; fix firmly; tie.

However, though the codes—here as elsewhere—are placed in the same order as in the tabular scheme, illustrative examples are not always arranged in a matching order. Nor are all the patterns always illustrated. This may be the result of competing illustrative priorities. In the case of the verb *rush* used intransitively, for instance, it is arguably vital to show a range of collocating prepositions. However, this has resulted in patterns 21 and 25 having no illustration:

(21) **'rush** . . . ❶ (P21, 23, 24, 25) go or come forward with violence; . . . *The bull rushed at him. The soldiers rushed forward. They rushed out of the room. Don't rush through your work.*

1.4.4.3. Countable and Uncountable Nouns

The distinction between 'countable' and 'uncountable' nouns—first recognized by Jespersen—had featured prominently in *GEW*, and Palmer had focused in his introductory comments on crucial differences, semantic as well as syntactic, between the categories (1938*a*: vi). Three points are of special interest in Hornby's handling of the contrast. As chief editor of a medium-sized, multi-purpose dictionary, Hornby was much more subject than Palmer had been to pressures of space, and it was Hornby who first introduced the abbreviations [C] and [U]. As for placement, the labels were positioned in a way similar to that of the verb-patterns. Thus, where a noun had more than one sense and these

---

[18] The first EFL dictionary to provide detailed information about syntactic transformations was the *Oxford Dictionary of Current Idiomatic English*, Volume 1 (1975).

differed in terms of countability, the relevant labels were inserted after the sense numbers, as here:

(22) **fresco** . . . ❶ [U] the method of painting pictures on plaster . . . ❷ [C] a picture made in this way . . . .

This was to become the standard method in later editions and titles—for VPs as for [U] and [C]—of dealing with syntactic contrasts which paralleled semantic ones. Where on the other hand, both or all of the senses in a given entry were uncountable, the label would precede the sense divisions, as in: 'friction . . . [U] ❶ . . . ❷ . . .'. This too became the standard way to deal with a recurrent relationship. However, it was only later that membership of the *countable* category by a noun in all its senses was regularly signalled by the omission of the label.

1.4.4.4. Definitions and Glosses

A hint is given in the introduction to *ISED* of its compilers' dependence on the *Concise Oxford Dictionary*, the third edition of which had appeared in 1934. There is a passage in which Hornby questions the suitability of a *COD*-style definition of *lobster* for foreign learners as against the effectiveness of a picture. There is also an acknowledgement that 'in general the COD has been followed' as an authoritative guide to hyphenation in compounds (Hornby *et al.* 1942: vi).

However, for reasons to do with the receptive needs of the advanced-level students for whom the dictionary was intended, *COD* 3 seems to have been drawn on much more extensively than those remarks suggest. It seems that the greater part of the macrostructure of *ISED* was produced by taking the *COD* 3 entry-list and deleting entries thought unsuitable for foreign learners at pre-university level. If we compare the run of entries **make²** to **mange** in both dictionaries, we find that the 115 main entries in *COD* 3 have been reduced by just under a half. Fifty-eight main entries—including such rare items as *mandola*, *mandragora*, and *manducate*, which are indeed unlikely to be useful to foreign learners —have been deleted from the *COD* 3 macrostructure and eleven compounds and derivatives added to that of *ISED*, producing a final total for the latter of sixty-eight entries. The fact that the included compounds (*make-believe*, *make shift*, *make up*, *makeweight*, *man-at-arms*, and *man-eater*) are present in the *COD* 3 entries for **make** *v.t.*, and **man¹** *n.*, respectively, points firmly to that edition as source. Further support is given to this supposition by the fact that four items from this run of entries which appear for the first time in the second edition of *ALD* (1963)—*maladjustment, maladroit, malaise*, and *malapropos*—were all in the macrostructure of *COD* 3. The assumption is that they were passed over, or put to one side, and retrieved subsequently.

A comparison of defining practice in *COD* 3 and *ISED* is informative also.

As well as confirming the former as the source of much in *ISED* that lies outside the core vocabulary of IRET research, it reveals the nature of the adaptations and replacements made to meet the special needs of its non-native users. Among the various patterns of imitation and adaptation the following are common.

In one type, the definition phrase has the same structure as in *COD* but uses simpler vocabulary:

(23) **malevolent**, a. Desirous of evil to others. (*COD* 3)
   malevolent . . . *adj.* (Cf. *benevolent.*) wishing to do evil to others; . . . (*ISED*)

But as Hornby knew, ease of understanding could depend as much on the grammatical structure of a definition as on the choice of words. In another quite common modification, illustrated here, a defining phrase containing a learned or technical abstract noun is replaced by a participial construction made up of simple words. (In this example *ISED* adds a crucial defining detail—'the right sort of food'—lacking in *COD* 3.)

(24) **malnutrition**, n. Insufficient nutrition. (*COD* 3)
   malnutrition . . . *n.* [U] not getting enough food or the right sort of food. (*ISED*)

Hornby was not tied down to the one-phrase analytical definition. Some definitions are made up of two parts, the second of which comprises a full sentence providing encyclopedic information or examples of the category being defined (cf. Cowie 1995: 289). In the entry for **malaria**, the supplementary sentence explains how the disease is transmitted. In the entry for **mammal** it provides examples of the class mammalia:

(25) **malaria** . . . *n.* . . . an illness in which there are periods of fever; it is caused by the bite of certain mosquitoes which introduce the disease into the blood. (*ISED*)

   mammal . . . *n.* . . . one of the class of animals which feed the young with milk from the breast. Human beings, dogs, bats and whales are mammals. (*ISED*)

An important difference between the two dictionaries is the much clearer marking of sub-senses in polysemous entries in *ISED*. This is achieved by the use of sharply defined white numbers in black circles: 1 2 3

(26) **manhood**, n. State of being a man (in any sense); . . . ; manliness, courage; the men of a country. (*COD* 3)
   manhood . . . *n.* [U] ❶ the state of being a man, . . . ❷ courage; the qualities that belong to a man. ❸ all the men (collectively), . . . (*ISED*)

A feature which does much to help with particular problems of definition is the attaching of parenthetical glosses to specific examples. This device was employed by Palmer in *GEW*, but is used more widely and for a greater variety of purposes by Hornby. Among the commoner functions of the gloss in *ISED* are the following:

- It may be added to an example to indicate a narrower or more specific sense than that conveyed by the definition, as in (27)(a).
- It may select one of several alternative definitions already given, as in (27)(b).
- It may serve to define the whole example rather than simply the headword (the example, in such cases, often containing, or consisting of, a compound, collocation, or idiom), as in (27)(c).
- In the latter case, the gloss may in addition include a contrasting compound, collocation, etc., as in (27)(d).

(27) (a) ¹discharge . . . ❷ give or send out. . . . *The Nile discharges itself* (i.e. flows; empties itself) *into the Mediterranean.*

(b) ¹discharge . . . ❻ send away from service or employment; dismiss; set free from duty; allow to leave. . . . *The members of the jury were discharged* (i.e. set free from their duties).

(c) ²disguise . . . ❷ [C] the clothes, false hair, actions and manner that are used. . . . *She made no disguise of her feelings* (i.e. she didn't hide them).

(d) ¹slow . . . ❷ taking a long time to cover a certain distance, as *a slow journey; a slow train* (i.e. one that stops at every station, contrasted with a fast or express train).

1.4.4.5. Synonyms and Antonyms

In an article which appeared in *English Language Teaching* in 1947, Hornby recommended a 'contextual' approach to vocabulary development based on the ideas of de Saussure. By this approach, he meant relating the teaching of a given lexical item to the systematic relations it contracted with other lexical items (e.g. synonymy and antonymy) and with its own derivatives and compounds. (It will be recalled that groupings of complex and compound words, clustered around a root, made up the structure of entries in the word-lists prepared earlier by Palmer and Hornby.) 'Paradigmatic' relations such as synonymy and antonymy were illustrated in some detail in the article, and methods proposed for presenting them in class (Hornby 1947*b*).

We have seen how this dimension of meaning was taken account of in Palmer's dictionary, where opposites of various kinds were often placed alongside headwords (1.4.2, above). However, it is broadly true that, until about the mid-1970s, Hornby largely ignored the paradigmatic relations of words (in their various senses), while attending with great thoroughness to their syntagmatic relations. Yet knowledge of words which are equivalent to, or contrastive with, a dictionary headword is every bit as essential for students wishing to write or speak in English as being informed of its collocational range or syntactic functions. (As we shall see later, Henri Béjoint in a well-known study (1981) found that 52 per cent of his student informants placed synonyms among the three most sought-after types of information.) However the treatment of synonyms (or antonyms) was not at first an urgent priority for Hornby.

So much is clear from a small-scale but revealing scan carried out of the first twenty pages from each of letters D, M, and R in *ISED/ALD 1*. In these pages, we find cross-references indicating equivalence, contrast, or inclusion in only 30 out of 993 entries, i.e. in just over 3 per cent of all the entries surveyed. The examples at (28) are from letter M, and illustrate some of the relationships represented: antonymy (*benevolent, malevolent; malign, benign*), synonymy (*manure, fertilizer*), and incompatibility among co-hyponyms (*map, plan, chart*):

(28) (a) **malevolent** . . . (cf. *benevolent.*)
           malign . . . (cf. *benign.*)
     (b) **manure** . . . (cf. *fertilizer.*)
     (c) **map** . . . (cf. *plan, chart*)

Even in such a modest spread of entries the treatment is far from consistent: several entries which the user is referred to fail to provide a cross-reference back (so, *benevolent* fails to refer the reader back to *malevolent*, and *benign* to *malign*); and as the various examples show, there is no system of labelling to distinguish one type of sense relation from another. But Hornby's fondness for an ad hoc approach to descriptive challenges as they arise can prove more of a strength than a weakness. Consider the entry for **man**. Here, Hornby skilfully illustrates the noun in its various senses by juxtaposing *man* and an appropriate converse term:

(29) **man** . . . ❹ husband (usu. in *man and wife*). ❺ a male servant or valet; a workman or employee (as in *masters and men*); . . . ordinary soldiers contrasted with their officers (as in *officers and men*); . . .

Elsewhere, Hornby conveys information about related entries through their definitions. Though there is no cross-reference between **fog** and **mist**, for example, the definition of each lexical unit is framed partly in terms of a modification of the other:

(30) **fog** . . . thick water vapour (thicker than mist) . . .
     mist . . . water vapour in the atmosphere at or near the earth's surface, . . . less thick than fog and not so light as haze.

This is learner-centred lexicography at its best, and closely reflects Hornby's 'contextual' approach to vocabulary teaching, an approach which, as we have seen, derived ultimately from the work of de Saussure.

1.5. Conclusion

The seven years which elapsed between the appearance of *NMED* and the publication of *ISED* had a longer prologue, in which—extraordinary though it may seem—a research project which had no dictionary as one of its stated objectives nonetheless produced structured lexicons which provided models for dictionary-makers to imitate and develop.

Palmer, Hornby, and West left learner lexicography permanently in their debt by adopting, during this critical period, a properly 'lexicological' approach to the study of words—insisting on rigorous categorization, resisting the lure of quantification uninformed by such rigour, and remaining alert to the possibility that every 'simple word' was part of a larger lexical complex. A principled approach to such complexes—to phraseology, in the broadest sense—was part of the legacy of Harold Palmer and A. S. Hornby especially, and it is with their contribution to this field that the next chapter begins.

2 Phraseology and the Learner's Dictionary

2.1. The Legacy of H. E. Palmer and A. S. Hornby

At one point in the Preface to the first edition of the *Concise Oxford Dictionary*, its compilers, H. W. and F. G. Fowler, referred to the difficulties posed for the writer or speaker of English by the commonest words, which were, they said,

(1) entangled with other words in so many alliances and antipathies during their perpetual knocking about the world that the idiomatic use of them is far from easy. (Fowler and Fowler 1911: v)

Here, in a memorable phrase, they identified a major obstacle to normal, native-like use of the language, and foreshadowed the intense theoretical and descriptive interest in collocations and idioms shown by later generations of dictionary-makers—though chiefly, it has to be said, by makers of dictionaries for foreign learners.

The first large-scale analysis of phraseology to be undertaken with the needs of such learners in mind dates from the 1920s. It was initiated in Tokyo by Harold E. Palmer, and later extended by his chief assistant, and eventual successor, A. S. Hornby. Its detailed findings were published as the *Second Interim Report on English Collocations* in 1933, with a revised and corrected impression following in 1935.[1] Like the *First Interim Report on Vocabulary Selection* (1930d) and the *General Service List* (1936), the *Report on Collocations* was destined to have a profound and enduring influence on EFL dictionary-making. It not only provided a detailed classification of word-combinations in English; it also with remarkable insight laid bare the widespread use of ready-made sequences in everyday speech and writing, and spelt out the implications of their prevalence for language learning and teaching. Writing on the usefulness of the *Report* for the language teacher, Palmer could justifiably claim that

(2) It will tend to confirm his impression that it is not so much the words of English nor the grammar of English that makes English difficult, but that that vague and undefined obstacle to progress in the learning of English consists

---

[1] A *First Interim Report* was issued, in mimeographed form, in 1931. Palmer later described it as 'a rough draft of a collection of collocations (culled for the most part from Saito's *Idiomological Dictionary*)' (1934d: 20).

for the most part in the existence of so many odd comings-together-of-words. (1933*c*: 13; cf. 1933*a*, *b*)

The *Second Interim Report on English Collocations* was a major landmark, and though its significance has been lost sight of at various times since, it shaped the treatment of phraseology in the highly innovative dictionaries of Palmer and Hornby, and then, in combination with other influences, formed the theoretical basis of the English 'phraseological' dictionaries of the 1970s and 1980s. Certain of its key ideas are also now present in an approach to language teaching which argues that since memorized word-combinations (the 'collocations' of the *Interim Report*) play a crucial part in language acquisition and use (Pawley and Syder 1983; Peters 1983) they are a vital element in any syllabus, reference work, or language teaching programme (Cowie 1988; Nattinger 1988).

Palmer's interest in what he informally termed 'comings-together-of words', but formally and technically referred to as 'collocations', dated back to the IRET Convention of 1927, at which it was decided that one aim of the Institute's research activity should be the compilation of a list of collocations (Palmer 1929*b*, 1933*c*: 1). It was this project that A. S. Hornby was invited to join in 1931. It was not, though, the only focus of interest in the partnership with Palmer which then began. As we have seen, Hornby was also interested in vocabulary selection and limitation, and collaborative work on the one-thousand-word list went ahead in parallel with the collocations research. Given the close association, in the experience of both men, between the selection of words and the analysis of their combinatorial possibilities, it was not surprising that a collection of idioms and phrasal verbs—contributed by Hornby—formed a major element in the 'General Service List' produced by Palmer, West, and others as part of the *Interim Report on Vocabulary Selection* of 1936, or that phraseology was to become a central feature of the earliest learners' dictionaries.

When A. S. Hornby joined the collocations project, some 5,000 collocations had already been gathered from Professor Hidesaburo Saito's *Idiomological English–Japanese Dictionary* (Palmer 1933*b*, 1934*d*).[2] According to the 1933 version of the *Report*, however, only 3,879 collocations of all types were eventually included in it. The discrepancy is probably explained by the fact that the initial 5,000 items (to which we must assume Hornby and his four fellow-researchers added many more between 1931 and 1933) contained numerous proverbs, catchphrases, and other sentence-like expressions (cf. 2.3, below), that were subsequently sifted out to give the much reduced total. What is clear beyond doubt is that Hornby (and his wife) were major contributors to the substantially

---

[2] The edition of Saito referred to must have been the first, of 1915. A revised edition did not appear until 1936.

enlarged revision of 1935.[3] According to the *IRET Bulletin*, Hornby and his wife were 'entrusted with the revision of the work on collocations' (words which suggest they were put in charge). Between 1934, when they took control, and the publication of the revised and corrected *Report* a year later, the total number of items grew from 3,879 to 5,749 (Palmer 1933*c*).

2.2. The *Second Interim Report on English Collocations*: The Descriptive Scheme

Palmer's approach to the definition of collocations tells us a good deal about his perception of himself as an 'applied' linguist. He was of course fully aware of the structural (and functional) diversity of word-combinations and recognized the need for a classification (1933*c*: 4). At the same time, his approach to the definition of the category as a whole was not linguistic but pedagogical. He defined these 'successions of words' in terms of the learning difficulty they represented and the approach that needed to be taken to mastering them. His terse formulation is proclaimed from the cover of the *Interim Report* and its title-page: 'A collocation is a succession of two or more words that must be learned as an integral whole and not pieced together from its component parts.' As his definition also shows, Palmer was careful to point out what collocations were not (as well as what they were). Free combinations were a manifestation of the language system and could be put together 'by dint of the application of the commonest and best-known rules of grammar' (1933*c*: 5).

Apart from the problem of definition, there was the question of a suitable choice of name. Despite the widespread use, then and since, of 'idiom' and its derivatives as generic terms (consider the 'idiomological' of Saito's title and the 'idiomatic' of *Idiomatic and Syntactic English Dictionary*), Palmer was unwilling to employ idiom as the term for his most inclusive category, since in his view this would have meant broadening its application to cover proverbs, sayings, and figurative expressions, all of which featured in the original IRET collection (Palmer 1933*c*: 5). By contrast, 'collocation' had no settled status as a generic label. Its use was already attested in the sense 'the arrangement of words in a sentence' (*OED*, s.v. **collocation**), though not yet as a technical term in modern linguistics (cf. Firth 1951).

The subsequent development of the term, however, took a different course from the one indicated by Palmer, and it will be part of the aim of this chapter

---

[3] In an interview given some 40 years later, Hornby recalled combing through the *Shorter Oxford Dictionary* and 'the big *Webster*' (Hornby and Ruse 1974: 3). As the *Shorter Oxford* was first published in February 1933, and the second edition of *Webster's New International Dictionary* in 1934, these resources are likely to have been drawn on during this second stage of enlargement.

to trace that course. For the moment, it is enough to say that few linguists would now apply collocation to the whole spectrum of items surveyed in the *Interim Report*. Many would now limit the term to word-combinations which are not idioms (i.e. not structurally invariable and semantically opaque) but which cannot be explained by general rules of combination either (Benson 1989; Cop 1990; Cowie 1981, 1986, 1994, 1998*a*; Hausmann 1979, 1989). According to this view, collocations are ready-made, memorized word-groups (e.g. *hold a conversation, a tidy sum*), in which one word—here the verb and adjective respectively—has a sense found only in combination with the other word, or with very few similar words (cf. *hold a discussion, a tidy amount*), a limitation which explains the 'restricted' of restricted collocation.[4] Collocations are midway between idioms and 'free combinations' (e.g. *buy a newspaper, the next house*), which fall outside the scope of the *Report* altogether. Because of the narrowing which the sense of collocation has undergone, it seems sensible, whenever confusion can arise, to use 'word-combination' in the all-embracing sense which Palmer gave to collocation (Ter-Minasova 1992; Cowie 1994).

These reservations, though, should not blind us to the virtues of Palmer's framework. One is that Palmer recognized the value of classifying the material along syntactic lines. Most of the major subdivisions of the *Report* are based on syntactic patterns ('colligations' in the Firthian sense) of which the listed collocations are specific instances. So, for example, subdivision number 3121.1 is headed by the formula VERB x SPECIFIC NOUN (x PREP x N3) and includes these examples:

(3) To earn one's living
     To enforce [the, *etc.*] law
     To entertain a belief
     To entertain a fear (x for N3)
     To entertain a hope [suspicion, doubt, *etc.*]

Here the material is analysed precisely and with an eye to different kinds of variable. When, for example, the combination is complete in itself but is optionally followed by a preposition and another noun, the appropriate preposition and 'N3' are added in parentheses, as in the fourth example. When, on the other hand, one or more alternatives may replace the specific noun (or another element), those choices are shown in square brackets, as in the second and fifth examples. These devices are simple and consistently applied, and were later to be used in learners' dictionaries by both Palmer and Hornby.

---

[4] The term 'heteroseme', as used by Palmer, comes closest to collocation in this sense, because 'at least one of the component words assumes a new and particular meaning by reason of being collocated with the other component or components'. Consider, in this respect, the *light* of *light-fingered* and the *Civil* of *Civil Service* (Palmer 1933*c*: 8).

Palmer spoke with some scorn of 'idiom lists' (1933*c*: 11) and clearly objected to the term itself because of its loose application to word-combinations of various types and even to 'peculiar construction patterns . . . likely to puzzle a foreign student' (Palmer 1938*a*: xii). This antipathy to an often misused label—and his own inclusive use of 'collocation'—may have helped to divert Palmer from a problem of definition which lurks on almost every page of the *Interim Report.* Consider, from the subsection just referred to, the examples 'To hold one's tongue' and 'To lose sight x of x N3'. The first has developed a sense ("be silent") which is no longer straightforwardly relatable to the literal holding of one's tongue (and is to that extent an 'idiom'), while the second seems to have two possible uses. In (4)(a), below, *lose sight of* is a collocation; in (4)(b), it is an idiomatic extension of that collocation.

(4) (a) Now don't lose sight of the rabbit!
     (b) She seems to have lost sight of the main purpose of the campaign.

The difference, as in those examples, between collocations in the narrow sense and idioms is of vital importance to foreign learners, and examples of both are mixed together in many sections of the *Interim Report.* However, failure to recognize this distinction in theory did not necessarily result in its being overlooked lexicographically. Like Palmer in *A Grammar of English Words*, Hornby in the *Idiomatic and Syntactic English Dictionary* was to have little difficulty in recognizing the most idiomatic word-combinations. More often, the problem for both lexicographers, as for the general run of language learners, was one of distinguishing collocations that were somewhat restricted from those that were open or free.

2.3. Phraseology in *A Grammar of English Words*

Harold Palmer's *A Grammar of English Words* (*GEW*), published in 1938, provided the first opportunity to use the material classified in the *Interim Report,* and to demonstrate in a practical form the importance he and A. S. Hornby attached to collocations in the learning and teaching of English. As we have seen, *A Grammar of English Words* included a great deal of specific information on the syntax, meaning, and phraseology of a core vocabulary of about 1,000 words, items which, until that time, had not been given the attention they deserved in either dictionaries or grammars (Palmer 1938*a*: iii), despite Henry Sweet's recognition, forty years earlier, of their fundamental importance to the foreign learner (Sweet 1899).

There was much to admire in the arrangement and presentation of word-combinations in *GEW*. Idioms in the strict sense were distinguished by the use of bold print and very few were not given due prominence by this means. The conventions of arrangement were close to, and possibly modelled on, those of *COD*. Idioms were placed within the entry for the principal open-class word they contained—usually the noun, if there was one—and arranged according to the sense of the headword to which they were judged to be closest. (In this respect, compare *bear in mind* and *so many men, so many minds* in the following entry.)

(5) **mind** [maind], **minds** [maindz], *n.*
   1. = consciousness, thought, memory
      Body and mind.
      An idea has just come into my mind.
      I don't know what to do to fix this in my mind.
   ¶¶ **bear [keep] in mind**
      You might bear [keep] this in mind.
   ¶ **out of one's mind**
      He is [has gone] out of his mind [He has become insane]. . . .
   2. = decision, opinion
   Phr. **So many men, so many minds.**
   ¶ **make up one's mind** (to . . .) [decide] . . .

We can also see from this entry that the same typographical conventions were used as in the *Interim Report* to mark optional elements (parentheses, as after **make up one's mind**) and alternative lexical material (square brackets, as in **bear [keep] in mind**). These devices were to be retained in the *Idiomatic and Syntactic English Dictionary*, and so too was the practice of placing idioms and collocations in those parts of the entry to which they seemed closest in meaning.

   As an additional phraseological category, *GEW* introduced the helpful and well-defined 'phrase' (abbreviated in the dictionary as *Phr.*), a class made up of word-combinations, usually of sentence length, which functioned as conversational formulae, sayings, and proverbs. Palmer had already written illuminatingly of conversational formulae, and produced a number of gramophone records illustrating their use (1933*a*). They include such expressions as *I beg your pardon* and *I must apologize*, which are recognized in the work of present-day phraseologists as 'speech formulas' (Pawley and Syder 1983) or 'routine formulae' (Gläser 1986).[5]

   Suitable labels and the use of bold print were helpful aids to location. However, unambiguous treatment of restricted collocations was hindered by the theoretical difficulties mentioned earlier, which sometimes led to collocations and free combinations appearing side by side in illustrative sentences without any distinguishing typography. In the following extract from *GEW*, the second,

---

[5] As we have seen, 'phrases' (or 'sentence-like' expressions) were not included in the *Second Interim Report*. However, Palmer returned in 1942 to the task of defining them and produced a detailed subcategorization. Regrettably, it has never been published in full (Bongers 1947).

third, fifth, and sixth examples represent free combinations of words, while the first and fourth contain restricted collocations (my italics):

(6) **hair** . . . *n*. . . . .
  That man has *red hair*.
  He had his hair cut.
  She is letting her hair grow.
  My dog has *a good head of hair*.
  I found a long black hair in my soup.
  She found two long black hairs on his coat.

The lack of some such distinctive marking could cause difficulties for a learner wishing to write in English, who might assume variation in, say, *a good head of hair* (*?a bad head of hair*) comparable to that in *have one's hair cut, trimmed, dyed, washed*, etc. However, a measure of the overall quality of *GEW* is that in a number of entries it provides a partial solution to the problem of indicating limited variation—grammatical as well as lexical—in restricted collocations. Consider the entry **harm** *n*. Here a number of collocations are presented in a maximally reduced form with a lower-case initial letter (thus, *do sy. harm, mean no harm*), and are then expanded into full sentences by way of illustration (*He did me no harm, He probably meant no harm*):[6]

(7) (a) **I. harm**
  do sy. harm . . .
  do harm to sy. . . .
  Did the storm do any harm to the corn?
  He did me no harm.
  mean no harm.
  He probably meant no harm.

I have suggested this is a partial solution, since the relationship between the 'skeleton' examples and their expansions is not made fully explicit. Italic print would have helped to make the learner aware of each minimal correct form (e.g. *do sy. harm*) while strict juxtaposition would have made clear the permitted expansions:

(7) (b) *do sy. harm* . . .
  He did me no harm.
  do harm to sy.[sth.] . . .
  Did the storm do any harm to the corn?
  mean no harm.
  He probably meant no harm.

---

[6] In a deeply perceptive paper published two years before *GEW*, Palmer had distinguished between 'skeleton-type' examples (of which *mean no harm* is an instance) and 'sentence-sample' examples (Palmer 1936*b*).

2.4. Collocations and Idioms in the *Idiomatic and Syntactic English Dictionary*

GEW was a specialized dictionary, one which, precisely because it focused on the core of the lexicon, provided an exceptionally rich treatment of word-combinations. The *Idiomatic and Syntactic English Dictionary* (*ISED*), by contrast, was a general-purpose dictionary for the advanced foreign learner. Yet it too gave great prominence to phraseology, and deserves close examination, both because it established precedents for the subsequent treatment of word-combinations in general EFL dictionaries and because certain of its features set a pattern for the phraseological dictionaries of the 1970s and 1980s.

2.4.1. *ISED*: Sources of Data

The phraseological research carried out by Palmer and Hornby, though originally intended for teachers of English and compilers of restricted vocabularies, was clearly too valuable to be ignored during the compilation of *ISED*, and there is evidence that extensive use was made of it, though material was drawn from other sources as well. Some idea of the use made of the *Second Interim Report* by Hornby and his fellow compilers can be gained by taking items from the *Report* and asking whether or not they are included in the dictionary. The left-hand column in Table 2.1 shows a random selection of 20 word-combinations from Pattern 3121.1 of the *Report* (the verb + object noun pattern). The right-hand column indicates whether the combinations appear in the dictionary, and if so in what form.

We can see that of the twenty items selected from the *Report*, seventeen also appear in the dictionary. Only one combination ('to clap one's hands') is not illustrated at all, while in two further cases ('to extend an invitation' and 'to follow someone's example') collocations present in the *Report* are matched by related ones (consider *extend a warm welcome to someone* and *follow a person's advice*).

A further point worth noting is the choice of bold print—reflecting Palmer's earlier use of the convention—to mark either idiomaticity, or an extreme degree of fixity, in given cases. The items **beat time, catch fire,** and **find fault (with)**, though not opaque and not in all cases fixed—the first two are relatable to *keep time* and *set fire to* respectively—are certainly more frozen than most of those appearing in italic.[7]

This then is the position when one moves from the *Report* to *ISED*: almost complete coverage of the (admittedly small) sample and an accurate reflection of degrees of idiomaticity. But if one starts from the dictionary and moves back

---

[7] The collocation *drop a hint* is also invariable, though not opaque.

TABLE 2.1. *Random choice of verb + object-noun combinations from the*
Interim Report

Verb + object combinations in the *Interim Report*	Examples (*italic*) and sub-entries (**bold**) in *ISED*
to beat time	**beat time**
to break the law	*to break a law*
to catch (a) cold	*to catch (a) cold*
to catch fire	**catch fire**
to clap one's hands	—
to drop a hint	*I dropped him a hint*
to earn one's living	*to earn one's living*
to extend an invitation	(*extend a warm welcome to someone*)
to find fault	**to find fault (with)**
to follow someone's example	(*follow a person's advice*)
to grant a request	*to grant a request*
to hold one's breath	*to hold one's breath*
to hold a conversation	*to hold a conversation*
to lay an egg	*Hens lay eggs*
to lend a hand	*Lend a hand*
to miss one's train	*He missed the 9.30 train*
to raise money	*to raise the money (for)*
to raise one's voice	*to raise one's voice*
to speak the truth	*to speak the truth*
to tell a lie	*to tell the truth* [*a lie*]

to the *Report*, quite a different picture emerges, as can be seen from Table 2.2. Here, twenty verb + object collocations gathered randomly from the entries for *break, catch, follow, miss, pass,* and *pay* have been listed. Of those twenty collocations, only five are also found in the *Interim Report*.

Two questions are raised here. First, why were such familiar collocations as *break a journey* and *break one's fall* not included in the *Interim Report*? And second, where were they eventually found by the compilers of *ISED*? The answer to the first question throws interesting light on the data-gathering methods of the early ELT researchers. Of the three sources of items then available to phraseologists—written texts, intuition, and other dictionaries—Palmer and Hornby seem to have depended largely, if not exclusively, on existing reference works for the items themselves but to have drawn later on personal intuition for supporting examples (cf. Drysdale 1987; Cowie 1989a). As we have already seen, Hornby's later recollections of his research refer only to dictionaries (Hornby and Ruse 1974). Choice, then, was determined by the works consulted. Were the missing items, then, culled from other dictionaries at a later stage? Saito's *Monograph on Prepositions* (1932), of which Hornby's own marked-up copy survives,

TABLE 2.2. *Verb + object-noun combinations in six selected verb entries in* ISED

Verb + object collocations in *ISED*	Present in (= ✓), absent from (=X), *Interim Report*
break a promise	X
break one's word	X
break a rule	X
break a journey	X
break one's fall	X
catch the train	✓
catch the post	X
catch someone's meaning	X
follow a trade	X
follow an argument	X
follow the fashion	✓
miss one's footing	X
miss the point	X
miss the target	X
pass judgement	X
pass an opinion	X
pass the time	✓
pay a compliment	✓
pay the penalty	X
pay a visit	✓

throws interesting light on this question.[8] The date 'Oct. 1st 1936', added in pencil at the end of the Publisher's Note, suggests that the copy was being used at least a year after the appearance of the revised *Interim Report*, i.e. that Hornby was still gathering material after the formal conclusion of his research. Some support is given to this view by the fact that, of the following set of collocations introduced by a preposition—none of which is in the *Report* but all of which are in *ISED* in the sequence *default* to *demand*—those to the left are all ticked in Hornby's copy of Saito:

(8) in default of   by default
     in defence of   in defeat
     in deference to   with deference
     in defiance of   in degradation
     to a degree   without delay
     on delivery   of some delicacy
     on demand   in [great, much] demand

---

[8] I am indebted to Simon Nugent, a former OUP editor, for kindly presenting me with this monograph.

It is possible, too, that a companion work compiled by Saito—*Studies in Radical English Verbs* (1933)—was the source of some of the verb + object-noun collocations included in *ISED* but absent from the *Report*. Certainly, all the collocations listed in Table 2.2 apart from *break a rule, catch the post,* and *miss the target* are listed in Saito's monograph (cf. Hornby 1937a).[9]

2.4.2. *ISED*: Collocations in Phrase and Clause Examples

Apart from the prolonged labour of gathering collocations, A. S. Hornby had to address the problem of presenting them in such a way that major structural differences—and the different learning problems they gave rise to—could be recognized and dealt with by the student. The solutions he arrived at, with their remarkable harmonization of descriptive and pedagogical needs, represent a major step forward in dictionary design.

As the *Interim Report* indicated, restricted collocations are of many structural types, but a helpful distinction can be drawn between 'lexical' and 'grammatical' collocations (Benson 1985; Cowie 1990). The former consist of two (or more) open-class words, such as the verb + object-noun combinations discussed earlier in this section (thus, *break a journey, miss the point*). The latter are made up of an open-class word (noun, verb, or adjective) and a closed-class word, and are represented by the preposition + noun collocations also noted earlier (e.g. *to a degree, on delivery*). The two types represent quite different learning problems. In the lexical type, both parts of the collocation need to be known. When one is writing in the foreign language ('encoding'), the verb has to be known because it represents, for the writer, an idiosyncratic choice (one 'pays' compliments just as one 'follows' a profession). But the noun also needs to be known because it may be one of a very limited set of options (the nouns *profession, trade,* and *calling*—but very little else—are possible collocates of *follow* in the appropriate sense) (Cowie 1981, 1986). In dealing with the grammatical type (say the preposition + noun pattern), knowledge of the appropriate preposition is essential for encoding, but it is often fixed (as in the examples shown). Even a limited set of alternative prepositions is unusual in such patterns. These differences, of course, have important implications for the treatment of lexical and grammatical collocations in EFL dictionaries.

When we examine the treatment of verb + noun (and adjective + noun) collocations in *ISED*, we come upon one of the most noteworthy design features of the dictionary. A recent analysis of examples in the first edition of the *Advanced Learner's Dictionary* (a photographic reproduction of *ISED* published

---

[9] I am grateful to Professor Mamoru Shimizu, a colleague of A. S. Hornby's and a former director of the English Language Exploratory Committee, for sending me a copy of *Studies in Radical English Verbs.*

by OUP in 1948 for distribution worldwide) has shown that Hornby consistently used examples of four basic structural types: complex and compound words, noun phrases, *to*-infinitive clauses, and full sentences, and that he tended to assign these to specific functions (Cowie 1995). Broadly speaking, phrase and clause examples in *ISED/ALD 1* are minimal lexicalized patterns (i.e. 'skeleton' examples) whose purpose is to assist in the interpretation or correct use of the headword. Sentences can fulfil this function too, but because of their grammatical completeness can come closer to simulating speech and writing and can convey cultural information more fully and explicitly (Cowie 1995: 286). Phrase and (subjectless) clause examples in *ISED* are distinguished by the use of introductory 'as', a device borrowed from the *Concise Oxford Dictionary* (1934), though in fact used by lexicographers as early as the eighteenth century. Consider, for example:

(9) **brew** . . . prepare, (by mixing, boiling, etc.) a drink, as *to brew tea* [*beer*].
   lusty . . . healthy and strong; full of vigour, as *a lusty young man; lusty cheers*
   luxurious. . . supplied with luxuries; splendid and comfortable, as *a luxurious hotel; . . . luxurious food*.
   ²**rear** . . . breed; grow; bring up; foster, as *to rear poultry*.

In the first and fourth examples here, we find a simplified clause structure consisting of a transitive verb in the active infinitive form, and a noun with minimal modification as direct object. The adjective + noun phrases (examples two and three) are similarly reduced. Simplification of this kind has parallels not only with the *Concise Oxford Dictionary* but also with dictionary traditions in other countries, and specifically with the French 'dictionnaire de langue', represented today by the *Petit Robert*, and the Italian 'dizionario scolastico', of which Palazzi's *Dizionario della lingua italiana* is a current example (Cowie 1996). The conventions in *ISED* also recall Palmer's use (in *GEW*) of 'skeleton-type' examples to indicate the minimal permitted core of a collocation.

Phrase and clause examples account for a high proportion of the examples in *ISED*. In the analysis referred to earlier, in which a continuous run of 506 entries and sub-entries was examined, there were 95 phrases, 34 clauses, and 115 sentences out of a total of 258 examples (Cowie 1995: 286). The prominence given to phrases and clauses in *ISED*—and their characteristic structure—give ample support to the view that Hornby assigned specific example types to particular functions and that the specific function of clauses and phrases was to serve as simplified lexical frames for comprehension and sentence building.

Cutting across the division between phrases, clauses, and sentences was another characteristic *ISED* device. Its purpose was to represent the 'collocational range' (the spread of lexical items) from which the individual collocations of a word are formed. The method (which has already been noted as a descriptive device in the *Interim Report* and in *GEW*) was to enclose a set of alternative words in square brackets at the end, occasionally in the middle, of an example phrase or clause:

(10) **gentle** . . . *a gentle nature* [*heart, look, voice, call, touch*]
     ²**love** . . . *to love comfort* [*golf, playing tennis, sea-bathing*]

The convention had certain drawbacks. It did not, for instance, point up the difference between a collocational range which was semantically mixed (as in the second example) and greatly extendable, and a range in which the words were related in sense and where there might be arbitrary limitations on choice (as in the first example: consider, for instance, ?*gentle feelings*, ?*gentle eyes*). But it is asking a great deal of a general EFL dictionary to expect it to provide detailed information on collocability, since many other types of information have equally strong claims on the available space (Cowie 1978*b*, 1983*b*). Though the need was not perceived until the late 1970s, there was scope for specialized dictionaries which could concentrate simply on collocations causing difficulties for learners wishing to speak or write English, including those (such as *conduct an experiment*, and *perform an operation*) where encoding problems were caused by arbitrary restriction on choice (c.f. *conduct a task and *perform a survey).

As regards the treatment of grammatical collocations—noun + preposition, verb + preposition, etc.—a method already existed in the third edition of the *Concise Oxford Dictionary* (1934) for indicating prepositions which were part of the complementation of nouns or verbs. These were included in the definition but marked off by means of italic print:

(11) **manage²**, *v.t. & i.* . . . place (person, thing) in competition *with*; . . .

As we have already seen, this edition of *COD* was used by Hornby and his colleagues in the compilation of *ISED*, and they would have been aware of this method of treating complementation. However, the method was not imitated. Instead, grammatical collocations such as *manage with* were illustrated by means of examples:

(12) **manage** . . . *v.t. & i.* . . . ❷ (P 21, 23, 25) deal with affairs; succeed in; con-
     trive. *I shan't be able to manage* (i.e. do what is necessary) *without help. If
     I can't borrow the money we shall have to manage without. We can't manage
     with these poor tools.*

There is much to be said for this approach—particularly when the various types of complementation allowed by the verb can all be illustrated. Here we are shown that *with* has an opposite in *without*, and that the latter can be used without a prepositional object (. . . *we shall have to manage without*). All the same, it has taken three natural examples to reflect this patterning, and there is nothing to show that the prepositions *with* and *without* are both deletable in cases where their objects are recoverable from the context. Consider: *I can't borrow the money so we shall just have to manage (without/without it)*. One way of reconciling explicitness with economy is to enclose deletable elements in brackets—as in this example—and in fact this was the solution commonly applied from the third edition of *ALD* (1974) onwards.

ISED marked a significant stage on the way to the specialized phraseological dictionary. Word-combinations, whether idioms, collocations, or speech formulae, make up a substantial part of its total word-stock—in the entry for the verb *break* alone, no less than 47 out of a total of 59 examples are 'phraseological'. In addition, and building on Palmer's pioneering achievement, Hornby gave a separate status—easily recognized by the learner—to lexical collocations, and developed the conventions already in existence for signalling limited variation. In these various ways, he was demonstrating his commitment to a model of the general-purpose dictionary which gave due weight to the *productive* needs of the foreign learner and, at the same time, helping to pave the way for the dictionaries of idioms and collocations of the 1970s and 1980s.

2.5. The *Oxford Dictionary of Current Idiomatic English*, Volume 1

The first response to the need for a specialized dictionary of word-combinations came in the late 1950s from Ronald Mackin, formerly an EFL specialist with the British Council but at the time teaching in the School of Applied Linguistics at Edinburgh University. Mackin had assembled—initially on paper slips—a corpus of some 30,000 citations from written texts with the aim of producing a dictionary of multi-word items that were in the broadest sense 'collocations'.

As an applied linguist who had professional links with A. S. Hornby, and who was later to edit two classic texts by Harold Palmer, Mackin was well aware of the analytical problems, on several levels, that faced anyone venturing into the domain of phraseology.[10] As the *Second Interim Report* had demonstrated, ready-made word-combinations occur in a broad spectrum of syntactic structures, of which *a busted flush, a running sore, spill the beans, give someone the eye*, and *come into money* are a modest sample. How could such a diversity of patterns be satisfactorily described in a phraseological dictionary for advanced learners? And there was the lingering problem of idiomaticity—the key theoretical issue that Palmer and Hornby had left unresolved. How were the more idiomatic items to be distinguished from the less idiomatic?

---

[10] Ronald Mackin collaborated with Hornby on a course for adult learners (Hornby and Mackin 1964) and knew J. R. Firth, whose colleague he was for a brief period in 1958 (Mackin 1983).

2.5.1. *ODCIE 1*: Problems of Grammar and Idiomaticity

At least part of the great range of expressions collected by Ronald Mackin lent itself to treatment in a separate volume (to appear in 1975 as Volume 1 of the *Oxford Dictionary of Current Idiomatic English*, or *ODCIE 1*, and in a later edition, in 1993, as the *Oxford Dictionary of Phrasal Verbs*). Combinations of verb + adverbial particle (e.g. *peter out, take someone off*) or verb + preposition (e.g. *run into someone, get somebody through something*), sometimes referred to collectively as 'phrasal verbs', can be related to each other grammatically in a systematic way. They were therefore gathered together by Mackin in a separate alphabetical list at an early stage (Mackin 1983). However, the scheme of linked construction-patterns that was to knit the first volume together had still to be elaborated. I devised such a system as part of a postgraduate dissertation in Edinburgh in 1964, and when in the same year Ronald Mackin invited me to begin with him the actual task of compiling *ODCIE 1*, this system was adopted for the volume (Cowie 1978a, 1993).

A brief description of 'phrasal' and 'prepositional' verbs—but one which was to prove influential—had already been published by the Firthian linguist T. F. Mitchell (1958). Mitchell recognized four structural types featuring a verb with an adverbial particle or preposition (see Table 2.3).

TABLE 2.3. *Phrasal and prepositional verbs (after Mitchell 1958)*

Categories	Examples
Phrasal verb intransitive	*The plane took off.*
Phrasal verb transitive	*Fred took off Jim/Fred took Jim off.*
Prepositional verb	*Fred took to Jane (in a big way).*
Phrasal-prepositional verb	*Fred took up with Jane.*

This analysis was firmly supported by syntactic evidence, but it could be challenged on two levels. First, it was arguable that two further patterns should be recognized (and incorporated in any 'phrasal verb' dictionary):

- a 'prepositional' type in which a noun-phrase object came between the verb and the preposition:
  Prepositional verb transitive   *Fred got both students through the test.*
- a 'phrasal-prepositional' type in which a noun-phrase object came between the particle and the preposition:
  Phrasal-prepositional verb transitive *Fred took out his irritation on Jim.*

But Mitchell's analysis could also be questioned at a deeper level. Part of his argument for recognizing the category 'phrasal verb transitive' (e.g. *The boss passed over my brother* (i.e. for promotion).) was that it contrasted syntactically with 'non-phrasal verb + preposition' (e.g. *The plane passed over the house.*). Now there is certainly a syntactic difference here. We can move the final noun phrase in front of *over* in the first sentence but not in the second. Compare:

(13) (a) The boss passed my brother over.
     (b)*The plane passed the house over.

Further evidence for the difference is the contrastive positioning of pronouns used in place of the noun phrases in the two cases:

(14) (a) The boss passed him over.
     (b) The plane passed over it.

It is on the basis of these contrasts that *over* can be said to function as an adverbial particle in (13)(a) and (14)(a) but as a preposition in (13)(b) and (14)(b) (Cowie 1975: viii). However, we cannot use this evidence, as Mitchell did, to support a claim that the first *pass over* ('not consider someone for promotion') is a unit of grammar and meaning (i.e. an idiom), as is implied by the term 'phrasal verb'. If we did, we would have to explain why *pass over* in the example

(15) Bill passed over the bread/Bill passed the bread over/Bill passed it over.

– which clearly is *not* an idiom—behaves syntactically in exactly the same way as the homonymous *pass over* (*my brother*)—which clearly *is* an idiom:

(16) The boss passed over my brother/The boss passed my brother over/
     The boss passed him over.

These conclusions had an important bearing on the way idiomaticity itself was regarded and defined in *ODCIE 1*. If the difference between particles and prepositions had little connection with whether the combinations they formed with verbs were idiomatic or not, the difference between idioms and non-idioms must have a different, lexico-semantic, basis. This could be determined in individual cases by applying the formal procedures or tests quite widely adopted by Firthian linguists in the 1960s and 1970s for identifying linguistic categories of various kinds (F. R. Palmer 1965; Mitchell 1966, 1971; Mackin 1978). The test of substitution, for example, would show that *passed* could be replaced by the synonymous *handed* in *Bill passed over the bread*, but not in *The boss passed over my brother*, and this would help to distinguish non-idiomatic from idiomatic *pass over*. Similarly, the test of deletion would show that the particle could be removed from the non-idiom, with little change of sense, but not from the idiom (cf. *Bill passed the bread.* and **The boss passed my brother.*) (Cowie 1993).

2.5.2. *ODCIE 1*: The Treatment of Grammar and Context

When it came to devising a method of presenting the syntactic contrasts between verbs with particles and prepositions to the foreign student, the compilers of

ODCIE 1 had a model in the *Advanced Learner's Dictionary* (second edition) with its scheme of number/letter 'codes' representing a variety of verb-patterns. Codes incorporating letters and numbers were also devised for *ODCIE 1*, to account for the different sentence patterns in which verbs with particles and/or prepositions could occur. However, it was possible to devise a set of codes that was simpler and more systematic than in *ALD*, since there were only two syntactic variables to account for: verb transitivity and the choice between particle and preposition. The letters A and B were chosen to represent intransitive and transitive patterns respectively (cf. *The bridge blew up, They blew the bridge up*), and 1, 2, or 3 were added to indicate whether the sentence pattern contained a particle, a preposition, or a particle *and* a preposition (see Table 2.4). The codes were then introduced singly, or in combination, into dictionary entries.

A number of abbreviations were also introduced into entries to indicate that they could undergo one or more specified transformations. (*ODCIE 1* was the first EFL dictionary to include in individual entries information about their transformational possibilities and restrictions.) In the code for the following entry, the letter 'i' indicates that the direct object may be placed on either side of the particle (cf. *leave on the fire/leave the fire on*), while the code 'pass' and the supporting example show that a passive transformation is also permitted:

(17) **leave on**[2] [B1i pass adj] allow to stay alight or keep burning . . . *The electric fire had been left on overnight.* . . .

There were other kinds of information which, though not grammatical themselves, had to be integrated with the grammatical description. The most important had to do with the collocability of entries, which, as we have seen, was conveyed by means of bracketed lists within examples in *GEW* and *ISED*. The verb-particle and verb-preposition combinations listed in *ODCIE 1* were idioms (or semi-idioms). But they in turn could collocate with nouns, adjectives, adverbs, etc., and from the outset it had been Ronald Mackin's intention to make the separate listing of collocates a special feature of the work—to combine, as he put it, 'original up-to-date citations with discrete meanings enlightened if not almost "defined" by listed collocations' (Mackin 1983: vii). As an example

TABLE 2.4. *Grammatical patterns and their codes in* ODCIE 1 *(1975)*

Codes	Examples
[A1]	*The electricity supply went off.*
[A2]	*We were banking on a change of heart.*
[A3]	*The committee fell back on an earlier plan.*
[B1]	*Fred tipped the police off.*
[B2]	*Peter foists all his problems on his unfortunate friends.*
[B3]	*You can put the shortage down to bad planning.*

of an entry enlightened by listed collocates, consider *take off* ("leave the ground") and the nouns *plane, jet, helicopter, glider,* all of which can combine with *take off* as its grammatical subject. But just as important was the need to set out these details in such a way that they could be used productively.

In the *Interim Report on English Collocations,* word-combinations had been classified according to the grammatical patterns, or constructions, to which they conformed. But the words which collocate with such combinations have syntactic functions also, and should be seen in all cases as forming part of a wider syntactic pattern. If *take off* (as in the example above) has the pattern 'intransitive verb + adverbial particle', the collocating nouns (*plane, jet,* etc.) function as its grammatical subject. This view of the relationship between dictionary entries and their collocates on the one hand, and syntactic patterns on the other informs the design of *ODCIE* (in both volumes) for practical as well as theoretical reasons. If, to take another example, we could show that *set up* (in the sense 'cause' or 'produce') collocated with *infection, swelling, rash* as possible direct objects, then it should be possible for the student to use that information to compose sentences (Cowie 1978*a*, 1993). The conventions that were chosen to demonstrate the connection between collocates and their functions can be explained using the combination just shown (*set up*). In the appropriate entry the user will find (after the definition) the abbreviation **O** (direct object), followed by a number of nouns:

(18) **set up**[4] . . . cause, produce. . . . **O**: infection; swelling, rash . . .

These three collocates represent a wider range of nouns which can combine acceptably with *set up* as its direct object. Any of the three collocates, and any of the larger set they belong to (e.g. *irritation, skin condition*), can therefore be substituted for the direct object in a sentence which the user wishes to reshape or compose from scratch (Cowie 1993). This method of indicating the collocates of an entry has the double advantage of setting out material which the student can use confidently for sentence building, while at the same time giving scope for the more advanced student to make personal choices by extrapolation from the items provided.

2.6. Dictionaries of English Idioms

The stress laid on grammatical classification in the phraseological research of Palmer and Hornby also influenced the design of two specialized idiom dictionaries, the *Longman Dictionary of English Idioms* (1979), and the *Oxford Dictionary of Current Idiomatic English,* Volume 2 (1983), later renamed the *Oxford Dictionary of English Idioms.* The *Second Interim Report on English Collocations* had encouraged the practice of allocating word-combinations to grammatical classes in dictionaries, and may have influenced the decision, taken by Oxford and Longman compilers alike, to assign phrasal verbs to separate volumes (Cowie 1990). But the influence went further. Once it had become the practice to classify word-combinations, it was a natural next step to describe their *elements* in more detail, specifying their functions and also their transformational possibilities and restrictions.[11] Such in-depth grammatical description was a feature not only of *ODCIE 1*, but also of the Oxford and Longman idiom dictionaries which we shall now turn to consider.

The compilers of both dictionaries were faced by a problem of definition that was as fundamental as, and more intractable than, any issue of grammatical description. We have seen how, in the *Interim Report*, word-combinations were defined in terms of learning difficulty, and that no criteria were proposed for separating the more from the less idiomatic cases. Also needed, then, was a categorization which would reflect not only the grammatical structure and function of word-combinations, but their phraseological status as well. One possibility was to adopt an approach that had begun to attract the attention of American, West German, and British linguists in the 1960s and 1970s (Weinreich 1969; Lipka 1974; Cowie 1978b). This was a movement pioneered by a group of Russian scholars, including V. V. Vinogradov and N. N. Amosova, who had been active up to twenty years earlier and whose influence had later spread to other parts of Eastern Europe (Klappenbach 1968; Zgusta 1971; Gläser 1986). In one respect, the systems developed by these linguists matched the framework of the *Interim Report*: they recognized a primary distinction between 'sentence-like' combinations (Palmer's 'phrases') and 'word-like' combinations (the latter corresponding to the spread of categories actually recorded in the *Report*). Sentence-like combinations were further divisible into sayings, catchphrases, etc., as shown in Table 2.5.

TABLE 2.5. *Sentence-like combinations*

Sentence-like combinations	Examples
Saying	*Many hands make light work.*
Catchphrase	*I don't mind if I do!*
Slogan	*All we do is driven by you.*
Speech formula	*That reminds me . . .*

The particular strength of the Russian contribution lay in recognizing that word-like combinations could differ in the *degree of idiomaticity* that they displayed. (Similar differences are discernible within the sentence-like category, but

---

[11] These new developments were also influenced by American work on the transformational restrictions characteristic of idioms (e.g. Fraser 1970; Newmeyer 1974).

these will not concern us here.) Word-like combinations of any grammatical type could be placed along a 'scale' of idiomaticity, from the free combinations that were in fact recognized by Palmer to opaque, invariable idioms (Cowie 1981, 1994, 1998*a*; Howarth 1996). Consider the shading-off from free to opaque as one runs down Table 2.6. As the table also shows, 'classical' Russian theory recognized four categories along the scale. I have preferred the terms indicated in the table, which incorporate 'idiom' and 'collocation'—themselves relatively familiar to Western linguists—to those originally employed by Vinogradov and Amosova. The point to note, however, is that the Russian scholars were careful to distinguish between idioms in the narrow sense (e.g. *spill the beans, a dead duck*) and 'figurative idioms', or dead metaphors (e.g. *call the shots, a sacred cow*), and also threw light on the nature of restricted collocations, which are more difficult to define than idioms and in many kinds of texts much more numerous.[12] Restricted collocations such as *break one's fall* or *meet the demand* were defined by Vinogradov as combinations in which one element had a figurative sense determined by its context—it was, according to his formulation 'phraseologically bound' (cf. 2.2, above). The binding or determining context was either a single word (e.g. the noun in *break one's fall*), or an arbitrarily limited set of words (e.g. the alternative nouns in *meet the demand/someone's need/someone's requirements*).

TABLE 2.6. *Word-like combinations and the scale of idiomaticity*

Word-like combinations	Examples: verb + noun; adjective + noun
Free combination	*open a window; a green wall*
Restricted collocation	*meet the demand; easy money*
Figurative idiom	*call the shots; a sacred cow*
Pure idiom	*spill the beans; a dead duck*

As we shall see, the precision with which these various distinctions were captured in dictionaries of idioms and collocations compiled in the 1970s and 1980s would be an important measure of their quality.

2.6.1. *Longman Dictionary of English Idioms*

2.6.1.1. *LDEI*: Scope and Organization

The compilers of the *Longman Dictionary of English Idioms* (*LDEI*) (1979) set about the task of defining and classifying idioms and related categories without reference to any specific analytical model. As a result, the dictionary lacked an

---

[12] The descriptive frameworks developed by Vinogradov and Amosova are discussed in greater detail in Cowie (1998*a*).

overall organizational framework. It did, it is true, recognize the important structural distinction between phrase idioms, such as *the salt of the earth*, and those which are 'almost full sentences', like *give up the ghost*. And it referred to the development of figurative from literal senses, as in *fall off one's chair laughing*, for instance, and the difficulties which such combinations created for foreign learners. Nevertheless, the development of a general framework of categories for *LDEI* was hampered and confused by lumping together structural, stylistic, and pragmatic criteria.

Nonetheless, the dictionary had several compensating strengths, chief among which was its approach to one of the most difficult organizational problems facing compilers of idiom dictionaries: how to arrange complex lexical entries so that they are easily accessed by users. The first ordering principle adopted in *LDEI* was that the first or only noun of a combination (if it contained one) was treated as the keyword under which the combination would be looked up, and was made the capitalized heading under which all expressions introduced by that word were grouped and defined. Thus, **the child is father of the man** and **child's play** (each with a full entry) appeared below the keyword **CHILD**. These entries also illustrate the second principle: that entries gathered under a specific keyword should—leaving aside articles, demonstratives, etc.—be arranged in strict alphabetical order. Compilers of idiom dictionaries are also obliged to introduce a mechanism whereby users looking up an idiom under a part of speech other than the first or only noun will nevertheless be guided to the appropriate main entry. Hence the third ordering principle: that under the keywords **FATHER** and **PLAY** (for instance), and within the alphabetical arrangements for those keywords, the user would find the above-mentioned idioms containing *child*, and cross-references to the headword **CHILD**, thus:

(19) **FATHER**
    the child is father of the man see at CHILD
    how's your father . . .
    like father/mother, like son/daughter . . .
    PLAY
    all work and no play makes Jack a dull boy . . .
    bring°/call° D into play . . .
    child's play see at CHILD . . .

2.6.1.2. *LDEI*: the Treatment of Grammar and Context

The authors of *LDEI* had, as a further noteworthy strength, designed a special scheme for treating the syntax of idioms and collocations. Indeed, the system was one of the most ingenious and satisfactory yet devised for a learner's dictionary. In essence, it employed a set of three capital letters denoting major clause functions, D for direct object, I for indirect object, and P for object of a preposition, and two superscript letters, ° to indicate that a word might inflect, and ᵐ to show that it could be transposed. The following examples illustrate various combinations of those symbols:

(20) **cut° D dead**
       give° I a piece of one's mind
       make° a man° of P
       put°/shove°/stick° inᵐ **one's oar°**

The capitals had a double value. Most obviously they indicated the syntactic functions of post-verbal and post-prepositional noun phrases, but they also showed that the place so marked was not a fixed part of the idiom, but a slot where open choice operated. (One could, as it were, give a colleague, a rival, or an employee a piece of one's mind.) As for superscript °, this was attached to verbs, nouns, or adjectives to indicate that they inflected normally. In **make° a man° of** P, for instance, the verb-forms *make, makes, making,* and *made* could all be used, as could the singular and plural forms of *man*. Superscript ᵐ was placed after a moveable element. In **put°/shove°/stick° in**ᵐ **one's oar°**, it signalled specifically that the particle *in* and the final noun phrase could be transposed, a fact which was confirmed by an example (*we will have to keep the arrangements a secret . . . because she'll only want to shove her oar in*). When either of the superscript letters was lacking at a point where the user might expect to find it, there was a syntactic or inflectional restriction. The absence of ° after the noun in **smell° a rat**, for example, indicated that **smell rats* was unacceptable.

As well as indicating the syntactic and inflectional restrictions which are characteristic of idioms, a phraseological dictionary must mark restrictions on the choice of specific words. As was shown in earlier discussions of *GEW*, such restrictions are of two kinds. At one or more points there may be a choice of words which is arbitrarily limited. Such limitation is illustrated by **bring°/call° D into play**, and here, in line with common practice, oblique strokes mark off the choices. The other common type of restriction is illustrated by **come rain or (come) shine**, where there is an optional element enclosed by parentheses.[13]

In an idiom such as *cut and thrust*, it is possible to specify items which, while not forming part of the idiom itself, can follow it as object of the preposition *of*. As we have seen in the discussion of *ODCIE 1*, such collocates often throw helpful additional light on the meaning of the idiom. Note, for instance, *the cut and thrust of debate, discussion, argument*. That such choices can be displayed separately from examples, and in relation to their syntactic functions, was shown earlier with reference to *ODCIE 1*. *ISED* made no attempt to indicate collocates separately, but as in the entry **cut and thrust**, sometimes did so in example

---

[13] As will be shown in Chapter 3, obliques and parentheses, as markers of alternative and optional elements respectively, were first introduced in *ALD 3* (1974).

sentences: *It was regrettable that such great issues had to be the cut-and-thrust of a general election.* The dictionary also occasionally indicated as part of the definition, but in general terms, the class of person or thing which the subject or object of the idiom could denote. In the following entry, 'another person, organization, etc.' indicates very general restrictions governing the choice of the object of *from*:

(21) **take° one's cue from** P . . . to use the practice of (another person, organization, etc.) as a guide to one's own actions . . .

However guidance of this kind appeared in relatively few entries, and arguably it would have been better to present users with a list of collocates since they could then work directly with lexical material—and possibly extrapolate from it —even though it might be limited in extent (Cowie 1978*b*: 136).

2.6.2.   *Oxford Dictionary of Current Idiomatic English*, Volume 2

2.6.2.1.   *ODCIE 2*: Scope and Organization

The second volume of the *Oxford Dictionary of Current Idiomatic English* (*ODCIE 2*) appeared in 1983.[14] Unlike *LDEI*, it was based on a specific analytical scheme—one which had its origins in Russian phraseological theory (Cowie 1998*a*). Like various East European descriptions (e.g. Gläser 1986), *ODCIE 2* included a broad spectrum of sentence-like expressions, including catchphrases (*if you can't beat them, join them*) and sayings (*patience is a virtue*), which were defined in the introduction. It also dealt prominently with speech formulae— such as *don't I know it* and *you can say that again*—which are used to structure exchanges and often indicate the speaker's attitude to an interlocutor's remarks (Cowie 1983*c*: xvii). The expression *do you know*, for instance, introduces (or follows) a statement, and points forward to an ironic or exasperated comment on it:

(22) **Do you know** *that's the first time I've heard of burglars having children. Makes them quite human doesn't it?*

   ODCIE 2 also recognized and applied the framework of categories developed by Russian phraseologists for 'word-like' combinations. This was broken down into pure idioms (e.g. *blow the gaff*), figurative idioms (e.g. *a close/narrow shave*), and restricted collocations (e.g. *jog someone's memory*) (Cowie 1981, 1983*c*). These types were described and illustrated in some detail in the introduction, but they also served as a yardstick against which possible entries were judged suitable for

---

[14] Isabel McCaig, who had not been involved in the first volume, made a major contribution to the second. As well as quarrying the Scottish daily and weekly press for material, she provided many examples of her own.

admission. In the case of restricted collocations, only those items were recorded which were absolutely fixed (e.g. *break one's fall, hold one's fire*) or which had limited internal variation (e.g. *carry/win the day, a chequered history/career*).

Unfortunately, the accessibility of entries in *ODCIE 2* does not always match the rigour with which they were categorized and described, and the chief focus of criticism in a number of reviews has been precisely the alphabetical arrangement of entries (Herbst 1986a). Leaving aside such items as the articles and possessives, entries in *ODCIE 2* were arranged in strict alphabetical order, taking account not only of major-class words such as nouns, verbs, and adjectives, but also of prepositions (e.g. *against, at*) and indefinite pronouns and determiners (*all, some, none*). These guidelines gave rise to sequences such as the following, in which one of the words that determines order is *another*:

(23)   **an angry young man**
       another cup of tea
       answer/obey the call of duty

The fact that **another cup of tea** was listed under **another**, rather than **cup** or **tea**, proved baffling to a number of users—perhaps understandably. The consequences of the approach were to some extent mitigated by the inclusion of an index at the back of the dictionary, in which groupings of items appeared under highlighted keywords. Indeed it has been suggested that the organization of entries could be improved first by including the index, with its keywords, in the body of the dictionary text, and then by grouping main entries under those keywords, according to the first or only open-class word which they contain.

2.6.2.2. *ODCIE 2*: The Treatment of Grammar and Context

ODCIE 2 (1983) covered a much wider spread of grammatical patterns than its companion volume, recording instances of many more of the types included in the *Second Interim Report*. Even if we limit ourselves to idioms and collocations in *ODCIE 2* that span subjectless clauses (e.g. *come clean, dish the dirt, paint the town red*, etc.), the structural range is still remarkably broad. Each entry falling within that range—and of course others too—is given a structural description, with element labels similar to those used in the grammars available during the

TABLE 2.7. *Clause-type idioms and collocations in* ODCIE 2

Clause patterns	Idioms and collocations
[V + Comp] verb + complement	*The suspects should* **come clean.**
[V + O] verb + direct object	*An article* **caught his attention.**
[V + O + Comp] verb + direct object + complement	*The boss* **caught** *Steve* **napping.**
[V + IO + O] verb + indirect object + direct object	*Mary* **sets** *us all* **a good example.**
[V + O + A] verb + direct object + adjunct	*The writer* **sells** *his characters* **short.**

period of compilation by Randolph Quirk and his associates (Quirk *et al.* 1972; Quirk and Greenbaum 1973). Those structural formulae constitute transparent codes. Table 2.7 shows the full set of codes, with examples, for subjectless clauses (cf. Cowie 1983c: xxix).

It has been suggested that it is 'unhelpful to attempt to analyse grammatically any portion of text which appears to be constructed on the idiom principle' (Sinclair 1991: 113). All the same, there may be a number of sound reasons for doing so in an idiom dictionary for advanced foreign students. Consider the last example in the table. The only strictly idiomatic parts of this sequence are *sells . . . short.* However, the intervening noun phrase is an integral part of the wider pattern, even though very many specific phrases can actually be substituted (*his aunt, her family, the economy, the country*). Now learners must be able to locate the point within the idiom at which these choices operate; but they need to be shown, too, that the substituted NPs are objects, and this is done by means of the conventional label 'O'. In this way the syntactic relationship to the idiom of an element which is strictly not part of it, and yet is important, can be made explicit.

Such guidance has the additional advantage that it helps to explain transfor- mations. A simple sentence such as *The boss caught Steve napping* is related to the passive *Steve was caught napping by the boss* in terms of general rules, and these can be specified by reference to the pattern V + O + Comp and its constituent elements.

A further advantage of specifying the syntactic structure of an idiom (including closely related elements in its context) is that it offers a clear and systematic way of spelling out its collocational range, or ranges. *ODCIE 2*, like *ODCIE 1*, set out to show that idioms could form collocational links outside their own strict limits with other sets of words. This was achieved by providing, in almost every entry, separate lists of collocates that were appropriate to its headphrase. In the case of *sell* (something or somebody) *short,* the single list included the items *country, economy, oneself, one's friends.* But these were preceded by the function label **O** to indicate that the collocates could function as the direct object in a sentence containing *sell . . . short.* In this way, the idiom, its grammatical structure, an important related element, and the collocates which could function at that point, were combined in one integrated statement:

(24) **sell sth/sb short** [V + O + A pass] . . . cheat sb in value or quantity; belittle oneself or sb/sth else O: . . . country, economy; oneself, one's friends . . .

2.7. Dictionaries of Collocations

While it is certainly helpful to advanced learners to specify the collocability of idioms, it is unarguable that they are in much greater need of guidance about the collocability of single words. Such information needs to be set out in special-ized collocational dictionaries, and it is a remarkable fact that before the early 1980s there were very few in existence that were reliable, compiled by native speakers of English, and readily available in most countries where English was taught as a foreign language. For the most part, seekers after reliability in such countries had to depend on general learners' dictionaries which, while gaining steadily in comprehensiveness since the 1960s, were unable to provide the wide coverage which advanced foreign learners required (Herbst 1996). Other learners fell back on such unsatisfactory guides as Friederich and Canavan's *Dictionary of English Words in Context* (1979) which contained not only collocations and idioms, but some free combinations, too, often in a haphazard arrangement (Cowie 1986, 1998*a*).

2.7.1. *Selected English Collocations*

The first dictionary of English collocations worthy of the name was published in Warsaw in 1982.[15] Entitled *Selected English Collocations (SEC)*, it had as one of its two compilers a native speaker of English (Christian Douglas Kozłowska) and the further merit that its collocations came from a wide range of written material, including academic books and journals, and British quality newspapers. As well as ensuring authenticity, this collection proved a rich source of informa-tion about the collocability of headwords. Though comparison with the coverage provided by general learners' dictionaries is misleading, since the latter must provide for a very wide range of reference needs, it is worth observing that whereas in the fourth and fifth editions of *ALD* the entry for *decision* contains six transitive verbs—*arrive at, come to, give, make, reach,* and *take*—in the corre-sponding entry in *SEC* we find not only these verbs but 42 other acceptable choices, including *abide by, acquiesce in, adhere to,* and *affect* (cf. Bahns 1996).

This relative abundance reinforces the point that the sole purpose of a collocational dictionary is to provide information about the combinatorial prop-erties of words, other information being stripped away and more space created for collocations. One notes, for instance, that *SEC* provides a bare minimum of grammatical labels, and no information on style or meaning. (The purpose of inserting a gloss ('notice') after the headword ATTENTION—see below—is simply to distinguish this sense from another ('care and attention') with a quite different collocational range.)

Each collocation in *SEC* contains at least one noun and a noun features in every case as the headword.[16] This 'orientation'—from noun headword to verb,

---

[15] An enlarged and revised edition appeared in 1988. All examples are taken from that edition.
[16] There is a companion volume, *English Adverbial Collocations* (1991), whose headwords are either adjectives or verbs.

adjective, or noun collocate, as in the following entry—reflects the 'encoding' (i.e. productive) function of the dictionary and the fact that, when writing, one's starting-point is normally the noun. This orientation is also justified by the relative difficulty, for the writer, of the two component elements. In a collocation such as *undivided attention* the noun is unproblematical: the problem is one of selecting an acceptable adjective collocate from an arbitrarily restricted set (Hausmann 1979, 1985, 1989; Cowie 1981, 1986).

(25) **ATTENTION** (notice)
       V. absorb, attract, call for, capture, . . . transfer ~
       V. ~ be taken up, flag, wander, waver
       Adj. close, finicky, full, . . . undivided, utmost, whole ~
       N. bid for, centre of, focus of ~

To help the user move quickly to the part of the entry where the appropriate collocate is to be found, two further design features are needed. The first of these is the grouping of collocates according to their parts of speech (verb, adjective, and noun in the above entry). Verbs are often arranged in two blocks, as the intransitive–transitive distinction frequently corresponds to a difference of collocability. This is the case in the ATTENTION entry, and accordingly the verbs are separately listed. A tilde (~), placed after the transitive and before the intransitive lists, indicates the functional difference economically. Adjectives appear in the third block and nouns in the fourth.

The second design feature that ideally should be present is the semantic grouping of collocates within those grammatical blocks. However, as is clear from the sequence *absorb, attract, call for, capture*, above, the arrangement in *SEC* is not semantic but alphabetical. Yet there is little doubt that learners would be helped by ordering words according to meaning, and introducing them by superordinate (or 'genus') terms as keywords (Hausmann 1979; Cowie 1986). To introduce the adjective collocates of *disaster* which denote 'highest degree', for instance, we might choose ABSOLUTE. (The collocates themselves would include *complete, sheer, total*, and *utter*.) Such a convention could help users who already know the meaning of a collocate to find the collocate itself.

This invaluable resource for advanced learners and translators prompts one final chastening comment. A dictionary may provide a less than satisfactory definition of the category it treats—indeed it may claim to deal with another category altogether, as is the case with *SEC*—and yet provide the very information that users require. *SEC* purports to deal not with restricted collocations, 'but "free" or "open" collocations, which means that a range of other words can be added at will' (1988: 8). Certainly, many of the collocates in the dictionary have synonymous substitutes (cf. *critical* and *crucial* as collocates of *phase*), but as a rule *SEC* excludes collocates which are free to occur in a wide range of contexts (e.g. *good*, *straight*, and *open* as collocates of *road*) and favours collocates which are contextually constrained or 'bound' (cf. *bumpy*, *impassable*, *winding*).

2.7.2. *The BBI Combinatory Dictionary of English*

Since its publication in 1986, the *BBI Combinatory Dictionary* has been widely and deservedly praised. True, dependence on the intuitions of its three American authors rather than a corpus of written texts puts *BBI* at a disadvantage vis-à-vis *SEC* in the coverage of many common-core words. For instance, *BBI* is admirable in its treatment of the collocability of *road*, where sensitivity to transatlantic differences plays a part (*trunk*, *ring*, and *slip* road representing British usage); but at *decision* ('judgement') *BBI*'s coverage of transitive verbs (*arrive at*, *make*, *reach*, *take*) falls far short of *SEC*'s list of over forty.

As one might expect from an editorial team familiar with Russian phraseological theory and Russian dictionary practice, several of the design features which characterize *SEC* also appear in *BBI*: an entry 'orientation' designed to favour the *writer* of English; the use of simple conventions to mark the transitive–intransitive distinction in collocate lists (note the use of the tilde in the following entry); and the arrangement of verb, adjective (and in this case prepositional) collocates in separate numbered sections:

(26) **controversy** *n*. 1. to arouse, cause, fuel, stir up (a) ~ 2. to settle a ~ 3. a bitter, furious, heated, lively ~ 4. a ~ about, over 5. a ~ between, with

However, *BBI* is a more complex dictionary than these remarks suggest, and in one respect goes outside the proper limits of a collocational dictionary altogether. Consider the following entries. Here, as in many other entries for nouns, adjectives, and verbs, there are codes and examples indicating the finite or non-finite clauses which function as their complementation:

(27) **conviction** *n*. . . . 3. a ~ that + clause (she expressed her firm ~ that television was harmful to children)
happy *adj*. . . . 3. ~ to + inf. (I'll be happy to attend the meeting . . .)
hate II *v*. . . . 3. (G) she ~s going to school

The complementation in each of these examples is of course a grammatical category, not a collocate, and to call the construction of which it is part (e.g. 'a conviction that + clause') a collocation is a misuse of the term. Such constructions belong in a valency dictionary, not a collocational dictionary.

The great bulk of material in *BBI* escapes these strictures, consisting as it does of lexical and grammatical collocations. These distinctions are illustrated by the entry for **controversy** (26), above, where collocations in the first three numbered sections are lexical and in the last two grammatical. Two points should be made about the way the grammar of both types of combination is presented. The dictionary contains quite a complex scheme of syntactic patterns (with appropriate codes), one which is reminiscent of the system in the *Longman Dictionary of Contemporary English* (*LDOCE 1*) (1978). The codes for grammatical collocations include G4, which denotes preposition + noun combination (thus, *by accident, in advance*), and G5, which refers to adjective + preposition combinations (e.g. *angry at, deaf to*). Among the categories of lexical collocation, pattern L2 is attributive adjective + noun (*a pitched battle*) while pattern L4 is subject noun + verb (*bees sting*). There are also codes referring to the types of clause complementation discussed above.

In the dictionary itself codes denoting *lexical* collocations do not appear, but as examples of their possible patterns are set out in a consistent order in entries, the user should soon learn where to find a collocation of a particular type—as in the following case, where lexical collocations precede grammatical ones, and where, specifically, transitive verb + noun collocations (at 1, 2, and 3) precede adjective + noun collocations (at 4):

(28) **supervision** *n.* . . . . 1. to exercise ~ of, over 2. to tighten ~ 3. to ease up on, relax ~ 4. lax, slack; strict ~ 5. under smb.'s ~

Unlike the compilers of *SEC*, Benson, Benson, and Ilson define with reasonable accuracy the kinds of lexical collocations that need to be included in *BBI*. They correctly rule out free combinations as being 'joined in accordance with the general rules of English syntax' and as allowing 'free substitution' (1986: ix). There is, however, uncertainty about the defining properties of restricted collocations, which may explain why, together with many collocations that are undoubtedly restricted, *BBI* includes several that are free. At the entry for *door*, for example, the user will find *close, shut,* and *open,* which occur with many other nouns, and *hang, slam,* and *break down,* whose specialized meanings are determined by very few (*door* and *gate*).

2.8. Conclusion

The analysis of phraseology was, for Palmer and Hornby especially, inseparable from their preoccupation with vocabulary control. As Palmer declared (1933c: 11), quoting I. A. Richards's Foreword to the two *Interim Reports on Vocabulary Selection,*

(29) Determinations of the relative frequencies of words in selected bodies of literature give us, at best, only raw material. . . . Each word must be re-examined in the light of the number and kinds of 'collocations' into which it enters.

The description of collocations and idioms, as developed at IRET, had certain characteristic features which, positively and negatively, were to influence the later treatment of phraseology in learners' dictionaries. One was concern for grammatical classification, conducted rigorously and in depth. This orientation did not at first affect the way individual combinations were set out in general EFL dictionaries, where the criteria of arrangement were influenced by those already adopted in native-speaker dictionaries. The grammar-centred approach of the pioneers was, however, one of the primary factors leading to the introduction of syntactic transformations into the specialized idiom dictionaries of the 1970s and 1980s. The treatment of word-combinations of various kinds, including phrasal verbs, in the multi-purpose EFL dictionary after *ISED* is a different strand in the general evolution, and will be taken up in the next chapter.

3 The Second Generation of Learners' Dictionaries

3.1. Introduction

The twenty-year period between the publication of *ISED/ALD 1* (1942) and *ALD 2* (1963) was one in which A. S. Hornby achieved a unique status and authority in learner lexicography—a position that was to remain unchallenged for a further fifteen years. Harold Palmer's involvement in dictionary-making had virtually ceased with the compilation of *GEW*—though his *English–French Phraseological Dictionary* (1943–4) showed that his interest in idioms and collocations was far from extinct after 1938—while Michael West—though subsequently involved in a number of dictionary schemes, including the radical recasting of *NMED*—never attempted to compile an advanced-level, general-purpose dictionary that could rival *ALD*.[1]

This chapter spans the period between the compilation and publication of *ALD 2* and the first appearance, in 1978, of the *Longman Dictionary of Contemporary English* (*LDOCE 1*). It describes the consolidation and further significant development of Hornby's classic work to the point where its dominance of EFL lexicography was first seriously challenged. Though the second edition of *ALD* is closer to the third than to the first in time, it is poised midway between *ALD 1* and *ALD 3* in content and structure, providing a broader coverage of scientific and technical terms than the former, and a greatly increased number of examples, but an unaltered verb-pattern scheme and unchanged principles of arrangement for idioms and most phrasal verbs. In *ALD 2*, the receptive needs of users were studied with as much deliberate care as, earlier, their productive needs had been.

The approach throughout this chapter is analytical, and in the two Oxford editions and *LDOCE 1*, attention is focused on the same aspects of dictionary design. These are, and have remained, features of vital importance in the learner's dictionary, but they are also aspects in which change and development were particularly striking over the fifteen-year period, taken as a whole. They are pronunciation, grammatical schemes (especially for verb, noun, and adjective

---

[1] The revised and updated version of the *NMED* was *An International Reader's Dictionary* (1965), by Michael West, with phonetic transcriptions by Roger Kingdon.

complementation), definitions and glosses, illustrative examples, and idioms and phrasal verbs.

3.1.1. A Guide to Patterns and Usage in English

When, in 1950, Hornby took up an offer from his publisher to work at home in the country, producing lower-level dictionaries based on *ALD 1*, and a number of language courses, he continued to draw on the grammatical descriptions on which he and Palmer had worked in the 1930s. He had not, to that point, produced a learner's grammar, but it was not altogether surprising when, in 1954, midway between the appearance of *ALD 1* and *2*, he published a small volume— *A Guide to Patterns and Usage in English*—which brought together some of the descriptive categories of the first edition, including the verb-patterns, while at the same time introducing a number of fresh insights which would go to shape the second. The *Guide* was in no sense a full pedagogical or reference grammar, but a selective work designed to emphasize certain key areas of the grammar considered important for language production. Its aims ran parallel to those of *ISED/ALD 1* and were broadly in line with numerous IRET publications of the 1930s. It was, for instance, syntactic rather than inflectional—it did not follow a traditional chapter organization based on word-classes—and it was synthetic rather than analytical, resorting to analysis only when this was 'helpful for synthesis, or sentence building' (Hornby 1954: v). The *Guide* also provided a further reminder that Hornby, like Palmer, and in accordance, too, with the tenets of American structuralism, considered 'a knowledge of how to put words together . . . as important as, perhaps more important than, a knowledge of their meanings' (ibid.) (cf. Strevens 1978*a*).

Apart from giving fresh prominence to certain topics thought crucial for encoding—including verb-patterns, the anomalous finites, and the determinatives (or determiners)—the *Guide* adopted an original approach to the treatment of modality and also dealt with types of syntactic pattern not hitherto examined and destined eventually to leave their mark on the second edition of *ALD*. I shall dwell only briefly on the treatment of modality in the *Guide to Patterns*, as in a dictionary the phenomenon will normally be dealt with from the standpoint of the individual modal verbs. In the *Guide*, however, Hornby's approach was to treat modality from the standpoint of the notions (e.g. of certainty or necessity) which the modal verbs expressed.[2] In a chapter headed 'Various concepts and how to express them', Hornby introduced such concepts as 'plans and arrangements' and 'promises and threats; refusals' and then set out the formal means used to express them. The similarity between these headings and those

---

[2] In *ALD 4* (1989), the modal verbs were to be gathered together in a number of 'usage notes' organized on a semantic basis.

of a notional and functional syllabus is very striking, though no reference was made to Hornby's innovative work in the most influential texts of the communicative movement (e.g. Wilkins 1976).

As for the types of structure introduced by Hornby for the first time, these were the complementation patterns of nouns and adjectives (e.g. *a decision to resign* and *certain to need help*). It so happened that, when compiling *ALD 2*, Hornby did not refer to those categories by means of the codes introduced in the *Guide* (NP1, AP1C, etc.). It was an omission which, despite the interest subsequently shown in the patterns themselves, and the efforts made to illustrate them more fully, seems to have escaped most commentators (e.g. Herbst 1984). Codes or no, however, there is clear evidence from *ALD 2* that Hornby's detailed analysis of noun and adjective complementation was used in its compilation, leading to a marked increase in the number of relevant illustrative examples, as will be demonstrated below.

3.2. *The Advanced Learner's Dictionary*, Second Edition

As we have seen, Hornby's energies were absorbed, in the late 1940s and early 1950s, not only by his work as a lecturer and adviser but also by the writing of textbooks, which drew on the same sound linguistic principles and employed the same methods of selection and grading as the teaching materials written in Japan (Stavropoulos 1978).[3] When eventually, in the late 1950s, he turned his attention again to *ALD*, he did so alone, as E. V. Gatenby had died in 1955, while H. Wakefield was fully occupied in teaching overseas until 1959 (Hornby *et al.* 1963: iii).[4] As well as entailing close scrutiny and substantial rewriting of the existing text, Hornby's revision also went a good deal further than its predecessor in meeting the receptive ('decoding') needs of the foreign student. As the Preface makes clear, care was taken to include words that had entered the language since 1942 and to admit technical and scientific terms known to the educated lay person—i.e. those 'that occur commonly in ordinary periodicals, but not those that rarely occur outside advanced textbooks and specialist periodicals' (1963: v–vi). We can judge how successful Hornby was in meeting those aims by a close comparison of a run of entries in the two editions. I have examined all entries in the parallel texts at letter L, noting not only which entries have been added to and deleted from the macrostructure of *ALD 1*, but also the sources of the additions and the destinations of the deletions. The breakdown is set out in Table 3.1.

---

[3] Hornby's three-volume *Oxford Progressive English for Adult Learners* was published between 1954 and 1956.

[4] Gatenby had been teaching at Robert College, in Turkey (Gatenby 1947), while Wakefield was headmaster of a boys' school in Penang, in what was then Malaya (David Neale, personal communication). Wakefield died in 1962, shortly after returning to England.

TABLE 3.1. *New and transferred entries at letter L in* ALD 2

ALD 2: new entries and transfers from *ALD 1* run-ons	75	New entries	63
		Main entries from *ALD 1* run-ons	12
ALD 1: deletions and transfers to appendices, etc.	105	Main entries to *ALD 2* run-ons	76
		To Appendix of Abbreviations	10
		To Appendix of Geographical Names[a]	2
		Deleted proper names	10
		Other deleted entries	7

[a]*ALD 2* contained nine appendices, to several of which encyclopaedic information from *ALD 1* was transferred.

If we look first at the bottom half of Table 3.1, it is clear that the number of entries removed altogether from *ALD 1* as a proportion of the total of deletions and transfers to appendices, etc., is very small (17 out of 105, or 16.2 per cent). In contrast, the number of new entries to *ALD 2* measured against the total of additions and transfers from *ALD 1* run-ons is very large (63 out of 75, or 80.4 per cent). Several of the additions reflect the priorities announced by Hornby in the Preface. Particularly prominent are words from scientific and technical fields such as geology (e.g. *laterite, loess*), music (*largo, legato, lento*), and botany (*liana, lobelia*). There are also a number of new items reflecting slang and regional usage (*loony, lor, lough*).

Though the removal from the headword list of *ALD 1*—as here at letter L—of many derivatives and compounds, and their absorption as run-ons, did not lead to any diminution of the content of *ALD 2*, it did of course greatly alter its macrostructure and microstructure. In the original version, complex and compound words were often given headword status, a practice in line with the design of American collegiate dictionaries (and, later on, the first edition of *LDOCE*). But beginning with *ALD 2*, and on through the later editions, the general tendency in the Hornby dictionary was to treat such items as defined run-ons. The difference of approach is illustrated by the following noun and adjective compounds, which appear as main entries in *ALD 1* in the following forms, but as a block of sub-headwords in bold print at the entry for **life** in *ALD 2*:

(1) **life=belt, life=blood, life=boat, life=buoy, life=guard, life=jacket, life-like, life=line, life-long**[5]

This policy was unevenly pursued. The compounds *lieutenant-colonel* and *lieutenant-general* were already embedded in *ALD 1*, while the derivatives *lawful* and *lawless*, which were main entries in *ALD 1*, remained main entries in *ALD 2*.

---

[5] The spelling conventions are those of *ALD 1*, where the equals sign indicates that the compound is to be written solid, but also marks the point where the form can be broken at the end of a line.

Moreover, in the absence of any clarifying statement from Hornby, it seems that the changes, when they were made, were prompted by the need to create space —certainly for new entries, but much more, as we shall see later, for additional examples.

3.2.1. Pronunciation

The treatment of pronunciation in the second edition of *ALD* was fuller and more explicit than in the first, as befitted a work 'adapted to meet more directly the special requirements of advanced students and teachers of English' (Hornby *et al.* 1963: v). There were no changes to the symbols used, except that, as in the *English Pronouncing Dictionary* (*EPD*), primary stress was now indicated by a short vertical stroke above the line, and secondary stress by a stroke below, as in:

(2) /ˌmisdiˈmiːnə*/
     /ˌregjuˈleiʃən/

Two minor conventions were introduced to reflect systematic changes to the forms of words in rapid speech and continuous speech. First, in order to show that in words such as *signal*, final /əl-/ could be replaced by syllabic /-l/, the transcription /ˈsignəl/ (with italicized 'schwa') was used, indicating that both /ˈsignəl/ and /ˈsignl/ are heard (1963: xxxii). The same device was adopted, as in the transcription of *regulation*, above, to indicate the alternation between final /-ən/ and syllabic /-n/. However, the convention was not applied in the dictionary in all cases that required it. Only transcriptions with syllabic /-l/, for instance, appear at **penal** and **pencil**.

As for linkages in continuous speech, Hornby had already, in *ALD 1*, indicated in the brief guide to pronunciation that in RP a final *r* was usually sounded if the next word in the sentence began with a vowel, as in *How far is it?* [hauˈfáːrizit] (1948: xxvii). As it happened, no regular marking was introduced in that edition in entries for words with linking *r*, but in the second, a final asterisk was added to the relevant transcription, thus:

(3) **square** [skweə*]
     squire [skwaiə*]
     stare [steə*]

The treatment of compounds was also changed. In *ALD 1*, as we have seen, a compound was fully transcribed when it was a main entry, but not when it was included (as a 'run-on') in the entry for its first element. A full phonetic transcription was not provided in the latter case in *ALD 2* either, but stresses were marked in the orthographic form of run-on compounds when they were written solid or with a hyphen, and (*a*) primary stress fell on the first element, with an unstressed second element (as in *'football*, *'foot-bath*), or (*b*) primary stress was followed by secondary stress (as in *'thought-,reader*, *'corn-ex,change*).[6] However, stresses were not marked in the many cases where one noun was modified by another as part of an 'open' compound, i.e. one written without a hyphen. Faced with forms such as **town crier** or **town hall**, the user could normally assume that the second element received primary stress. However, there is no strict correlation between open spelling, on the one hand, and 'phrasal' stress, on the other, and to omit stress marking from compounds such as **corn pone** and *field events*—both stressed on the first element—was to risk misleading the foreign student.

3.2.2. Verb- and Adjective-Patterns

Except for a few minor changes to examples, and the replacement, when introducing patterns in entries, of 'P' by 'VP', the verb-pattern scheme in *ALD 2* remained what it had been in *ALD 1*. So here, too, we find the clarifying division into two major blocks, transitive and intransitive; the helpful cross-references between related patterns (as, for instance, between the variant indirect-object structures at VP18 and VP19); and the practice, in some cases, of juxtaposing VPs whose final constituents are the same. (Compare *I hope (that) you will come* (VP 11) and *I told the man (that) he was mistaken* (VP 12).)

And yet, the time had perhaps come for some critical stocktaking. There was clearly a need, for instance, to assign the constituent elements of patterns overtly and consistently to functional categories (such as direct object and object complement). In some parts of the scheme, functional similarity was suggested by the way two or more patterns were juxtaposed, but such hints were not always confirmed by the structural descriptions heading the tables, or by the notes accompanying them. Consider:

(4) (VP 7) *Subject* x *Verb* x *Object* x *Adjective*
        Don't get your clothes dirty.
    (VP 8) *Subject* x *Verb* x *Object* x *Noun*
        They elected him king.
    (VP 9) *Subject* x *Verb* x *Object* x *Past Participle*
        You must get your hair cut.

Here, the functions of the first three elements in each case are indicated. It is left to the notes, though, to point out that the final adjective (in VP 7) and noun (in VP 8) both function as object complements, while, in the case of VP 9, the

---

[6] In *ALD 2*, as subsequently in *ALD 3*, the headword of a given entry was replaced by a tilde in examples, idioms, derivatives, and compounds. For clarity of presentation, the headword is restored to the compounds discussed here.

fact that the final constituent has the same function as in the two previous patterns is not indicated at all.

One advantage of providing overt and consistent functional descriptions is that, as in the above case, they may point to similarities of meaning (it will be noted that the object complement in each of VPs 7–9 denotes the end-result of a process). Another advantage of such analyses is that they help to explain transformational behaviour. Consider a case where differences of *constituent* structure, as indicated by *ALD 2*, are much more marked than in the above set of patterns:

(5) (VP 12) *Subject* x *Verb* x *Noun or Pronoun* x (that) x *Clause*
            I told the man (that) he was mistaken.
     (VP 14) *Subject* x *Verb* x *Noun or Pronoun* x *Conjunctive* x to x *Infinitive, etc.*
            They told him when to start.

Despite their superficial differences, these patterns are alike in having two objects (neither as it happens revealed by the notes), the first of which in each case is arguably indirect and the second direct (cf. *She told the man the answer to the riddle*). This analysis helps to explain the transformation, common to all three examples, by means of which the direct object becomes the *what*-element in a *wh*-question:

(6) What did I tell the man? That he was mistaken.
     What did they tell him? When to start.
     What did she tell the man? The answer to the riddle.

Such needs would, in time, require a new approach to the syntactic analysis of verb complementation. But one area of the grammar in which Hornby already had fresh analysis to draw on was the complementation of nouns and adjectives. If we confine our attention to adjective-patterns (APs) with a post-modifying *to*-infinitive clause (as in *happy to help you*), we find three sub-categories, differentiated in the *Guide* on the basis of their respective syntactic analogues (1954: 136–42):

- **AP 1A**   Here the basic pattern (a) has two analogous patterns, (b) and (c). (Cf. Quirk *et al.* 1972: 826–7, where this is Type I.)

    (a) You were unwise to accept his offer.
    (b) It was unwise of you to accept his offer.
    (c) How unwise of you to accept his offer!

- **AP 1B**   In the basic pattern here, as in (a) above, the subject of the sentence is also that of the *to*-infinitive. However, in contrast with AP 1A, a pattern (b) can occur in which 'the infinitive has its own subject, different from that of the main verb' (1954: 139). (Cf. Quirk *et al.* 1972: 828–9, where this is Type IV.)

    (a) The children were impatient to start.
    (b) The children were impatient for the bus to start.

At **AP 1C**, there are in fact three subclasses, identified here as **AP 1Ci, 1Cii,** and **1Ciii**, respectively. Hornby, it should be noted, provides evidence for the differences, though without using it as the basis for a finer sub-categorization (1954: 140–2).

- **AP 1Ci** In the first subclass, as Hornby demonstrates by an informal para-phrase, the basic pattern has an analogue (b) containing a finite verb, corre-sponding to the infinitive of (a), and an adverb, corresponding to the adjec-tive *quick*. There are two acceptable exclamatory patterns (c). (Cf. Quirk *et al.* 1972: 828, where this is Type III.)

    (a) He was quick to realize his advantage.
    (b) He quickly realized his advantage.
    (c) How quick he was to realize/quick of him to realize his advantage!

- **AP 1Cii** In the second subclass, the basic pattern has an analogue in which the infinitive clause is replaced by a prepositional phrase (1954: 140):

    (a) The old man is unfit to work.
    (b) The old man is unfit for work.

- **AP 1Ciii** In the third subclass, the subject of the whole sentence at (a), 'this room', is the direct object of the infinitive, as demonstrated at (b). Analogue (c) shows the adjective in attributive position (1954: 142). (In Quirk *et al.* 1972, this is a subtype of Type III.)

    (a) This room is difficult to heat.
    (b) It is difficult to heat this room.
    (c) This is a difficult room to heat.

In order to determine how far and in what ways these various patterns are taken account of in *ALD 2*, I examined entries in the dictionary for all the adjectives of which examples are provided in the *Guide* within each of the five categories analysed above. I also examined the parallel entries in *ALD 1* with a view to deter-mining what progress had been made in the treatment of the relevant patterns.

If one begins with the 15 adjectives illustrated at AP 1A, and compares the evidence of the two editions, it is clear that progress has been made on three levels. First, as Table 3.2 shows, the number of entries in which at least one pattern is illustrated has gone up (from 4 to 11). Second, the number of pattern examples has also risen (from 6 to 15). Third, and perhaps most significantly, each of the analogues shown as characteristic of AP 1A in the *Guide* is now illustrated in at least two entries (8 in the case of pattern (b)). On the evidence of these entries, the analysis has led to greater depth of treatment over a much wider range of cases.

As regards the 16 adjectives illustrated at AP 1B in the *Guide,* the evidence of the two editions is less impressive. Of the entries for those adjectives in *ALD 1,* 9 contain a pattern example—a total which rises to 12 in *ALD 2.* On the other hand, only basic pattern (a) is represented in the first edition, and it dominates the second, where (a) appears 12 times but (b) only twice.

A characteristic feature of the treatment in *ALD 2* of patterns AP 1Ci and 1Cii is that Hornby provides no examples of analogues of the basic patterns, though it is worth noting that he does, in several entries, offer two or more examples of the basic pattern itself, as here:

(7) **quick** . . . *quick to understand;* . . . *quick to make up one's mind (to seize an opportunity);* . . .

The reason for the lack of structural variety in examples is chiefly that, in the *Guide,* Hornby did not make fully explicit the structural differences between subclasses AP 1Ci and 1Cii—though he did, we should note, often helpfully include the relevant analogues in the *Guide* as glosses within parentheses, like this:

(8) *You are certain to need* (= will certainly need) *help.*
    The old man is unfit to work (= unfit for work).

As for AP 1Ciii, the adjectives in the *Guide* which conform to this pattern are *difficult, easy, painful, hard, dangerous, impossible,* and *pleasant.* The entries for these items in *ALD 1* and 2 are quite suggestive. Already in the first edition we

TABLE 3.2. *Adjective-pattern 1A in the* Guide to Patterns, ALD 1, *and* ALD 2

Adjectives of type AP 1A illustrated in the *Guide*	Examples in *ALD 1*	Examples in *ALD 2*
unwise	No entry	No entry
kind	(a) (b)	(a) (b)
stupid	No examples	(a)
foolish	No examples	(b) (c)
naughty	No examples	(b)
clever	No examples	(c)
wrong	(b)	(a) (b)
careless	No examples	No examples
ill-natured	No examples	No examples
polite	No examples	No examples
considerate	(b)	(b)
impudent	No examples	(a)
brave	No examples	(b)
good	(a) (b)	(a) (b)
wicked	No examples	(b)

find instances of the three variants later recognized in the *Guide*, with more than one example of some patterns. The corresponding *ALD 2* entries then mark a further step forward by providing almost twice as many examples (15 as compared with 8), and some increase in the representation of the three variant structures. The reason for this fullness of treatment may be that, in the *Guide to Patterns*, the analogous patterns of AP 1Ciii are consistently arranged, as shown below, making this subpattern easy to distinguish and to represent in dictionary entries:

(9) *This nut is hard to crack. This is a hard nut to crack.* (It is hard to crack this nut.) *That question is hard to answer. That is a hard question to answer.* (It is hard to answer that question.)

On the whole, adjective complementation in *ALD 2* provides a good example of how grammatical research can systematically extend the dictionary treatment of a particular feature. When, as at AP 1Ci and 1Cii, there is a lack of examples illustrating analogous patterns, this is because the analysis has not made explicit their status as analogues. Arguably, too, the handling of adjective complementation in *ALD 2* would have been further strengthened by the inclusion of AP codes, which could have indicated the range of permitted variation without the need for full illustration in all cases.

3.2.3. Definitions and Glosses

As he contemplated the task of reorganizing senses and rewriting definitions for *ALD 2*, Hornby was faced by two conflicting requirements. On the one hand, and quite apart from the need to include new meanings of existing entries, he recognized that it might be necessary to alter the arrangement of senses in certain polysemous entries, and to assign some definitions (within complex groupings of definitions) to numbered sub-entries, with the aim of achieving a clearer and more logical arrangement. Such changes would of course tend to lead to expansion, not contraction. On the other hand, there was a need to create space, not only to make way for new entries, but also to accommodate additional examples.

So as to be able to analyse Hornby's editorial methods across a variety of entries, I have examined 'lexical units' in the run **dervish** to **devolve** in both *ALD 1* and *ALD 2* (cf. Cowie 1995). By lexical units, I mean (*a*) defined but unnumbered main entries, whether for simple words (e.g. **descry**), or derivatives (e.g. **descriptive**); (*b*) numbered senses of a main entry, again whether for simple words (e.g. **describe**) or derivatives (e.g. **description**); (*c*) defined run-on derivatives (e.g. **detectable**) and zero-derivatives (e.g. **devilish**, as adverb), with numbered senses as appropriate.

Analysis shows that out of 36 new lexical units, 12 are new senses in polysemous entries, as at **descent**, where the legal sense 'handing down (of properties, titles, qualities, etc.) by inheritance' is included, or as at **devil** (verb), where both senses appear for the first time:

(10) ²**devil** . . . **1**. . . . grill with hot condiments . . . **2**. . . . work (*for* a barrister) . . .

At the same time, there is a good deal of reorganization of existing definitions, sometimes leading to the recognition of separate numbered senses. In five (mostly polysemous) entries, this amounts to recognizing in a complex sub-entry in *ALD 1* major differences of meaning and structure. Notice, for instance, how in the following extract from **describe** in the first edition, the last two examples conform to a special pattern ('describe sb. as (being) sth.') and have the meaning 'say that (sb. or sth.) has certain qualities', and how these syntactic and semantic properties form the basis of a separate sense in the second edition.

(11) (a) **describe** . . . ❶ . . . *Can you describe it to me? Please describe what you saw. He was described as being very clever* (i.e. people said that he was very clever). *He describes himself as a doctor* (i.e. says that he is a doctor). (*ALD 1*)

   (b) **describe** . . . **1** . . . . say what (sb. or sth.) is like; give a picture of in words: *Words cannot ~ the beauty of the scene. Can you ~ it to me? Please ~ what you saw.* **2**. (VP 10, with *as*) qualify; say that (sb. or sth.) has certain qualities: *I hesitate to ~ him as really clever. He ~s himself as a doctor.* (*ALD 2*)

Though the changes include the removal of the parenthetical glosses, the overall result is a much closer correspondence between meaning, syntax, and entry structure.

There is an editorial practice, characteristic of *ALD 2*, which (conversely) often leads to greater conciseness in the layout and wording of definitions, thus serving the strategic needs of economy, as the above revision does not. What is involved is the combining in one sub-section of definitions which, in *ALD 1*, appear as separate numbered senses. Compare the extracts from **desolate** (adjective) in *ALD 1* with the matching parts of the corresponding entry in *ALD 2*. Arrows are included to facilitate comparison between parts of the definitions in the two texts:

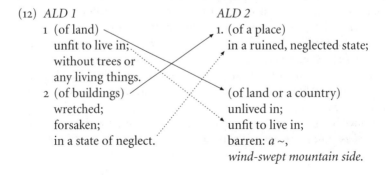

(12) *ALD 1*   *ALD 2*
      1 (of land)   1. (of a place)
         unfit to live in;   in a ruined, neglected state;
         without trees or
         any living things.
      2 (of buildings)   (of land or a country)
         wretched;   unlived in;
         forsaken;   unfit to live in;
         in a state of neglect.   barren: *a ~,*
                                          wind-swept mountain side.

There are three points especially worth noting here. The first is that references (in parentheses) to the categories of noun which the adjective modifies, i.e. '(of land)', '(of buildings)', become in *ALD 2*, less narrowly specific. The second is that some formal and difficult defining vocabulary ('wretched', 'forsaken') is removed. A further point is that despite the loss of specificity in the second *ALD 2* definition, it is supported by a highly specific example. The approach discussed here is an important aspect of Hornby's defining strategy for *ALD 2*, being applied in 10 entries. Generally, as here, sacrificing clear separation of the senses is offset by the greater simplicity of the defining language.

There is one further aspect of Hornby's defining method in *ALD 2* that deserves mention. This is much more widely applied than in *ALD 1* and chiefly affects pairs of homonymous entries, one of which is a zero-derivative of the other (cf. **design** (noun), **design** (verb)). In such cases one or more senses in the verb entry are defined with reference to numbered senses in the noun entry. Compare, in *ALD 2*:

(13) ¹**design** . . . *n.* 1. [C] drawing or outline from which sth. may be made: ~*s for a dress* (*a garden*); . . . 3. [C] pattern; arrangement of lines, shapes, details, as ornament (e.g. on a bowl or carpet) . . .
      ²**design** . . . *v.t. & i.* 1. . . . make designs (def. 1) for: *to ~ a garden* (*a dress*); . . . make designs (def. 3): *He ~s for a large firm of carpet-manufacturers.*

This is a strategy with interesting implications. Usually there is a gain in conciseness. (Compare with 1 in the verb entry the corresponding definition in *ALD 1*: 'make a plan or outline; draw patterns or shapes'.) Furthermore, since understanding of the verb definitions requires reference to the corresponding noun definitions, the learner's sense of the relatedness of roots and their derivatives (in their various meanings) is strengthened. This is chiefly of advantage for encoding (Cowie 1983*b*). But there is a corresponding disadvantage. Students typically turn to their dictionaries for remedies to specific, single problems of communication, especially when decoding, and expect all relevant information to appear at the particular place of reference. Hornby's strategy was perhaps a sign that, while preparing an edition that would meet the needs of the *reader* more fully than before, he had not lost sight of the needs of the *writer*.

3.2.4. Illustrative Examples

It is perhaps only to be expected that, having given prominence to grammatical classes and structures in the Introduction to *ALD 2*—as in that of the first edition—Hornby should devote more space, and often more ingenuity, to the exemplification of grammatical than lexical words in the dictionary itself. This was broadly the case. Yet progress in the illustration of familiar open-class words in a range of functions was often striking. As a comparison of the entries for twelve common adjectives in the two editions shows (see Table 3.3), there was a rise—of just over 20 per cent—in the total number of examples. Yet, when allowances are made for the modest size of the sample, there was an appreciable shift, too, in the types of pattern being illustrated. Though the numerical difference between attributive examples such as *a heavy blow, a heavy fall, a heavy heart* and predicative or postnominal examples—cf. *His literary style is still rather raw* and *cherries not ripe enough to eat*—is still extreme (at 199 to 29), the percentage of the latter types has almost doubled (8.6 per cent to 14.5 per cent).

TABLE 3.3. *Adjectives with attributive and predicative function in* ALD 1 *and* ALD 2

Adjective entry	Examples in *ALD 1*			Examples in *ALD 2*		
	Total	Attributive	Predicative	Total	Attributive	Predicative
able	5	2	3	5	3	2
bright	7	5	2	7	5	2
broad	8	7	1	13	10	3
dark	9	7	2	18	14	4
fresh	22	18	4	21	18	3
heavy	15	14	1	21	19	2
high	42	40	2	49	45	4
light	37	37	0	25	24	1
raw	8	7	1	12	10	2
ripe	6	6	0	12	9	3
rough	17	17	0	21	19	2
small	10	10	0	21	20	1
TOTALS	186	170	16	225	196	29

If we now turn to grammatical entries in *ALD 2*, and specifically to the sub-entry devoted to the positional and directional meanings of the preposition *on*, we find first a marked increase in the number of examples as compared with *ALD 1*. While *ALD 1* offers 8 examples, in an entry occupying half a loosely packed column, *ALD 2* provides, as part of a much denser two-column entry, 20 examples of the corresponding sense. Even in the earlier version, the organization of the entry is helpfully systematic, arranging examples according to the referents of the prepositional object. Note, for instance, the following sequence of three, where the object nouns denote, respectively, a lower horizontal surface, a vertical surface, and an upper horizontal surface—all inside a house:

(14)   *a carpet on the floor*
        a picture on the wall
        a mark on the ceiling (ALD 1)

This arrangement of examples is extended and diversified with great skill in the second edition. The principle of organization to which I have just referred is carried over, and in some cases this means simply providing further examples of the same type of referent:

(15) *pictures on the wall*
      the words (written) on the blackboard (ALD 2)

However, new types of referent are introduced (here 'body parts' and 'means of transport') and useful alternatives added as appropriate:

(16) *have a hat on one's head (a ring on one's finger)*
      carry a coat on (or *over*) *one's arm*
      be (go) on board a ship
      have lunch on the train (ALD 2)

In a number of cases, too, as in this set, a further collocational link is set up between the head of the complex noun phrases (*hat, coat,* etc.) and an appropriate verb. Such examples are of immense value, as they illustrate a complex network of conventional links:

(17) preposition to noun: [*on one's head*]
      noun head to prepositional phrase: [*a hat* [*on one's head*]]
      transitive verb to noun object: [*have* [*a hat* [*on one's head*]]].

3.2.5. Idioms and Phrasal Verbs

A characteristic feature of the treatment of idioms in both *ALD 1* and *ALD 2* was their positioning in the entry for the most 'prominent' constituent word—or 'keyword'—often, though not always, the first or only noun in the idiom. Idioms were not gathered together in a special section but spread throughout the numbered sections of the selected entry according to the sense that their keyword seemed closest to. If one considers *look someone in the face, show one's face,* and *face to face,* then *face* is at least partially interpretable in terms of 'the front part of the head'. Those idioms accordingly appear (in both editions) in the first numbered sub-entry of **face** (noun), the one in which that sense is treated. Similarly, *face* as used in the idiom *keep a straight face* can perhaps be understood in relation to 'expression' or 'look', and the idiom is positioned accordingly.

This approach is designed to help users to understand idioms by reactivating the figurative or literal meanings (consider again *face to face*) from which the idiom derives. Unfortunately, however, it is not always possible to help learners to interpret an idiom by ascribing a meaning to its keyword. The sense of *pull a face,* for instance cannot be arrived at in this way, and in practice, as at **face**, a 'wastebasket' must be provided to receive idioms whose meaning cannot be construed from an understanding of their chief components.

The other problem which this approach gives rise to is accessibility. Given such an arrangement, the user wishing to access a particular idiom must decide first which is its keyword, since this will determine the entry in which the idiom is to be found. (There is no declared policy in either dictionary on which words rank as keywords, though in all the cases we have considered, the keyword is the first or only noun (*face*).) Beyond the problem of identifying the keyword, there is that of deciding in which sub-entry the idiom has been placed. In practice—and in both editions—users may have to read through an entire entry before finding the idiom that interests them.

A solution in fact lay to hand in the way it had been decided to rearrange phrasal verbs in the entries for the major (or 'heavy-duty') verbs (e.g. *come, bring, go, put, take*) in the second edition. In the smaller entries, say those for *catch* or *rub*, verbs with particles or prepositions continued to be positioned at various points in the entry—very much as idioms were—according to the meaning of the verb. So at **catch**, for instance, *catch out* (the cricketing sense) is placed early as it reflects a common literal meaning of the verb. This is the procedure in the shorter entries. In the entries for heavy-duty verbs, however, all phrasal verbs were allocated to a special numbered section headed 'in various senses with advv. and preps.'. There, they were listed alphabetically according to the only (or first) particle or preposition, and their senses (where there was polysemy) were given and illustrated in subsections headed by letters. Nouns formed by zero-derivation from phrasal verbs appeared at the ends of the appropriate subsections:

(18)   **come** . . . **11.** (in various senses with advv. and preps.): . . . ~ **away**, become detached: *The door handle came away in my hand.* ~ **back**, (a) return. (b) recur to the memory: *Their names are all coming back to me now,* I'm beginning to remember them. (c) (of fashions) become popular again: *Will ankle-length skirts* ~ *back again?* . . . '~ -**back** *n.* (esp. of boxers, politicians) return to . . . a former position: *Can he stage a ~-back?*

This is an admirably clear and systematic method which inspired the style of presentation for phrasal verbs adopted in the third edition. At the same time, it also suggested a way forward for the treatment of other types of idiom. The solution to the user's retrieval problems which it surely indicated was: first, to adopt a sensible policy towards the selection of a keyword (or keywords), and then apply it consistently; second, to arrange all items containing a given keyword in a single block within its entry—thus obviating the time-consuming and sometimes fruitless process of searching an entry from end to end for a single idiom; and third, to ensure that all items within the block were arranged in strict alphabetical order (cf. 2.6.1.1). How far that solution was adopted in subsequent compilations, and with what success, we shall see when considering the treatment of idioms in *ALD 3* and *LDOCE 1*.

3.3. *Oxford Advanced Learner's Dictionary*, Third Edition

The decade following the publication of *ALD* 2 was one in which the teaching of English as a Foreign Language in Britain became increasingly professionalized. From the early 1960s onwards, courses of advanced training for teachers of English as Foreign Language became available in a number of British universities, a development which went hand in hand with the emergence of applied linguistics as an academic subject. Professional organizations such as the British Association for Applied Linguistics (BAAL) were set up during the same period. These were all developments that H. E. Palmer and A. S. Hornby had helped pave the way for.

Significantly, this was also a period in which a major programme of grammatical research at the Survey of English Usage, at University College London, began to bear fruit. Its first major publication was also the first comprehensive grammar of contemporary English to be published in Britain (Quirk *et al.* 1972). Such developments would inevitably have a profound effect on the dictionaries that were shortly to be produced, and it was very much in keeping with them that, for the revision and updating of *ALD* 3, A. S. Hornby assembled a small team of linguists from the University of Leeds to help with the treatment of phraseology (A. P. Cowie), phonetics (J. Windsor Lewis), and scientific and technical English (Loreto Todd).

In part, *ALD* 3 continued the movement already begun by *ALD* 2 towards broad and up-to-date lexical coverage. It captured at many points the political, economic, and social changes of the previous decade, mirroring the cultural revolution of the 1960s and early 1970s (with entries for *acid, disco, flower power,* and *pop festival*) and proclaiming its awareness of the social and environmental issues of the time (with *aggro, drop-out, defoliation*) (Cowie 1995: 293). Its illustrations included for the first time a number of photographs, and legibility and ease of reference were served by the introduction of a bold sanserif type-face for headwords and sub-headwords. *ALD* 3 was mainly important, however, for addressing some of the chief descriptive and organizational problems left unresolved by the second edition. These problems and the attempts made to resolve them will be our chief concern in the following sections.

3.3.1. Pronunciation

Plans drawn up for the revision and updating of *ALD* 2 included a scheme for the treatment of pronunciation prepared by Jack Windsor Lewis, at the time a member of the Phonetics Department at the University of Leeds. Windsor Lewis had reviewed *ALD* 2 in 1965 and had remarked favourably on the inclusion of many compounds with appropriate stress markings which were not so marked in other dictionaries or in the *English Pronouncing Dictionary* (*EPD*). But he had also noted the absence of stress marking (cf. 3.2.1, above) from 'open' compounds such as *bank clerk* and *child's play* (1965: 15)—where the first element, misleadingly for the foreign student, carries primary stress—and resolved to make good the omission. It was also his intention to indicate the stress values of idioms in those cases where they were not predictable—as in *to be 'coining money* and *a 'pretty kettle of fish*—where nuclear stress falls, in both cases, not on the last full (or lexical) word, but on an earlier one.

However, Windsor Lewis also had in mind more radical, and as it later turned out, more controversial, changes. These chiefly concerned the symbols chosen to represent simple vowels. Windsor Lewis inherited from *ALD 2* the following set of symbols representing the contrasted vowels in the pairs *bead, bid; fool, full; bard, bad; cord, cod; bird, cupboard*: /iː, i; uː, u; ɑː, æ; ɔː, ɔ; əː, ə/. As he recognized, however, this notation can be misleading as it 'obscures the more significant qualitative differences between the pairs' (Gimson: 1981: 257), while emphasizing the quantitative contrasts by the inclusion or omission of length marks. In now introducing into *ALD 3* the symbols /ɪ/ for /i/, /ʊ/ for /u/, and /ɜ/ for /əː/, and abandoning the length marks, Windsor Lewis was consolidating a movement towards the highlighting of quality distinctions between vowels already begun in his own *Concise Pronouncing Dictionary of British and American English* (1972). His use of the symbol /o/ in place of /ɔ/ was part of that movement. When his transcriptions of the key vowel contrasts are set out, thus: /i, ɪ; u, ʊ; ɑ, æ; ɔ, o; ɜ, ə/, one can see that they were 'quite unambiguous and economical' (Gimson 1981: 257).

As for the omission of length marks after /i, u, ɑ, ɔ, ɜ/, this was prompted by a wish to give due prominence to qualitative contrasts, and to avoid 'misleading the unwary as to the durational value of the English vowels' (Windsor Lewis 1978: 185). As Gimson was to point out in his later (1981) appraisal of the *ALD 3* scheme, this was an entirely defensible change.[7] There was, it was true, a slight loss of simplicity resulting from the introduction of a new non-orthographic symbol (/ɜ/ for the vowel of *burn*). However, in fairness to Windsor Lewis, it should be added that, in order to represent the qualitative difference between the vowels in *port* and *pot*, Gimson would, in *EPD 14* (1977), introduce the equally non-orthographic /ɒ/.

For the most part, criticisms of the transcriptions in *ALD 3* were pedagogical. They were directed first at the replacement of /ɔ/ by /o/, thought by some overseas teachers of English to encourage in such words as *pot, hot* the pronunciation of the vowel found in German *ohne, bohne*, etc., which in a German

---

[7] Earlier, in his Preface to Windsor Lewis's *Concise Pronouncing Dictionary*, Gimson had gone further, stating that the author's 'decision to emphasize the differences of quality rather than of quantity between vowels is especially welcome, since the former have a greater practical relevance for the foreign learner' (1972: v).

transcription was represented by the same symbol. In addition, Windsor Lewis's slanting primary stress mark (shown in /ˈmɑstə(r)/, /ˈpeɪmənt/) 'was judged by many to be too readily suggestive of a specific tone' (Gimson 1980: vii), and in a revised and reset impression of *ALD* 3, published in 1980, the vertical primary stress mark of *ALD* 2 was restored. Users were even more firmly opposed, however, to the removal of length marks after /i, u, ɑ, ɔ, ɜ/, and in a revised and reset impression of *ALD* 3 (1980), these were restored in face of the tenacity with which teachers worldwide clung 'to this familiar symbol' (Gimson 1981: 257).

3.3.2. The Verb-Pattern System

For the new edition, some radical changes were made to the verb-pattern scheme. There were several organizational improvements, the new framework being more systematic and more soundly based than the one it replaced. At the same time, a good deal of complexity was introduced, since many of the patterns were divided into subpatterns, often on the basis of a single transformational difference between them. Above all, the pressing need was not met for a fully mnemonic coding system.

Though the total number of VPs in *ALD* 3 remained the same as in the previous editions (25), the number of subdivisions was greatly increased (from 13 to 38). Much more importantly, though, the arrangement of the patterns was changed, so that, taking account of the major verb-classes represented, they now followed the order copular and intransitive (VPs 1–4E), monotransitive (VPs 6A–10), di-transitive (VPs 11–21, though with some wrongly allocated monotransitives), and complex-transitive (VPs 22–25).[8] This categorization of patterns according to major verb-types clearly owed a great deal to the framework in the *Grammar of Contemporary English*, which had appeared in 1972 (Cowie 1989*b*, 1992*b*).

These major groupings were not made explicit by setting out subsets of VP tables under appropriate headings. However, Hornby continued to demonstrate the relatedness of various minor groupings of VPs within those major categories. This he did by juxtaposing patterns whose differing post-verbal constituents had the same function (cf. 3.2.2, above). Such a juxtaposition exists at VPs 8, 9, and 10—all monotransitive, and all with a different type of clause functioning as direct object:

(19) [VP 8] I couldn't decide what to do next.
       [VP 9] I suppose you'll be leaving soon.
       [VP 10] She asked why I was so late.

As has already been pointed out, the VP scheme was sometimes made more complex by creating subpatterns on the basis of transformational differences

---

[8] VPs 4F, 5, and 7B contained modals or semi-modals (e.g. *have to*) treated as main verbs.

between subclasses of verbs. For instance, the division of VP 6 into A and B was made on the grounds that while some transitive verbs with noun-phrase objects allowed passivization, others did not. Furthermore, some patterns were divided to account for the fact that, after verbs of a specific semantic class, different constituents might be substituted for one another. VP 18A, for example, is set up for verbs denoting 'physical perceptions' and taking a bare infinitive construction, as in *We felt the house shake*. The point is then made that these verbs are also used in VP 19A, which features a present participle (*-ing* form) construction (cf. *We felt the house shaking.*).

A further point has to do with the relationship between the redesigned VP scheme and the individual dictionary entries. Ideally, when the patterns corresponding to the major verb-groupings (intransitive, monotransitive, and so on) were rearranged in the tables for the third edition, they should have been given a matching arrangement in the individual verb entries. However, the old ordering of patterns was left untouched in a number of cases, only the codes themselves being altered to reflect the listing of patterns in the new system (Cowie 1992*b*: 345). There were numerous anomalies. In the entry for **love**[24], for instance, the patterns followed the same order as in the revised framework [VP 6A, D, 7, 17B], while at **marry** 1, they followed the order of the old scheme [VP 6A, 2A, 4A].

Yet the chief focus of criticism, as *ALD 3* was put to the test of constant use throughout the 1970s and 1980s, was undoubtedly the letter/number codes linking individual verb entries and sub-entries to the explanatory tables (Heath 1982; Cowie 1984; Lemmens and Wekker 1986). Codes such as VP6A and VP9 simply reflected the ordering of patterns in the scheme. They told the user nothing about the structure of the individual patterns, nor (as I have already indicated) did they signal any larger category, based on a classification of verbs, to which those patterns might belong. The absence of any mnemonic element in the VP codes additionally made them very difficult to learn, and no doubt deterred many students from even making the effort.

3.3.3. Definitions and Complement Frames

While a number of policy decisions led to regular changes in the treatment of verb patterns, examples, and idioms in *ALD 3*, there were no all-embracing plans to change the arrangement of senses or the structure of definitions. Moreover, as can be shown by examining the heavy-duty verb **break** and the sequence **dervish** to **devolve**, few individual changes were made either, except where entirely new senses were introduced.[9]

---

[9] Neither edition was consistent in marking (by means of parentheses) the direct objects of transitive verbs. In the first sense division of *describe*, in both editions, the first definition has a specified object, but not the second, viz.: 'say what (sb. or sth.) is like; give a picture of in words'.

There was, however, one readily noticeable new feature which deserves mention, as it served as a link between headword and definition and invariably had implications for the form of the latter. It is illustrated in the following two entries from *ALD 3*:

(20) **descend** . . . 4 . . . ~ *upon,* attack suddenly . . .
 despoil . . . ~ *sb (of)*, rob, plunder . . .

Here we are concerned chiefly with a preposition, made prominent by bold italic, which introduces the complementation of a verb. (It may occasionally introduce the complementation of a noun or adjective, as in **devoid** . . . *adj* ~ *of,* without; empty of: . . .).

We have met such patterns before, when discussing exemplification in *ALD 1*. In *ALD 2*, the relevant preposition normally appears as part of the VP code:

(21) **despoil** . . . (VP 1, 18 with *of*) rob, plunder.

However, the preposition is occasionally included in *ALD 2* entries as part of the definition (a convention also used in the *Concise Oxford Dictionary*):

(22) **deter** . . . discourage, hinder (sb. *from* doing sth.): *Failure did not* ~ *him from trying again.*

Most interestingly of all, the preposition is sometimes made, in *ALD 2*, to form part of a 'skeleton' example (Palmer 1936*b*), which *precedes* the definition:

(23) **discourage** . . . 2. (VP 18) ~ *sb. from doing sth.*, put difficulties in his way; . . . try to persuade him not to do it: . . .

What are the merits of these various strategies in relation to the definitions they precede or form part of? Linking the preposition with the verb code, as in (VP 1, 18 with *of*), at (21), is probably the least satisfactory, as it fails to reflect the close relationship between headword and preposition, and the obligatory or optional nature of the latter. Inclusion of the preposition and its object—as in the **deter** entry, above—as part of the definition is better, as it marries up synonyms ('discourage', 'hinder') of the headword with the complementation to form a natural sentence, which can then be echoed by the example. This is the model that would later be favoured by the *Cobuild 1* editors, and there is much to commend it (Sinclair *et al.* 1987).

Perhaps, though, the third arrangement, as at (23), is the best. The entity being defined is, after all, the headword as part of a larger lexico-syntactic pattern (note again *discourage sb. from doing sth.*) and it is fitting that this whole pattern should precede the definition. This, at any rate, was the convention adopted for *ALD 3*.

Individual 'complement frames' were made to differ according to whether there was one preposition or a choice of two. Compare:

(24) **derogate** . . . ~ *from,*
      descant . . . ~ *on/upon,*

However, *ALD* 3 was not always successful in distinguishing cases in which there was a direct object preceding the preposition from one in which there was none. In the frame for the following entry, for example, *sb* should ideally have appeared before *from*:

(25) **deter** . . . ~ *from,* discourage, hinder . . .

Finally, the problem was not solved, in all cases, of marrying such frames satisfactorily to definitions. In the following sub-entry, the definition 'attack suddenly' is equivalent to the verb + preposition as a unit, and this is correctly conveyed:

(26) **descend** . . . 4 . . . ~ *upon,* attack suddenly: *The bandits ~ed upon the defenceless village.*

The same, however, cannot be said of the definition 'set apart' in the following entry—and even less of 'decide or ordain in advance'—in relation to **destine** . . . **for:**

(27) **destine** . . . ~ *for,* set apart, decide or ordain in advance: *He was ~d from birth for the army.*

These were problems of analysis and presentation that would have to await resolution in the fourth edition.

3.3.4. Illustrative Examples

Clause and phrase examples in the first two editions of *ALD* were, as we have seen, for the most part 'minimal lexicalized patterns', whose function was to help in the understanding and correct use of the headword. 'Minimal', in the case of clauses, meant the use of verbs in the bare infinitive (or 'base') form, and of object nouns with little or no modification, as in the examples *grasp sb's hand, grasp an argument.* Beginning with the third edition, however, the characteristic structure of such examples began to change. While a number of the newly introduced phrase examples, for instance, were of the familiar type (e.g. *discriminatory legislation, disposable nappies*), a growing number were more fully developed and closer to simulated instances of language in use (Cowie 1995: 290). This is borne out by considering noun-phrase examples in entries for nouns and adjectives in *ALD* 3. The examples may be found in main entries for those two parts of speech, or in run-ons dealing with noun or adjective derivatives of verbs, as here:

(28) **disengage** . . . *vt, vi* . . . **~ment** *n* . . . *the military and economic ~ment of the USA from SE Asia.*

In the sequence of entries from **make²** to **market¹** in *ALD 3*, there are in total 79 noun phrase examples, of which 13 are entirely new (just over 16 per cent of the total). Of these, six have complex post-modification of the head (with a prepositional phrase or non-finite clause):

(29) **malaise** . . . *years of ~ in industrial relations*
  malformation . . . *a ~ of the spine*
  mandarin . . . *the ~ prose of civil servants*
  mandate . . . *the ~ given to us by the electors*
  mania . . . *a ~ for collecting china ornaments*
  manufacture . . . *goods of foreign ~*

I have suggested elsewhere that this extended type of pattern confers a double advantage (Cowie 1995: 291). First, its structure can indicate collocation at several points and deepen understanding. (Compare *mandarin prose* and *the mandarin prose of civil servants*.) Second, if the phrase contains a non-finite clause, the whole can often be converted to a simple sentence structure. In other words there is added flexibility for sentence building:

(30) *the mandate given to us by the electors* ⇒
  the electors have given us a mandate

Finally, examples of this type (consider again *the mandarin prose of civil servants*) provide for a fuller and more convincing expression of cultural information.

If we now turn to the conventions used to denote collocability (or collocational range) in *ALD 3*, we find that parentheses are reserved for marking off optional words or phrases, while the oblique stroke is used to indicate alternatives, as here:

(31) *The argument still holds (good/true).*[10]
  a tea/dinner service of 30 pieces.

However, no systematic attempt was made to distinguish between 'open' and 'restricted' collocability—the problem identified when discussing collocational ranges in *GEW* and *ALD 1*, where they were marked off by square brackets. True, in some cases, restricted collocational range was implied in the new edition. In a case such as *hold a meeting/debate/examination*, for instance, the specialized sense of *hold* was determined by a fairly narrow range of nouns (of which *reunion*, *discussion*, and *review* might also form part), and this range could appropriately be signalled by obliques. In other cases, though, the same device set off a series of semantically unrelated nouns which could easily be extended

---

[10] In *ALD 2*, parentheses were used in examples to indicate alternatives, as here: 'efficient . . . *an ~ secretary (staff of teachers)*'. Square brackets had been used for this purpose in *ALD 1*.

(as in: *have a sensation of warmth/dizziness/falling*). Some attempt would be made to deal with this problem in the fourth edition.

3.3.5. Idioms and Phrasal Verbs

Work on the third edition of *ALD* proceeded in parallel with the compilation of the first volume of the *Oxford Dictionary of Current Idiomatic English* (*ODCIE 1*), which was to appear a year after *ALD 3* itself. Its authors drew extensively and fruitfully on the Palmer-Hornby tradition in phraseology, as we have already seen, but some items from *ODCIE*, and above all a more rigorous approach to the definition of idioms, fed into the revision of the major work.[11] We have seen how one result of failing to distinguish sharply between collocations and idioms was that some of the latter lay undetected among examples illustrating non-idiomatic uses of the headword. Of the following set of three examples from the entry for *account* (noun) in *ALD 2*, for instance, the first is non-idiomatic, while the second and third are idiomatic:

(32)   **account** . . . 6. . . . *Don't always believe newspaper ~s. By his own ~, . . . By all ~s, . . .*

In *ALD 3*, however, items that were clearly invariable, or variable to a limited degree—and possibly figurative or opaque as well—were made prominent by means of bold print, as follows:

(33)   **account** . . . **6** . . . *Don't always believe newspaper ~s of events.* **by one's own ~, . . . by/from all ~s, . . .**

The use of the oblique to mark off alternatives in idioms, and of parentheses to indicate their optional elements, was standardized in this edition, and some progress was made (within particular numbered sections) towards alphabetical arrangement, as here in the entry for **ear¹**:

(34)   **ear**[1] . . . 1 **be all ears, . . . fall on deaf ears, . . . feel one's 'ears burning, . . . give one's ears (for sth/to do sth), . . . go in (at) ,one ear and out (at) the 'other, . . .**

There was also some improvement in the presentation of phrasal verbs in the new edition, though, as in its predecessor, this chiefly affected combinations featuring one of the 'heavy-duty' verbs (e.g. *bring, come, lay, make, send, take*). The new edition drew on some of the design features of *ODCIE 1*, which dealt specifically with phrasal verbs. For example, combinations of verb + particle which contained a fixed noun-phrase object (e.g. *lay down one's arms, lay down*

---

[11] As joint compiler of *ODCIE 1*, I was invited by Hornby to take responsibility for the treatment of idioms and phrasal verbs in *ALD 3*.

the law) were positioned immediately after the simple verb + particle combination (here, *lay sth down*):

(35) **lay sth down,** . . . **lay down one's arms,** . . . **lay down the law,** . . . **lay down one's life**

The use of a prominent bold-italic face for phrasal verbs and their alignment with the edge of the column (with a fresh paragraph for each new particle or preposition combining with a given verb) was intended to facilitate access:

(36) **lay sth aside,** . . .
      lay sth back, . . .
      lay sth in, . . .
      lay off, . . .

One helpful new convention, introduced into *ALD 3*, though not adopted by the authors of *ODCIE 1*, was the systematic insertion of **sb** ('somebody') and **sth** ('something') between verbs and particles, or their omission, to indicate the transitive/intransitive contrast. In the above series, the first, second, and third items are transitive, while the last is intransitive.

   Not all the presentational shortcomings noted in *ALD 2* were put right in *ALD 3*. No attempt was made in the new edition to settle on a specific class of word as keyword to ensure ease of reference to individual idioms, and with few exceptions no move was made to arrange idioms in blocks, whether in specially designated sub-entries or not.[12] Nor was the new method of setting out phrasal verbs applied to all the verb entries which contained them. Both these deficiencies would be made good in the fourth edition of *ALD* (1989).

3.4. *Longman Dictionary of Contemporary English*, First Edition

The monopoly enjoyed for over thirty years by A. S. Hornby's *Advanced Learner's Dictionary* was broken in 1978 by the publication of the *Longman Dictionary of Contemporary English* (*LDOCE*). Though not such a revolutionary work as was claimed at the time, nor—as our survey of investigations undertaken in the 1920s and 1930s has shown—the first to make use of the findings of linguistic research, it did achieve the desirable end of bringing the learner's dictionary into line with more recent developments, especially in grammar and semantics (Procter 1978: viii). Significantly, two senior editors, Robert Ilson and Janet Whitcut, had worked on the Survey of English Usage, whose resources lay behind two major descriptive grammars which had appeared just before the

---

[12] In certain larger entries in both *ALD 2* and *ALD 3* (e.g. **head** *n*), idioms were placed in a special section headed 'various phrases'. However, this procedure was by no means uniformly applied.

dictionary itself (Quirk *et al.* 1972; Quirk and Greenbaum 1973), and on which the *LDOCE* team were able to draw so fruitfully. Yet, despite the acclaim that it deservedly attracted—for an early, close analysis see Stein (1979)—*LDOCE* was noteworthy not so much for breaking entirely new ground as for extending with skill and rigour two design features which can be traced back to the very beginnings of the learner's dictionary—a system of construction-patterns linked to entries by a letter/number coding system and a controlled defining vocabulary (Cowie 1990). Our appraisal of a major landmark in EFL lexicography focuses especially on those two features.

3.4.1. Pronunciation

The treatment of pronunciation in *LDOCE 1* reflects the linguistic professionalism of its editors. It is more detailed than in *ALD 3*, and more fully described in the introduction, though some of the guidance provided there is likely to be of greater interest to the teacher or advanced student than to the ordinary learner. All aspects of the scheme, however, are clearly explained and fully illustrated. The comparative table which shows the sets of vowel and diphthong symbols used in *LDOCE*, Windsor Lewis's *Concise Pronouncing Dictionary of British and American English* (*CPD*) (1972), and the 13th edition of the *English Pronouncing Dictionary* (*EPD 13*) (1969) is a helpful reference point for teachers needing to adjust from one familiar system to another, less familiar, scheme. It should be noted, incidentally, that the pronunciation adviser, A. C. Gimson, recommended for *LDOCE* the system of vowel symbols that he had introduced in the 14th edition of *EPD* (1977) and that he was later to incorporate in the revised and reset impression of *ALD 3* (1980). This differed from Windsor Lewis's 1972 system only in the replacement of /o/ by /ɒ/ and in the restoration of length marks, as in /iː/, /ɑː/, etc.[13]

As regards the marking of stress, *LDOCE* employed the same vertical strokes (placed before the relevant syllable and respectively above and below the transcription) to indicate primary and secondary stress that were used in *ALD 2* and *ALD 3*, as here:

(37)   /ˌkɒnsəˈtiːnə/
        /kəˌmɪzəˈreɪʃən/

In some longer words (e.g. *contraindication* and *incompatibility*), two levels of stress were present other than primary stress and arguably these should have been marked as secondary stresses, as indeed they were in the case of *contraindication*: /ˌkɒntrəˌɪndɪˈkeɪʃən/. However, not to provide a similar marking for

---

[13] There were also differences in the representation of diphthongs in *bite* and *now*. Cf. /aɪ/, /aʊ/ (*CPD* and *ALD 3*) and /aɪ/, /aʊ/ (*EPD 14* and *LDOCE*).

incompatibility on the grounds that the third syllable in this word, though not in the other, contained a vowel, /æ/, that was always 'strong', was to fall into the trap of requiring the dictionary user to apply predigested rules, rather than recover information explicitly set out at the point of entry (cf. Gimson 1981).

Whether written solid (**trade·mark**), with a hyphen (**touch-type**), or open (**town hall**), compounds were entered in *LDOCE* as main entries.[14] Editorial policy for the treatment of stress in compounds of the first type was to provide a full transcription. However, when they were hyphenated or open, and both parts of the compound also appeared in the dictionary as separate main words, the policy was not to provide a full transcription, but to indicate the stress pattern alone. Each syllable was represented by a centred dot, and a raised stroke was placed before the dot representing the syllable with primary stress. Secondary stress marks were also used where necessary:

(38)   **touch-type** /ˈ· ·/ **town hall** /ˌ· ˈ·/

This was a type of treatment which, unlike *ALD 3* in its treatment of open compounds, left nothing for the user to determine by rule. However, it is arguably more difficult to interpret than marks placed above or below the full orthographic form (cf. ˈtouch-type, ˌtown ˈhall).

A valuable feature of the *LDOCE* pronunciation scheme was the introduction of a special mark to indicate stress shift in compounds when they are used as modifiers of nouns. When a compound such as *long-range* is pronounced independently, or at the end of a sentence, it has the stress pattern /ˌ· ˈ·/. But in a phrase such as *long-range forecast*, primary stress shifts to *forecast*, with *range* becoming unstressed and *long* acquiring secondary stress in the phrase as a whole: /ˌ· ·ˈ ·/. In the entry for **long-range**, this shift is indicated by a black arrowhead placed after the syllable carrying primary stress: /ˌ·ˈ·◄/

3.4.2. The Grammatical Scheme

The grammatical scheme devised for *LDOCE 1* was a bold and imaginative attempt to deal in one comprehensive system of categories and 'codes' with the syntax and inflectional morphology of the major (open) word-classes in English. The scheme was set out in some detail in the introduction. (Closed-class categories such as personal and relative pronouns and auxiliary verbs were treated in a separate set of tables.) The outstanding feature of the system was that it codified a wider range of syntactic structures than *ALD 3*, and that at least part of the set of codes was mnemonic. As well as codifying verb-complementation, for

---

[14] The centred bold dot (as in **trade·mark**) indicates the point at which the compound may be broken at the end of a line.

instance, as all three editions of the Hornby dictionary had, *LDOCE* introduced codes for several subclasses of nouns and adjectives and for the types of phrase and clause constructions which could occur as their post-modifiers. The codes accompanying the following examples, for instance, indicate not only the predicative function of the adjective (F) but also possible differences in the choice of post-modifier (3 = *to*-infinitive, 5 = *that*-clause):

(39) [F3] *John is* **eager** *to please.*
      [F5] *He was* **sure** (*that*) *she knew.*

Yet despite its success in bringing this much wider range of word-classes and complementation patterns within a systematic framework, the *LDOCE* scheme had serious weaknesses, both analytical and presentational. The system was over-elaborate, involving no less than three levels of analysis, each with its own labels, and was liable to defeat all but the most sophisticated or determined user. Incomprehensibly, given the appearance, shortly before, of two major grammars from the same publishing house, the compilers failed to make use of their more familiar and manageable approach to clause structure and noun subclassification (cf. Quirk *et al.* 1972; Quirk and Greenbaum 1973).

The difficulties which the scheme presents for the dictionary user are, as I have suggested, linked to the elaborate, multi-level approach to analysis. First, there is an attempt to explain the syntactic functions of nouns, adjectives, verbs, and to a more limited extent adverbs, by reference to a frame in which four numbered positions (I, II, III, IV) indicate *both* the modifying functions of adjectives and nouns in noun phrase structure, *and* the clause functions of objects and complements (see Figure 3.1).

My summary statement is perhaps already indicative of the likely confusion

```
                        POSITION
                           I
          She gave him a  new   coat.
                    His   new   coat was black.
                           II
       The wood was 3 inches  thick.
                The president  elect  visited the factory.
                           III
                    She was  happy.
             He gave the  boy  a boat.
             He kicked the  ball.
                           IV
          He made him a  king.
          He gave the boy a  boat.
```

FIG. 3.1. Positional Frame in *LDOCE* (1978)

in the mind of the user, since 'slots' I and II have to do with phrase structure—and within phrase structure chiefly with modifiers, not with heads—while slots III and IV are concerned with clause structure.[15] Moreover, while positions III and IV are said to 'show the position of OBJECTS and COMPLEMENTS after a verb' (Procter 1978: xxix), what the diagram in fact illustrates in those positions is the functioning of adjectives and nouns (*happy*, *boy*, etc.), as *the heads of adjective and noun phrases*—which then in turn operate as clause elements.

After the positional diagram, the user is introduced to a list of capital letters designed to act as codes for various functionally and inflectionally defined sub-classes. (Letter F, denoting predicative adjectives and adverbs, is illustrated at (39), above.) Here we reach a second level of analysis, and a further weakness, which is that of 32 letter-codes referring to the major word-classes, only 9 are defined in relation to the positional diagram. Many of the letter codes refer to noun subclasses defined (more satisfactorily) in terms of subject-verb concord and inflectional anomalies (e.g. *trousers, dramatics*). Arguably, the scheme would have been better for dispensing with the positional frame altogether, especially as clause-functions such as direct object or object complement could have been defined in relation to the newly published *Grammar of Contemporary English*. Failure to draw fully and explicitly on that model is all the more inexplicable when one realizes that the verb-classes copular, intransitive, (mono) transitive, di-transitive and complex-transitive—though dispersed throughout the alphabetically arranged list of letters instead of being helpfully placed together—are nonetheless present in the grammatical scheme.[16]

A third key feature of the scheme is by contrast a source of strength. This is a set of numbers (1–9) designed to indicate the class of constituent that follows a given verb (say, as its direct object), or a particular noun or adjective (say, as its post-modifier). A given number always refers to the same constituent class, irrespective of its function. For instance, nouns, verbs, and adjectives followed by a *to*-infinitive construction all have the code 3, as follows:

(40) [P3] **qualifications** *to do the job*
      [T3] *I* **want** *to go.*
      [U3] *There is some* **reason** *to believe it.*

The first two editions of *ALD* pointed out more or less systematically, in notes accompanying the relevant verb-patterns, which of them allowed the passive and how the passive was variously formed. Yet, no system of passive codes was developed, and coverage by example was somewhat hit and miss. Here too was an

[15] In the third example, *The wood was 3 inches thick*, *thick* is the head of an adjective phrase functioning as subject complement.
[16] The term 'di-transitive' is not used in the scheme, though the relevant category is labelled 'D'. 'Complex-transitive' verbs (e.g. *consider* as in *They considered him a fool*) are again not referred to as such. Here the label used is 'X'.

area where the Longman dictionary broke fresh ground. As Stein has shown, labels were devised which allowed for four possibilities—'often passive', 'usually passive', 'passive rare', and 'no passive'—and these were introduced into entries on a generous scale (Stein 1979).

3.4.3. The Controlled Defining Vocabulary

The notion of a controlled defining vocabulary (or CV) dates from the earliest days of the learner's dictionary and derives ultimately from the limited definition vocabulary of Michael West's *New Method English Dictionary* (1935), to which reference was made in Chapter 1. The defining vocabulary of *LDOCE*, however, was modelled on a later compilation by West, the *General Service List* of 1953. As Paul Procter acknowledged, all definitions in the new dictionary were 'written in a controlled vocabulary of approximately 2,000 words which were selected by a thorough study of a number of frequency and pedagogic lists . . . particular reference having been made to *A General Service List of English Words* . . . by Michael West (Procter 1978: viii–ix). Furthermore, 'a rigorous set of principles' was designed to ensure that only the most 'central' meanings of those words were used. Finally, it should be noted that the CV was used not simply for framing definitions but also for composing illustrative examples (Cowie 1990).[17]

The *LDOCE* scheme has prompted a good deal of analysis, and much favourable and critical comment. Among those who have analysed the scheme in some detail, Gabriele Stein asks whether the range of grammatical functions and meanings actually exploited by the dictionary compilers exceeds the stated total of 2,000 words (Stein 1979). The CV contains, for instance, a number of affixes such as *-al*, *-ate*, and *-en*, each of which helps to form words of more than one class and with more than one sense. (Compare, for instance, *nation* ⇒ *national* and *arrive* ⇒ *arrival*.) Should these various uses be included in the overall total? Partly in order to suggest that the learning burden represented by a CV is lighter than in fact it is, there is a tendency on the part of their designers to conceal their actual size. Stein opposes this tendency, arguing that 'it is more important that [the CV] be semantically self-sufficient than that it be restricted to an arbitrary fixed number of items' (1979: 6).

A more extensive investigation based on the machine-readable version of *LDOCE 1* sought to test the claim made by its chief editor that, in the controlled vocabulary (CV), 'only the most "central" meanings of these 2,000 words, and only easily understood derivatives, were used' (Procter 1978: ix). The researchers —three computational linguists at the University of Liège—concentrated specifically on ambiguities due to the use of polysemous words, phrasal verbs, and

---

[17] In the second edition of *LDOCE* (1987), only the definitions were written within the limits of the CV.

idioms in the CV and on how they might be remedied, and concluded that, partly as a result of those ambiguities, the use of the CV caused difficulties for the foreign user of the dictionary (Jansen, Mergeai, and Vanandroye 1987).

By creating a CV-subfile containing all the entries describing the *LDOCE* CV-items and a list of all the dictionary headwords, and then adapting the CV-subfile to an information retrieval package, the investigators were able to show that some words (e.g. *amusing, anyone*) were listed in the CV but did not appear in the dictionary as headwords, while others (e.g. *business, hole,* and *whose*), though occurring quite frequently in definitions and examples, were not included in the CV-list. Given the special interest of the investigators in phrasal verbs, they were surprised to discover that the only phrasal verb in the CV-list was *wrap (up)*, thus suggesting that all other occurrences of phrasal verbs in definitions were transparent combinations of verbs + adverbs/prepositions. In fact, idiomatic phrasal verbs were quite often used in a defining role.

Focusing on the possible ambiguity of simple verbs in their definition contexts, the researchers examined occurrences of five of the most polysemous verbs and showed that though 74 occurrences of *run* (for instance) referred to the notion of fast movement, no less than 19 uses were more or less idiomatic (1987: 88). As for the verb *break*, a number of its uses in definitions consisted of restricted collocations, in which the sense of the verb was far from straightforward, thus: *break the habit, break the law, break the flow, break the rules,* and *break a record.* As regards phrasal verbs in definitions, the analysis showed that there were as many (idiomatic) phrasal verbs incorporating *run* (16) as there were non-idiomatic uses of the verb with an adverb or preposition, while about a quarter of all occurrences of *break* were as components of phrasal verbs (1987: 89).[18]

As for the practical effectiveness of the Longman CV, investigations which have been carried out with foreign students have shown that, when asked to compare a selection of *LDOCE* definitions with corresponding ones from *ALD* and/or a mother-tongue dictionary, students had ranked *LDOCE* first for 'comprehensibility' (MacFarquhar and Richards 1983; Herbst 1986*b*). However, simplicity and comprehensibility are, arguably, not the only properties that definitions written within a controlled vocabulary need to possess. It is also important that they should be accurate, concise and written in natural English, and *LDOCE* provides some evidence that, in striving to be simple and comprehensible, compilers can sometimes lose sight of one or more of the other criteria. Lack of precision is especially evident in definitions of scientific and technical

---

[18] As a means of dealing with the constant use of definition words with multiple meanings, the researchers proposed that such items should be cross-referenced to the appropriate senses in the dictionary by means of superscript numbers. The absence of a superscript would denote reference to the first (i.e. literal) sense.

words, such as the names of plants, animals, and substances (Stein 1979; Herbst 1986*b*). In the following definition of *lobster*, for instance, there is no reference to claws, while in attempting to avoid the use of the generic term 'shellfish' the drafter has fallen back on the awkward and misleading 'sea animal'. In these respects it may be compared with the corresponding definition in *ALD* 3:

(41) **lobster** . . . a type of large 8-legged sea animal with a shell, the flesh of which may be eaten after boiling, when it turns bright red (*LDOCE 1*)
      lobster . . . shellfish with eight legs and two claws, bluish-black before and scarlet after being boiled. (*ALD 3*)

A problem that is posed by many words—and not simply technical terms—is that to obtain satisfactory definitions, it is necessary to include references to words outside the radius of the CV (Herbst 1986*b*). Moreover, as West had shown in *Definition Vocabulary* (1935), if such words are included in definitions, there is the further problem of whether they should be glossed there as well as at their own point of entry. In the first of the following two definitions, the capitalized item (GOLF CLUB) serves simply as a cross-reference, but in the second, the item in capitals (ELEMENT) is preceded by a definition ('a simple substance') which, though helpful, is hardly economic:

(42) **wedge** . . . a GOLF CLUB with a heavy metal head for driving the ball high out of sand or rough ground
      sulphur . . . a simple substance (ELEMENT) that is found in different forms (esp. a light yellow powder) and is used in the chemical and paper industries and in medicines

The earlier reference to 'sea animal' is a reminder that, in attempting to steer clear of superordinate terms that fall outside the CV, the editor may either invent a term or—perhaps worse—use a word which is more familiar than the definiendum but not a true superordinate. This criticism can be applied to 'screw' in the following definition, one which is made additionally imprecise by suggesting that the bolt is fastened to the nut, rather than the nut to the bolt:

(43) **bolt[1]** . . . a screw with no point, which fastens onto a NUT[1] (2) to hold things together

3.4.4. Illustrative Examples

A fact of some importance to keep in mind when examining the choice and presentation of illustrative material in *LDOCE 1* is that it is composed within the same controlled vocabulary as the definitions (Procter 1978: viii–ix). That this does not necessarily result in the use of unnatural English is borne out by the following examples from the entry for **for[1]** (preposition). The informal or neutral style represented here goes hand in hand with a brevity which is desirable in sentences whose chief functions are—besides illustrating sense—to convey the possibility of choosing between an animate or inanimate prepositional object (viz. *your sister* vs. *the office*) and to indicate collocation with verbs (cf. *save . . . for, buy . . . for*):

(44) **for**[1] *. . . prep* 1 that is/are intended to belong to, be given to, or used for the purpose of: *This parcel isn't for you, it's for your sister.* | *They've bought some new chairs for the office.* | *Save some of the cake for Arthur . . . .* | *What's this money for? It's for buying some food for dinner.* | *. . .*

The same qualities of brevity, naturalness, and fitness for purpose can be seen in many verb entries, where a key function of examples is to illustrate verb-patterns. In the following sense-division of the entry for **forget**, the examples cover all the relevant patterns, almost exactly in the same order as in the table of codes:

(45) **forget** *. . .* 1 [T1, 3, 4, 5a, 6a,b; IØ] *. . . I'm sorry, I've forgotten your name.* | *Don't forget to bring the cases.* | *I'll never forget finding that rare old coin in my garden.* | *I'm sorry, I was forgetting (that) you don't like beans.* | *I forget who it was who said it.* | *I forget where to go.* | *"What's her name?" "I forget"*

As it happens, none of the examples in these entries indicate possible variation, whether lexical or grammatical. In *ALD 3*, as we have seen, alternative complementation patterns, marked off by obliques, are often included in the same example sentence, as here: *I have forgotten how to do it/where he lives/whether he wants it.* Part of the collocational range of a headword can of course be indicated by the same means:

(46) **piece**[1] *. . .* 2 a ~ *of news/luck/advice/information, etc.* . . . . 4 *a fine* ~ *of work/ music/poetry . . . (ALD 3)*

Now the same device is sometimes employed in *LDOCE* also, and for the same purposes, i.e. indicating alternative constructions (*the Americans were fighting for/fighting to gain their freedom.*) and lexical (or grammatical) substitutes (*Where did you pick up that book/your excellent English/the habit/such ideas?*). However, use of the oblique is not widespread in *LDOCE*, and this is possibly a weakness. Especially where the choice is between single lexical items, as at **piece**, use of the oblique allows the editor to pack a good deal of information into a small space, and as I have indicated elsewhere, some idea can also be given of the semantic range of substitutable items and even of restricted lexical choice (Cowie 1978*b*, 1989*a*).

Does the use of the controlled vocabulary sometimes act as a constraint on the Longman editors when composing examples? It is true that longer examples in *LDOCE 1* are sometimes artificial, but this is not necessarily a consequence of using a limited vocabulary. Unnaturalness is much more likely to be due to uncertainty over the precise collocability of a word and/or its appropriate level of use. Consider, for example, *a deadly (powerful? telling?) argument against his plan, I tried to deal justice to all men* (a blend of *dispense justice to* and *deal justly with?*) and *a debatable (disputed?) border area*. Another source of artificiality is the attempt to include within the limits of one example sentence information that would, in normal discourse, be spread over two or more. Take, for example, *That very sick man is at death's door, I'm afraid.* Here, *at death's door*, which has end focus, will be interpreted as 'new' information. In contrast, *That very sick man* is in a position associated with 'given' information—information that the reader is assumed to possess already. Yet full modification of a noun phrase (as in *that very sick . . .*) is more typical of new than given, and in normal discourse the detail provided here would probably be given end focus in a separate clause (*He's a very sick man.*). In fact, *LDOCE 1* packs the information into one sentence, so sacrificing naturalness to economy (cf. Cowie 1989*a*: 60).

3.4.5. Idioms and Phrasal Verbs

In the General Introduction to *LDOCE 1* some attempt was made to tackle the problems of idiom arrangement identified earlier in this chapter, and specifically the questions of which word (or perhaps word-class) was to be regarded as the keyword, and of how individual idioms were to be arranged within the entry for the keyword. As it happened, no one criterion was referred to in *LDOCE 1* when deciding which the keyword was to be. It was decided that the keyword would vary according to whether the whole or a part of the idiom was 'idiomatic' (in the sense of semantically opaque):

(47) . . . a **bone of contention** is under **bone** because *bone* is used in a more
IDIOMATIC way than *contention*. If all the words are IDIOMATIC the idiom
will be included under the most unusual word. Thus **a pig in a poke** is
under **poke**. If you cannot find the IDIOM under the first word you
choose, then look under the other words. (Procter 1978: xxvi–xxvii)

Here the *LDOCE* editors are shown to have fallen into the same trap as Hornby and his colleagues: that of supposing that dictionary users are capable of breaking down the semantic structure of an expression which we must surely assume they are largely ignorant of. It is arguably as futile to expect learners to determine whether the whole or a part of an unfamiliar word-combination is 'idiomatic' as it is to expect them to know which sense of a constituent word provides the best clue to its overall meaning. Any approach to the location of idioms in EFL dictionaries, and possibly in dictionaries for native speakers also, must begin with recognition of that simple truth. And also with its corollary: that at most we can expect a learner to recognize the words of which an idiom is composed —and possibly the parts of speech of some of them. These truths were not fully grasped, nor the right conclusions drawn, until work began on the EFL dictionaries of the third generation.

As far as the arrangement of idioms within entries was concerned, however, *LDOCE 1* was already taking a significant step forward. Though idioms were not drawn together to form a single block, a method was adopted which was just as effective. This was to order idioms alphabetically in a series of numbered subsections towards the end of the entry for their keyword, as in this entry, where the idioms begin in the third sub-section:

(48) **ease¹** . . . *n* [U] **1** the state of being comfortable . . . **2** the ability to do something without difficulty: . . . **3 at (one's) ease** without worry or nervousness **4 ill at ease** worried and nervous **5 put someone at his ease** to free someone from worry or nervousness **6 (stand) at ease** (*used esp. as a military command*) (to stand) with feet apart . . . **7 take one's ease** rest from work or effort

This admirably clear arrangement put idioms on the same level within the structure of the entry as numbered senses of the headword. It is worth noting, too, that the oblique and parentheses were introduced (with the same functions as in *ALD 3*) and that in some entries examples were provided:

(49) **pocket¹** . . . **9 be/live in each other's pockets** *infml* (of two people) to be always together . . . **13 out of pocket** *BrE* having paid a certain amount, usu without good results: *I bought a new cigarette lighter and it broke; now I'm £10 out of pocket*

The treatment of phrasal verbs in *LDOCE 1* was less successful than that of idioms, particularly in regard to placement (later to be the object of radical revision). As far as arrangement was concerned, phrasal verbs were treated as main entries and listed in strict alphabetical order. The same ordering principle was applied to zero-derived nouns, whether printed solid (e.g. **blackout**) or with a hyphen (e.g. **foul-up**). The implementation of this policy naturally gave rise to alphabetical sequences in which phrasal verbs alternated with simple words, nominal compounds, and derivatives (consider: **riderless, ride up, ridge¹, ridge², ridgepole, ridge tile**), but there seemed to be no reason why the user, once the principle was grasped, should have any more difficulty in retrieving **ride up** from this sequence than from the entry for **ride**. The strategy had, after all, an American pedigree which included the great *Webster's Third* itself. However, the approach did pose a number of problems, both of analysis and retrieval. The chief problem had to do with where the line was to be drawn, analytically, between idiomatic and non-idiomatic phrasal verbs. We could be sure that fully idiomatic phrasal verbs would have main entry status in *LDOCE 1* (so, for instance, *carry* *out* in the sense 'fulfil' or 'complete') and equally that non-idiomatic cases would not (e.g. *carry out* in the sense 'bear or convey from a place'). But what of *whip up*, as in *whip up the cream*, where the particle has an intensive or completive sense, and the whole combination may be perceived as a unit? This is recorded neither at **whip** nor at **whip up**—unlike the precisely parallel *beat up* (*the eggs*), which appears in the entry for **beat up**, alongside two more idiomatic senses. What is called for here is precise identification of several marginal types, and probably the decision to include them as main entries (Stein 1989*b*).

One final problem of analysis and organization is interestingly handled. Some phrasal verbs feature in more complex combinations, in which a noun is also part of an idiomatic whole (cf. 3.3.5). Consider, for example, *let off steam* and *pull out all the stops*. Will users regard such items as extensions of the simplex phrasal verb (and consult the entries for **let off** and **pull out**)? Or will they regard them as idioms involving problematic senses of *steam* and *stops*? On the whole, *LDOCE* inclines to the first assumption, entering **let off steam**, for instance, as a subentry at **let off**. In other cases, including *pull out all the stops*, there is a belt and braces approach, with full treatment at the appropriate noun entry (here **stop**) and—at the entry for the phrasal verb—a cross-reference in which STOPS (with its relevant entry and sense numbers) is highlighted:

(50) **pull out** *v adv* . . . —see also . . . **pull out (all) the** STOPS[2] (10)

3.5. Conclusion

EFL lexicography in the middle and late 1970s was characterized both by steady advance within established guidelines, and by radical innovation. *ALD* 2, a decade earlier, had already shifted the balance within the content and design of the general-purpose dictionary, thus ensuring that it would cater even-handedly for the learner's receptive and productive needs. This movement was consolidated by *ALD* 3, which also made major changes to its verb-pattern scheme and to the treatment of pronunciation, idioms, and phrasal verbs. The appearance of *LDOCE* 1 towards the end of the decade was an important turning-point, breaking the monopoly enjoyed by Hornby's classic work and, especially in its introduction of a controlled defining vocabulary, ensuring that the 1980s would be a period of profound re-evaluation and further substantial change.

The publication of *LDOCE* 1 also represented a significant extension of the role of the computer in EFL dictionary-making. Though as early as 1959 a database system had been designed in the United States for encoding on computer the major information categories—pronunciation, grammar, and so on—of dictionary entries (Bailey 1986), *LDOCE* 1 was the first EFL dictionary to be reconstituted as an electronic database. The encoded, computer-stored dictionary not only transformed the processes of compilation, editing, and revision but also —as references to research using the machine-readable version of *LDOCE 1* have shown—became a versatile resource for pure and applied research and further development (Cowie 1990). Nothing less than a computer revolution had taken place in lexicography, and it is with its impact on lexical research and dictionary development in the 1980s that the next chapter will be concerned.

4 The Role of the Computer in Learner Lexicography

4.1. Introduction

Without doubt, the most important single development in learner lexicography from the mid-1970s onwards has been the steadily increasing involvement of the computer at all stages of the dictionary-making process, from data gathering and analysis at one end, to compilation, production, and revision at the other. The first use of computers in learner lexicography dates from the early 1970s, and specifically from the compilation of *ALD 3* (1974). This was the first edition of any MLD to include a computerized stage, one which made it possible to turn the text into a printed book, but which did not reflect—as it had not involved—the use of the computer in the data-gathering, analytical, or editorial stages of production (Meijs 1992).

Since that time, the computer has come to play an indispensable role in dictionary-making of all kinds, while computerized resources have continued to grow in size and complexity. In the mid-1980s, these varied in scale from the computerized text files of the Oxford English Dictionary Archive and the five million-word Longman newspaper corpus (Summers 1993) to the COBUILD[1] corpus—assembled at Birmingham specifically for dictionary-making—of over seven million words of written and spoken English (Clear 1987; Renouf 1987). In different ways, and to varying degrees, these resources were drawn upon when compiling the major general-purpose EFL dictionaries of the late 1980s. By the late 1990s, they had given way to, or expanded to form, the Longman–Lancaster English Language Corpus, of 50 million words, the British National Corpus, of approximately 117 million words, and the Bank of English, an enlargement to over 320 million words of the earlier Birmingham Collection of English Texts (Summers 1993; Clear *et al.* 1996).

The dictionary which, in learner lexicography, most fully represented the new computational developments of the 1980s was the *Collins Cobuild English Language Dictionary* (*Cobuild 1*) (1987). It was—as we shall see in greater detail in Chapter 5—revolutionary both in structure and content. It introduced a definition style in which the headword featured as part of a sentence; it used

[1] i.e. Collins–Birmingham University International Language Database.

unmodified—or minimally edited—corpus extracts as illustrative examples; it depended on frequency of occurrence as the principal—if not the sole—criterion determining the inclusion (and sometimes the ranking) of items, senses, and forms; and it stressed frequency of co-occurrence as a means of identifying collocations, idioms, and speech formulae. One might add that, in the 1990s, all of *Cobuild*'s competitors have followed the lead of its first edition in one or more of these respects (Clear *et al.* 1996; Herbst 1996). At the same time, some of the theoretical assumptions which underlay the *Cobuild 1* approach have been called in question in the more critical and competitive climate of the 1990s.

This chapter sets out to survey a decade of extraordinarily rapid change:

- It begins by showing in brief how the use of computers in learner lexicography evolved between the late 1970s and the late 1980s by comparing the machine-readable version of *ALD 3* with those of *LDOCE 1* and *Cobuild 1* (4.2). It then deals in some detail with progress in corpus building (4.3) and in the development of data-processing tools (4.4) to the end of the 1980s.
- We then turn to look critically at how theories that developed within corpus linguistics during that period affected views of what needed to be included in a learner's dictionary, how it was to be organized and how best it could be illustrated. Here we shall focus largely on the COBUILD project in lexical computing, which, as I have just mentioned, pioneered an approach to these questions that has proved highly influential (4.5). We shall limit ourselves to developments in theory and analysis to the point where *Cobuild 1* appeared (1987), challenging a number of assumptions underlying its compilation, and arguing that for learner lexicography, as for a range of other applications, we cannot depend on descriptive theory developed within corpus linguistics alone.
- Finally, we shall consider some alternative approaches to the analysis of corpus data as evidence of progress during the 1990s (4.6). Specifically, we examine recent work which combines insights from semantic theory with the accessing of machine-readable dictionaries and large-scale corpora, and consider the potential value of this research to learner lexicography.

4.2. Learner Lexicography and the Evolution of the Machine-Readable Dictionary

Some idea of the growing involvement of computers in EFL dictionary-making over the past twenty-five years can be gained by comparing the first machine-readable versions of three well-known monolingual learners' dictionaries, *ALD 3*, *LDOCE 1*, and *Cobuild 1*, whose printed versions appeared in 1974, 1978, and 1987, respectively (Meijs 1992). These works were similar in that all were designed for advanced-level students and all provided much the same range of detailed linguistic information (i.e. on pronunciation, irregular inflection, meaning, verb sub-categorization and complementation, collocations, and idioms).

ALD 3 was a machine-readable dictionary (MRD) in the narrow sense that while it included all the information (e.g. numbers signalling font changes and special characters denoting phonetic symbols) needed to produce a printed text, it did not identify the various categories of linguistic information which the dictionary contained. In other words it did not, and could not, reflect the use of the computer at the level of *linguistic* categorization and labelling.

The computer tape of *LDOCE 1* (made available just after the *ALD 3* tape) was much more than an MRD in this limited sense (i.e. more than a 'typesetting tape'). Indeed, as Michiels (1982) was the first to demonstrate, it was the first truly computerized dictionary. It marked an advance in sophistication from a development in American lexicography some twenty years earlier, when Laurence Urdang, then working on the *Random House Dictionary*, had designed a database system for 'encoding all the separate elements of the dictionary entries' i.e. marking the information categories with special symbols or 'flags' (Bailey 1986: 125). A more complex system was designed by the *LDOCE* editors, who in addition flagged details not intended for publication in the printed dictionary, including, in some cases, details of register and regional origin (Meijs 1992).[2] The fact that in *LDOCE* all categories of information ('fields') were preceded by numerical markers meant that the MRD had now evolved into a lexical database (LDB), a computerized resource which, as well as being capable of further linguistic enrichment, was a flexible editorial and research tool (Calzolari *et al.* 1987). As far as practical dictionary-making was concerned, it was now possible, using simple search procedures, to locate and gather together all members of an appropriately coded sub-set (e.g. pronunciation) for intensive checking or even for the production of specialized dictionaries (Knowles 1984; Cowie 1990). As for the benefit to research of such resources, various studies have shown what can be extracted from the machine-readable *LDOCE*, especially from its grammar-code fields and definitions (Akkerman 1989).

Cobuild 1, published almost a decade later than *LDOCE 1*, marked a further and substantial advance, as the computer was now involved at several stages of compilation, including data-gathering, entry-selection, and entry-preparation (Clear 1987; Renouf 1987). The first stage was the assembly of a large body of language data on computer from a variety of written and spoken sources. The material thus stored could then, by means of a concordance program, be presented on screen in a display suitable for scrutiny and analysis. Access to concordance data helped the lexicographers to discriminate between senses,

---

[2] The additional information also included semantic markers (e.g. + HUMAN, + MALE) to encode the semantic nature of deep subjects and first and second objects (Thierry Fontenelle, personal communication).

to detect recurrent collocations, and to select suitable examples. Third, the results of the lexicographers' work, which was guided by standardized entry formats on screen that prescribed typography and layout for each category of information, was fed back into the computer in the form of a structured database (Clear 1987: 41).

4.3. Computer Corpora and Lexicography

The progressive computerization of dictionary editing in the 1980s (and 1990s) has gone more or less hand in hand with the transformation of an activity that had long been the essential prelude to large-scale dictionary-making along traditional lines. This was the gathering of large bodies of authentic examples, often from literary sources and, in the case of the *OED*, by amateur readers (Landau 1984; Cowie 1990). Computerized data-gathering has speeded up this process enormously and, in so doing, corrected the bias in traditional gathering techniques towards the unusual or idiosyncratic and encouraged due respect for those more humdrum items that carry the chief burden of communication (Meijs 1992: 146). It has also placed the computer corpus at the centre of EFL dictionary-making.

Computer corpora are essentially bodies of textual material stored in machine-readable form. Being composed and stored electronically, they can be accessed by a computer user, who may automatically search, copy, or transfer the material they contain (Leech and Fligelstone 1992). Corpora are created by inputting text into a computer through a number of channels, of which the most familiar to the ordinary computer user is the keyboard of a microcomputer. The corpus compiler may develop at least part of a corpus in this way, but more often his or her task is one of capturing machine-readable text which already exists as a result of word-processing by others.

Material captured in this way may consist of computerized files originally created for uses quite unconnected with lexicography. These have ranged from mass-circulation newspapers to transcriptions of NASA investigations and the (bilingual) proceedings of the Canadian parliament. Such material, however, does permit searches for specific lexical items with the help of special retrieval systems (Bailey 1986) and had been used by Oxford lexicographers before the setting-up of the *New Oxford English Dictionary* project (in 1982–3) to search for items of special interest (Weiner 1987).[3] A large and constantly expanding source of data is of course the daily and weekly press, and since major British

---

[3] Corpus search and retrieval tools have grown enormously in power and flexibility since the late 1980s. Atkins describes (among others) a tool that can 'receive, record and display lexical entries and amendments to these' (Atkins 1992–3: 7).

and American newspapers are now printed with the aid of computer-driven composition systems, such material can be supplied to the lexicographer in machine-readable form (Cowie 1990).

When a corpus is being built up from scratch, data-gathering can be enormously speeded up by the use of a high-speed optical character reading machine (OCR), which scans written material, converts it to digital form and stores it on tape or disc. A further refinement is the Kurzweil Data Entry Machine (KDEM) which, provided it is confronted with good-quality paper and print, can be trained to recognize and input not only a wide variety of typesizes and fonts but also some exotic scripts (Knowles 1984; Renouf 1987; Butler 1990). Its overriding advantage, however, is its speed of operation: a KDEM can read whole books into the computer far faster than they could be typed via a keyboard (Leech and Fligelstone 1992; cf. Burnard 1992).

4.3.1. Corpora of Written English and French

Present-day corpora vary greatly in size, from the small body of text read or keyed into a PC by a single researcher to the more than 320 million words—in the late 1990s—of the (COBUILD) Bank of English. A number of older corpora, though, need to be mentioned, as they are well-documented and have been widely used in linguistic research, and I shall refer briefly to these before moving on to the much larger corpora of English texts now available to lexicographers, and to EFL lexicographers in particular.

Two long-established resources are the Brown corpus, compiled from one million words of written American English, and the Lancaster–Oslo–Bergen (LOB) corpus, designed as a British-English equivalent to Brown, and also consisting of one million words of written text (Butler 1990; Leech 1991). These collections have proved invaluable to analysts of high-frequency (especially grammatical) words, and they have helped to establish the principle of the 'balanced' corpus. In the case of Brown, this meant subdivision into '500 text samples of about 2000 words each, randomly sampled with fifteen text-type categories (or "genres") from material published in 1961' (Leech and Fligelstone 1992). As a further enhancement, both Brown and LOB are available in tagged versions which have been widely used in research. However, because of their modest size, these corpora have been of limited usefulness to analysts interested in the frequencies and distribution of 'lexical' words—and hence of little interest to lexicographers.

Interestingly, it was in France and the United States that efforts were first made to assemble the much larger bodies of data needed for the compilation of even a 'desk-size' dictionary. A major initiative was taken in the 1960s by French lexicographers embarking on a multi-volume historical dictionary of French (the *Trésor de la langue française*); in furtherance of this aim, they gathered on computer a corpus of 70 million words (Rey 1977). Later, Clarence Barnhart proposed a central archive for lexicography in English which would contain 25 to 30 million quotations covering half a million possible lexical items (Barnhart 1973), and at about the same time Laurence Urdang produced a newspaper corpus of 20 million edited words from machine-readable material supplied by publishers (Urdang 1973).

4.3.2. The COBUILD, Longman–Lancaster, and British National Corpora

Corpus development on a scale and with the representativeness needed to support major dictionary projects came later in Britain. However, since 1980, a large-scale corpus—consisting of both spoken and written material, though in different proportions—has been developed in stages by a research team led by John Sinclair at Birmingham University. This originated as the Birmingham Collection of English Text, which with 20 million words in the mid-1980s supported the first set of COBUILD publications, including *Cobuild 1*, and which in the 1990s, as the Bank of English, consists of 320 million words of tagged and parsed data (Clear *et al.* 1996). The Birmingham Collection was, incidentally, the first large-scale corpus to be built largely with the help of OCR technology (Leech and Fligelstone 1992).

The resources initially built up at Birmingham, with substantial funding from Collins Publishers, marked a breakthrough in the development of computer corpora as a data source for dictionary-making, and this initiative was followed by Longman in its establishment of the 50-million word Longman–Lancaster Corpus and by a collaborative venture led by Oxford University Press, involving the British Library, the publishers Longman and Chambers and the Universities of Oxford and Lancaster, and leading to the creation of the 117-million word British National Corpus.[4] Because of the lexicographical interests of the publishers involved, the latter two corpora included spoken as well as written material.

Beyond these corpora lies what Geoffrey Leech has called the 'third generation', measured in hundreds of millions of words, and exploiting the technologies now widely used in commercial offices and publishing houses, 'whereby huge amounts of machine-readable text become available as a by-product of modern electronic communication systems' (Leech 1991: 10). Leech does not provide examples, but it is arguable that the Bank of English, with just under 43 per cent of its written text drawn from British newspapers and magazines, ranks as a 'computerized archive', rather than a balanced collection of samples, designed to be representative of standard varieties of English (Ooi 1998). It is important to

---

[4] And with funding from the Department of Trade and Industry and the Science and Engineering Research Council (Burnage and Dunlop 1993).

bear in mind, too, that the development of computer-processing tools lags some way behind the accelerating expansion of computerized data.

4.3.3. The 'Balanced' Corpus

In stressing the importance of balanced corpora in lexicography, I had in mind especially the foreign student's need for dictionaries based on carefully measured samples of a range of varieties and discourse types. As an example of such resources, we shall focus on the Birmingham Collection, as initially conceived and developed, since the design and assembly of the 'main' and 'reserve' corpora intended to provide data for *Cobuild 1* are well documented (Renouf 1987; and cf. Clear *et al.* 1996).

Plans formulated at the launch of the COBUILD project, in 1980, provided for the creation of a Main Corpus of six million words. This was to be the primary task, but the team also envisaged the establishment of a technical corpus of 26 million words, covering 26 disciplines, which would supplement the information given in the dictionary. Work towards this was held in abeyance, however, so that effort could be concentrated on the basic task (Renouf 1987: 2), a point that may help to explain the relatively low level of illustration of technical and scientific terms in *Cobuild 1*—whether highly specialized or not. (Of the 47 entries for compounds in *Cobuild 1* with the initial element *air*—e.g. *airline, airliner, airmail* —25 have no example. Of these, perhaps five, i.e. *air brake, airlane, airlock, air pocket, airspeed*, are 'specialist' terms.)

By keyboarding almost all the spoken material, and optically scanning written texts of adequate print quality, the team succeeded in gathering on computer by late 1982 a Main Corpus of approximately 7.3 million words—considerably more than at first envisaged.[5] However, the amassing of data continued beyond that point, though the resulting Reserve Corpus was not intended to extend scientific or technical coverage in the strict sense. The aim rather was to draw on topic areas that had been thinly represented in the Main Corpus. Several of these reflected themes of current interest, e.g. ecology and conservation, and would inevitably throw up some specialist items. Nonetheless, the Reserve Corpus 'was not built with attention to the parameters of register and discourse' (Renouf 1987: 11).[6]

The COBUILD team sought to make a selection of texts that were 'relevant to the needs of the international user', and in doing so they singled out parameters which were defining of standard, adult, non-technical, current, predominantly British English, spoken as well as written. A strength of the accumulating

[5] According to Clear *et al.*, this initial collection was used for 'our first, tentative analysis' (1996: 303).

[6] Its vital importance, in the event, lay in providing additional data at a fairly advanced stage of the compilation process to illustrate less common (though not necessarily semi-technical) vocabulary.

material was that the transcriptions of spoken material supplied by university departments and the BBC were rich in specific types of vocabulary (including that of the arts and current affairs) 'but suitably slanted towards a non-technical audience' (Renouf 1987: 5).

In summary, then, in building up their Main and Reserve corpora in the early 1980s, the COBUILD team laid particular stress on coverage of a current, standard, core vocabulary, while taking care to ensure that texts representing a number of subject areas, often quite specific and of current interest, were also sampled. In contrast to the much smaller Brown and LOB corpora, however, there was no attempt to provide systematic coverage of scientific or technical varieties as such.

4.4. Computer Processing of Corpus Data

4.4.1. Concordancing

If a corpus is to be useful to lexicographers, they need to be able to search it quickly, find instances of a particular word or phrase, sort the examples systematically, and display the results in a convenient form (Leech and Fligelstone 1992). The type of program which performs these tasks is a concordancer, and its output a concordance. The best-known concordancer is the KWIC (Key Word in Context) program, which scans the corpus for all occurrences ('tokens') of a specific 'target item' ('type') and displays them, with a little preceding and following context, one above the other in the centre of the computer screen. A type of KWIC display which has proved particularly useful to lexicographers is one in which the right-hand contexts of the target item are arranged alphabetically, thus:

(1)   . . . 'Would you mind checking up?' . . .
     . . . own inner needs, often mind children when . . .
               . . . She didn't mind cigarette smoke any more. . . .
                                                  (Renouf 1987: 36)

This type of display, drawing (as here) on the resources of the Birmingham Collection, was used for compiling *Cobuild 1*. It should be stressed, however, that the data in such outputs was 'raw', and that the visibly separate units were orthographic words, or 'spelling-forms' (Calzolari *et al.* 1987). It was, of course, still possible to access as target items combinations such as *on leave* or *beneath contempt*, or even a complex item in which there were variable elements corresponding to the inflected forms of nouns, determiners, and verbs. Such complex items could be retrieved with the help of sequences in which the variable elements were replaced by '*', the so-called 'wildcard' symbol. Thus *ke*p* * * *nose* to the grindstone* would match with and retrieve the following (among other possible variants):

(2) Keep his nose to the grindstone
     Kept their noses to the grindstone
     Keeping Peter's nose to the grindstone (Leech and Fligelstone 1992: 128)

As we shall go on to show, more sophisticated tools than were available to the *Cobuild 1* lexicographers make it possible, in the 1990s, to lemmatize the forms of a given lexeme, enabling the various inflected forms of 'keep', for example, to be grouped together in a concordance display.

4.4.2. Corpus Annotation

Idioms convey clearly the difficulty of retrieving essential lexical data when the only information accessible to the analyst is what is immediately available in the raw corpus, i.e. orthographic forms and punctuation marks. To provide access to the formal or functional categories underlying such data, a variety of tools have been developed corresponding to various levels of linguistic abstraction—inflectional, word-class, syntactic, and, more recently, semantic (Eyes and Leech 1993). One such tool is the lemmatizer, designed to recognize and gather together inflected forms of the same 'lemma' (or lexeme). Without special intervention, the computer will treat two or more identical strings of letters as the same, whether they represent different inflectional forms of the same lexeme (*come* as 'base' form, *come* as 'unmarked' present-tense form, *come* as past participle), or simply different occurrences of the same inflectional form. Conversely, it will treat as 'different' visibly distinct forms of the same lemma. Using a lemmatizer, the investigator can bring together a set of inflected forms (e.g. *give, gives, giving, gave, given*) as realizations of the same lemma ('give').

At a further level of analysis, a grammatical tagging program—one which adds a grammatical category label to each word token in the corpus—can be brought into play. Once such annotation is complete it is possible to use a concordance program to retrieve data via tagged target items. It can, for instance, retrieve all examples (with appropriate contexts) of *mind* as verb or *mind* as noun. Equally it can search for instances of grammatical abstractions, such as the perfect aspect or the passive voice (Leech 1991: 19).

For certain more complex tasks, such as the recognition of various classes of subordinate clause, tagging cannot help us. We need a corpus which has undergone a syntactic analysis of higher-level units such as phrases and clauses—in other words a 'parsed' corpus. To date, because of the time and effort involved in syntactic analysis, only parsed sub-corpora or 'treebanks' have come into existence (Leech 1991; and cf. Grefenstette *et al.* 1996). As regards the British

National Corpus, for instance, which a team at Lancaster has the responsibility for tagging (using a probabilistic word-tagging system), only a more limited core corpus will be tagged 'with a more fine-grained tagset, partly skeleton-parsed, and annotated at other levels (such as cohesion analysis)' (Eyes and Leech 1993: 123–43).[7]

Lemmatization and grammatical tagging are already transforming the lexicographical analysis of corpus data, so that analysts have moved beyond the stage reported in the COBUILD literature of the mid-1980s, where concordances permitted access to raw data only, and categorization had to be supplied by the individual lexicographer (Sinclair 1985a). Lemmatization alone enables analysts to assemble within the same on-screen display different inflected forms of the same word or expression (e.g. *come to grief, coming to grief, came to grief*), which in the kind of concordance output already quoted from might be widely separated. Since the collocational ranges of different inflected forms of a given lexeme in a particular sense are typically the same, similarities of collocation across the total range of occurrence of the target item would also be thrown into relief.

Severe problems are created for corpus linguists and lexicographers by the sheer quantity of data now being gathered by computational text processing, and for certain analytical purposes reduction is essential, as the BNC team at Lancaster have shown. But lexicographers may also have to reduce, by systematic selection, the number of quotations to be treated (Calzolari *et al.* 1987: 62). One possibility is to search through a previously tagged corpus for collocates of a given target word fitting one or more predetermined constructions. Thus, for the verb *glance* one could limit the search to co-occurrence with the adverbial particles *away*, *up*, and *down*, which are incidentally indicative of the verb in a particular sense.

4.4.3. The Lexicographical Workstation

Reference was made earlier to constant interaction, in the compilation of *Cobuild 1*, between the lexicographer and various kinds of computer-stored information. Indeed a major advance of recent years, chiefly in commercial publishing houses, has been the setting up of 'lexicographical workstations', whereby a lexicographer preparing dictionary entries can interact with different information sources, including concordanced corpus text, archives built up by traditional methods, and pre-existing dictionaries (or editions) in machine-readable form (Knowles 1983). The central element in such a constellation of resources is a lexical database (LDB) associated with the work being compiled or revised, 'with

---

[7] The Skeleton Parsing System developed at Lancaster enables the analyst to annotate such 'higher-level' syntactic units as adverbial, comparative, and relative clauses (Eyes and Leech 1993).

structured and formalized information, both at the entry level and . . . at the level of relations between entries' (Calzolari *et al.* 1987: 67). In the case of a new edition of an existing work, the LDB may possibly be an elaboration of an MRD initially designed for the photocomposition of the previous edition.

The conversion of the machine-readable form of a dictionary such as *ALD 3* into an LDB (for the purpose of preparing a fresh edition) entailed the codification of information at each of a number of linguistic levels, including phonetic, inflectional, syntactic, semantic, and stylistic information. In the case of *ODCIE 1*, the LDB prepared for its recent revision and updating had to codify for most entries collocate lists with their respective syntactic functions (as subjects, objects, adjuncts, etc.), and an elaborate cross-reference system. The actual task of revising existing entries, or preparing new ones, was also computationally controlled, in the sense that the editor was guided on screen by standardized entry formats prescribing specific fonts and layouts for each category of information (Cowie and Mackin 1993).

4.5. Corpus Linguistics and Lexical Theory

Since the publication of *Cobuild 1*, in 1987, the theory and methodology which gave rise to it have had a considerable impact on the development of EFL lexicography as a whole. One effect, as we have seen, has been to encourage other leading dictionary publishers, singly or in collaboration, to establish large-scale computer resources of their own. Another result, deeper and more pervasive, has been to transform the view which many EFL lexicographers take of the data on which their accounts of meaning and structure are based. Even in the late 1990s, there is a strong tendency for dictionary editors—rather less so linguistically trained lexicographers—to regard frequency of occurrence in a properly constituted large-scale corpus as a crucial, if not the chief, factor governing the inclusion and ordering of words, expressions, and meanings. (That statistics are considered to be of value to learners—for example, when deciding which of the adverbs *approximately*, *about*, or *roughly* to use in written or spoken English—is shown by the inclusion in the most recent *LDOCE* edition (1995) of a diagram showing the comparative frequencies of those items, in written and spoken material, in terms of hundreds of occurrences per million.) Ironically, the stressing of frequency of occurrence as a major determinant of inclusion or non-inclusion has had the effect of giving pride of place, in *Cobuild 1*, to the core vocabulary of grammatical items and heavy-duty words which, for quite different reasons, were prioritized in the 1930s by Palmer and Hornby (cf. Moon 1998).

The COBUILD project of the early and mid-1980s is not the whole of corpus-based lexicography, but it has played a vital pioneering role in the field, and certain of its theoretical assumptions have been supported by a number of leading computational linguists (Knowles 1983; Butler 1990; Meijs 1992). For these reasons, COBUILD research is the obvious starting-point for an examination of the theoretical cornerstones of corpus linguistics as applied to EFL lexicography.

We shall examine four assumptions in particular, limiting discussion to publications of the 1980s and chiefly to statements by the project leader, John Sinclair. First, we shall examine the claim that the availability of large-scale text corpora such as the Birmingham Collection (now the Bank of English) has brought to light a great deal of new information about English—information that we would otherwise have remained ignorant of. Second, we shall consider Sinclair's view of context as the chief determinant of semantic differences. Third, we shall examine the dichotomy proposed by Sinclair between the 'open-choice' principle and the 'idiom' principle, noting especially the challenging suggestion that much of 'normal text' is context-determined. Lastly, we shall consider the relationship between corpus data and dictionary examples, asking whether there is a place for simplification and abstraction, as well as straightforward reproduction, in preparing illustrative examples, and whether this is an issue that lexicographical theory needs to address.

4.5.1. Corpus Data as a Source of New Linguistic Information

At various times over the past ten years or so, John Sinclair has stressed the newness of much of the linguistic information that COBUILD's corpus data has brought to light. Two years before the publication of *Cobuild 1*, he declared:

(3) . . . there is now ample evidence of the existence of significant language patterns which have gone largely unrecorded in centuries of study . . . on the other hand there is a dearth of support for some phenomena which are regularly put forward as normal patterns of English.   (Sinclair 1985*b*: 251)

It followed from this observation that EFL teachers were teaching in ignorance of a 'vast amount of language fact', while dictionary-makers were employing categories and analytical methods inappropriate to the new material. Indeed, in the light of the new evidence, so Sinclair argued, our descriptive procedures were in need of a radical overhaul.

Perhaps, in statements such as these, more was being claimed for the new evidence than it could reasonably supply. Classes and structures about which the COBUILD material yielded information in such abundance—for instance, the complementation patterns of nouns, verbs, and adjectives, including optional or obligatory prepositions—were already well covered in a number of learners' dictionaries published before *Cobuild 1*. (We saw earlier, for instance, how remarkably thorough Hornby was in his treatment of 'adjective patterns' in *ALD 2*.) In this regard, Sinclair's critical references to 'conventional dictionaries', though vague, could only have been directed at some (unspecified) mother-tongue dictionaries—though by no means all of those. The value of Sinclair's published analyses based on corpus data in fact often lay in providing more in-depth evidence of distributional differences which were already recognized in other dictionaries. For example, the indeterminacy which Sinclair notes between the 'grow smaller' and 'deteriorate' senses of the verb *decline* is also recorded in *LDOCE 1* (1978). He is simply able to back up his analysis with a much broader spread of data (Sinclair 1985a).

Then there was the claim that new categories were coming to light. It was certainly helpful to be told that the frequency ratings of such routine formulae as *You see* or *I see* were greater than those of supposedly more basic senses of the simple verb *see* (Sinclair and Renouf 1988). Though no longer neglected in EFL dictionaries, formulae are given less than their due in vocabulary teaching, and data showing their prevalence in speech may help to make syllabus design-ers more aware of their importance as discourse structuring devices (Nattinger and DeCarrico 1992). All this was positive and helpful, but the category itself was not new. Harold Palmer was well aware of the importance of speech formulae and even persuaded Columbia Tokyo, in the early 1930s, to issue a number of gramophone records demonstrating their use in conversation (Palmer 1933a).

Turning back to the prominence given to certain words, or classes of words, by their frequency of occurrence in the COBUILD corpora, perhaps too much stress can be laid on frequency as a measure of the importance to learners of certain words. Technical terms with a low frequency rating may be of vital inter-est to advanced readers of English, as several studies of dictionary use have shown, and as is demonstrated later in this volume (Chapter 6). This brings us to the much broader issue of the relationship between even a large text corpus and the decoding needs of the advanced foreign learner. As Sinclair points out in the Introduction to *Cobuild 1*, the dictionary provides a great deal of informa-tion about the commonest words—those lying at the heart of the language. This is undoubtedly true. But as we have already seen, the dictionary does not give a high level of illustrated coverage to semi-technical words which are familiar to the average educated native-speaker. Thus it does not always meet the decoding needs which, as user studies have again shown, are of paramount importance to foreign students at various levels of proficiency.

4.5.2. The Role of Context

In the analysis of phrasal verbs which formed part of the volume of essays published in the same year as *Cobuild 1*, John Sinclair laid great stress on the vital role of context, both in distinguishing one meaning from another and in providing suitable illustrations:

(4) Each sense of the phrase is co-ordinated with a pattern of choice that helps to distinguish it from other senses. . . . The distinguishing criteria are commonplace features of grammar or semantics, . . . Instead of individual words and phrases being crudely associated with a meaning, we could see them presented in active and typical contexts.   (1987*b*: 158)

Here there are two key points: the reference to the crucial role of context in marking off one sense from another; and the implied dismissal of an alternative approach which 'crudely' assigns meanings to words and phrases. The first point is unchallengeable, as far as it goes, though perhaps the practical help often provided by other dictionaries in drawing up a preliminary checklist of meanings might have been mentioned. (Cf. Sinclair (1985*a*), where the use of the *Collins English Dictionary* (1979) for this purpose is acknowledged.)

The second point is somewhat disturbing, because it conveys a quite misleading impression of how lexicographers, within various national traditions, actually proceed. There is clear evidence from the early part of this century, not to go beyond, of lexicographers taking full account of context in the actual process of compilation. Indeed, we have already seen in the case of the Fowler brothers how two self-taught but deeply perceptive lexicographers could recognize that analysis was made difficult by the very 'entanglement' of entry words with their contexts.

Nearer our own time, we have the example of Jean Dubois' learners' dictionary for French native speakers—strikingly original in its day—the *Dictionnaire du français contemporain* (1966). This is firmly grounded in an analysis of the vocabulary of French which distinguishes between senses not simply on the basis of their syntagmatic relations (i.e. collocations and syntax) but also according to their paradigmatic relations (i.e. sense relations, such as hyponymy and synonymy) (Dubois 1962, 1981). A similar approach was adopted to sense discrimination in *ODCIE 1*, where for example the phrasal verb *think of*, in the meaning 'consider or examine (sth) to see if one should take action', is distinguished from the same item in the sense 'propose, suggest (sth)' on the grounds that while the first has the synonym *think about* and is often associated with continuous aspect, the second has the synonym *think up* and is not associated with continuous aspect. Compare: *Margot, are you thinking of marrying Jim?* and *We're still trying to think of a suitable title for the book* (Cowie and Mackin 1993).

The assumed inadequacies of 'traditional' dictionaries are addressed at various points by other COBUILD analysts. In an approach to the analysis of meaning in *Cobuild 1* which is very broadly based, taking account of formal criteria such as word-formation and phonology, as well as collocation and syntax, Rosamund Moon uncharacteristically dismisses some unidentified rivals and predecessors. 'Dictionaries traditionally record vocabulary,' she states, 'as if meaning is something independent, inherent and unique to an item, and serving to distinguish it from all others' (Moon 1987: 86–7).

The question of dependent and independent meaning is more fully taken up in the next section, but it is perhaps worth noting that if dictionaries faithfully reflect the way meaning arises from words, or from words in context, then they are right to indicate that in *some* cases meaning is indeed independent and inherent. Monosemous words, a category which includes many scientific and technical terms, typically convey meaning independently of the contexts in which they are used. Consider, in this respect, *helium, phlebitis, piccolo.* If these items are recorded in either a mother-tongue or foreign learner's dictionary with a definition but no illustrative example, the editors have done all that can reasonably be expected of them.

4.5.3. The Open-Choice Principle and the Idiom Principle

John Sinclair first put forward in 1987 the notion that two principles of interpretation were needed to explain how meaning arises from language text—the 'open-choice' principle and the 'idiom' principle (Sinclair 1987c). The open-choice principle, he suggested, represented text as resulting from a large number of complex choices. 'At each point where a unit is completed (a word or a phrase or a clause), a large range of choice opens up and the only restraint is grammaticalness' (1991: 109).[8] However, and as he goes on to suggest, we would be unable to produce normal text simply by operating the open-choice principle —which, incidentally, according to Sinclair, forms the basis of 'virtually all grammars'. We also require the idiom principle, which by contrast represents text as being composed of 'a large number of semi-preconstructed phrases that constitute single choices, even though they might appear to be analysable into segments' (1991: 110).

The first comment to make about this dichotomy is that it is a familiar one. Harold Palmer, almost sixty years previously, drew attention to the widespread occurrence of ready-made word-combinations in speech and writing, and to the implications of their pervasiveness for language learners (cf. 2.1). Palmer was also aware of the operation of an 'open-choice' principle: he recognized, in other words, that there were 'free combinations' which could be put together by application of the commonest grammatical rules (Palmer 1933c).

The range of phenomena covered by the idiom principle is, however, very broad and it is helpful to find in the same article discussion of indeterminate categories. Referring to possible contexts for the expression *set eyes on*, Sinclair asks 'How much of this is integral to the phrase and how much is in the nature of collocational attraction?' This is a pertinent question, but again, Sinclair is not the first to ask it. In fact all of the restrictions which are pinpointed as representing the 'fuzzy' nature of idiomaticity have been noted at various times by

---

[8]   The article was later included, in a modified form, in Sinclair (1991). References are to that version.

other phraseologists and lexicographers (e.g. Aisenstadt 1979; Cowie *et al.* 1983; Pawley and Syder 1983; Bolinger 1985; Benson *et al.* 1986).

If Sinclair is often unconvincing in dealing with categorization, he can be persuasive when commenting on the relationship between concepts such as delexicalization and the frequency ratings which he is in a good position to supply. Here, there are three theoretical claims worth noting. The first is that there is a correlation between the frequency of occurrence of a word and the relative lack of an identifiable independent meaning. The meanings of those 'frequent words are difficult to identify and explain' (1991: 113).[9] (So-called delexical verbs such as *get, give, set,* and *take,* in certain of their uses, spring readily to mind.) The second claim is that such non-independence of meaning 'correlates with the operation of the idiom principle to make fewer . . . choices' (1991: 113). If Sinclair is claiming here that delexicalized senses are determined by narrow and arbitrary sets of collocates, he is surely right. (Consider *make* in collocation with *room* or *way* as object nouns.) The third suggestion, also persuasive, is that the 'core' meaning of a word will not normally be delexical, the explanation being that the core meaning (e.g. *run* in its movement sense, *touch* in the physical rather than the emotional sense) is the most frequent independent sense, i.e. the most frequent sense that does not need to be disambiguated by reference to context.

Two further stages in Sinclair's argument are interesting and challenging, but cannot be fully sustained, given what we know of restricted collocations. Here is Sinclair on the constituency of 'normal text':

(5) Most normal text is made up of the occurrence of frequent words, and the frequent senses of less frequent words. Hence, normal text is largely delexicalized, and appears to be formed by exercise of the idiom principle, with occasional switching to the open-choice principle. (Sinclair 1991: 113)

While we may agree that a very large proportion of words in normal text are frequently occurring words, and that many of those will be delexicalized, it must also be recognized that a large proportion of those will also form restricted collocations with 'independent' items. (Consider the nouns in *break one's journey, lay the table, cut one's losses.*) As recent studies of collocations in news stories in the quality press and academic essays in the social sciences have shown, collocations of delexicalized and core items (of the pattern verb + object noun) make up well over 30 per cent of all instances of that grammatical type in those genres (Cowie 1991, 1992*a*; Cowie and Howarth 1996; Howarth 1996).

Whether the two models of language proposed by Sinclair are 'incompatible

---

[9] Speaking of delexicalized words such as *quite,* Hornby commented: 'Definition is often inadequate for words of this type, words of which the primary or original meanings have faded or changed' (1965: 108).

with each other', as he goes on to suggest, is somewhat doubtful. There may be 'sharp switches', as one moves sequentially through a text, between language formed now according to the idiom principle, now according to the open-choice principle. However, it is undoubtedly true that idiomatic and non-idiomatic principles of composition and reception interact both diachronically and in the course of everyday language use. It is a commonplace observation that, over time, phrases formed according to the open-choice principle may petrify into idioms. (In this respect consider *go off the rails* and *reach the end of the line*.) Conversely, in word play, idioms can be manipulated so that the literal senses of their components are once more brought to the surface (Moon 1998*a*, *b*).

4.5.4. Authentic and Made-Up Examples

No issue to do with the involvement of computers in EFL lexicography has aroused fiercer debate than the question of whether examples based on corpus data are necessarily superior to those made up by the lexicographer, or whether, at least for some purposes, made-up examples are preferable. The question has naturally attracted the attention of researchers into dictionary use, and to date attempts have been made to determine whether teachers—non-native as well as native—can distinguish between unidentified authentic and concocted examples, and which they prefer (Maingay and Rundell 1990); and also to decide which type of example provides better support in the production and comprehension of new words (Laufer 1992).

The issue was also of interest to A. S. Hornby. In an article which appeared shortly after the publication of *ALD 2*, Hornby came out strongly in support of invented examples. His argument was that in made-up phrases and sentences the lexicographer could include detail, grammatical or lexical, which threw light on the meaning or use of the headword (Hornby 1965). Invented examples could, as it were, be judiciously shaped to meet the learner's needs (cf. Cowie 1978*b*: 129; 1989*a*: 58).

The question is naturally of crucial concern to corpus lexicographers. In his Introduction to *Cobuild 1*, John Sinclair identified two possible functions for examples in learners' dictionaries—providing explanations and serving as models for speaking and writing—and denied that invented examples could fulfil the productive function. Authentic examples, on the other hand, could do both:

(6) [They] support the explanations and they illustrate usage. They provide a reliable guide for speaking and writing in the English of today. In contrast, invented examples are really part of the explanations. They have no independent authority or reason for their existence; and they are constructed to refine the explanations and in many cases to clarify the explanations. They give no reliable guide to composition in English and would be very misleading if applied to this task.   (Sinclair 1987*a*: xv)

As I have argued elsewhere, such claims give an incomplete and distorted view of the respective roles of invented and authentic examples in learners' dictionaries (Cowie 1989*a*: 58). In practice, made-up examples are not confined to the supportive roles of clarifying and refining definitions—nor should they be. Certainly, invented examples can serve those purposes. But, in addition, editors are constantly constructing examples (or adapting them from corpus excerpts, as the *Cobuild 1* editors themselves occasionally do) to help students wishing to write in English. This was one of the most noteworthy achievements of the earliest learners' dictionaries, and we saw (in Chapter 3) how the early patterns were developed in more recent publications.

Dictionary examples, then, wherever they originate, may have to be adapted to the particular study needs of learners. They may also have to be adjusted to fit the physical limits of the dictionary. In a typical advanced-level work of about 55,000 entries, the average length of an entry is seven lines in a half-page column. The consequent need for economy has two effects. The first is that an example sentence is made to fulfil two or more functions at once—for example clarifying meanings and illustrating grammatical patterning (Cowie 1978*b*, 1989*a*). The second effect is on the typical length of an example in terms of the grammatical units spanned. Though lexicographers occasionally go beyond the limits of a single sentence or phrase when illustrating a word or sense, most examples are isolated and self-sufficient sentences or phrases.[10] The key word here is 'self-sufficient': whilst naturally occurring sentences often reveal their full meaning by reference to a wider context, it may not be possible, for the reason just given, for the dictionary example to refer outside itself for complete elucidation (Cowie 1989*a*: 59).

A complementary problem is illustrated by authentic examples such as those at (7), below. Here the problem is not so much that the sentence requires reference outside itself for complete understanding, but, rather, that certain of the words and expressions making up the sentence may be as difficult as, or more difficult than, the item being defined. Consider for example *brassy*, *blatant*, *venal*, and *loose* in the first example (where *be any man's money* is being defined) and *cooped up* and *procured* in the second (where the definiendum is *at short notice*):

(7) (a) Barmaids were brassy, blatant, loud-voiced, impudent, vulgar, venal, and, above all, loose: they *were any man's money.*

   (b) The children hadn't been well, cooped up in a London flat she had procured *at short notice.*[11]

---

[10] There may, of course, be more scope for extended examples in specialized learners' dictionaries.

[11] These examples are taken from the 30,000-excerpt collection built up by Ronald Mackin to provide illustrative material for *ODCIE* (1975/1983/1993).

The need for economy was in fact recognized by Sinclair, as was the possible need for an example to be 'edited to make it easier to understand when it is removed from its context' (Sinclair 1987a: xv), a statement that is in line with the first of the two problems identified above. Both problems, however, raise quite complex questions concerning the relationship between raw data chosen for illustrative purposes, on the one hand, and its grammatical structure and possible user functions, on the other, and these questions need to be addressed.

I suggested earlier that examples might have to be specially adapted to meet the needs of learners wishing to write, and added that helpful guidelines had been laid down by the earliest EFL dictionary-makers (Palmer 1936b). Two widely-used techniques can be briefly recalled here. The first, *listing* (cf. 2.3), is well known; the other, *simplification* (cf. 2.4.2), though found in very many dictionaries, including dictionaries of languages other than English, has been less widely discussed (cf. Cowie 1996). Both methods can take corpus data as a starting point, but may then depart quite radically from it. In fact, a degree of artificiality is inevitable in both cases.

Listing, as its name implies, involves the introduction into a phrase or sentence of a list of alternative words or phrases, usually separated by commas or oblique strokes, as in the following examples from *ALD 3*:

(8) (a) the field of politics/art/science/medicine
     (b) a historic spot/event/speech
     (c) summon/adjourn Parliament; Parliament sits/rises

In learners' dictionaries, as we have seen, this technique originated with H. E. Palmer and *A Grammar of English Words* (1938a), though there the alternative items were marked off by commas and enclosed in square brackets.[12] Either way, the convention was designed to indicate choice, including limited choice, at various points, and to encourage sentence or phrase building (Palmer 1936b).

The notion of simplification, with particular reference to *ISED* (1942), was discussed briefly in Chapter 2. There it was shown that simplification involved the reduction of a predicate or phrase pattern to a structural minimum. So, a predicate pattern, for example, would normally consist of a main verb and noun-phrase object (itself structurally minimal) or prepositional complement (e.g. *to repay kindness; to shiver with cold*). Such simplification had the effect of stripping away distracting lexical detail and throwing a significant collocation into relief (cf. Cowie 1995).

Note that this too had a practical purpose. For simplification, like listing, recognizes and provides for a process that often takes place when users refer to

---

[12] There were earlier precedents, for example monolingual French dictionaries of the seventeenth century and bilingual English–French dictionaries (e.g. Boyer) of the eighteenth (Noel Osselton, personal communication).

a dictionary for help with production. At such times, users may simply wish to know which word, or words, function at *one structural point* other than that of the headword consulted. In the case of the headword *Parliament*, for example, they may need to know that *summon* and *adjourn* are the transitive verbs used to refer to the beginning and ending of a session. The first set of examples at (8)(c), which is reduced to those essentials, may be more effective than a phrase that provides superfluous detail in the name of authenticity.

The lexicographer's approach to the use of corpus data for examples needs to be flexible. There is certainly a place for full-sentence examples which show no abstraction or alternation at all—what Palmer called the 'sentence-sample' type (1936*b*). On the other hand, the encoding needs of the student may also call for maximally reduced examples—'skeleton-type' examples according to Palmer—as these give prominence to collocations.

Throughout the 1990s, corpus linguists have tended to move beyond the position taken up by COBUILD researchers in the 1980s, when analysis was strongly data-oriented and there were certainly expectations on the part of some investigators, notably Sinclair himself, that a radically new categorization— phraseological as well as grammatical—would emerge. There is a new flexibility of approach apparent in the present widespread collaboration between lexicographers, theoretical linguists, and corpus linguists. Partnership of this kind is reflected in the use or development in the 1990s, by several teams of analysts, of data-processing tools designed to identify categories at the word-class, syntactic, and semantic levels. The following section will describe some of the results— significant for dictionary-makers and language learners alike—which can be achieved by such means.

4.6. Expanding Resources for Dictionary-Making

As well as enabling linguists to identify and remedy weaknesses in existing EFL dictionaries, the availability of databases, text corpora, and sophisticated software programs has encouraged them to undertake the fundamental research needed for further substantial progress. Of particular interest are a number of recent projects which bring particular theoretical models to bear on information extracted from text corpora and existing machine-readable dictionaries, and which store the results in computerized lexicons 'so that [they] may be exploited by traditional dictionary builders as well as by automated language processing' (Grefenstette *et al.* 1996). Two of the most interesting projects—both funded by the European Commission—are described briefly below. Both have implications for EFL lexicography, though neither was set up with the monolingual learner's dictionary specifically in mind. The first has added significantly to the resources of dictionary-makers, bilingual as well as monolingual, while the second is helping to transform our ideas of the scope and precision of dictionary definitions.

4.6.1. Extracting Collocations from Bilingual Dictionaries and Corpus Data

The DECIDE project, which ran from 1994 to 1996, was a computational linguistics project funded by the European Commission which involved collaboration between researchers in Belgium, Germany, and France. It took as its starting point an encoding difficulty often faced by bilingual dictionary users—that while they might know the translation in the L2 of one word in a collocation, they were often uncertain about the appropriate choice of lexical partner. Given *examination* (easily translated into French as *examen*), for example, they might be unsure how to translate *sit*. As we saw in Chapter 2, attempts have been made in recent years to design specialized dictionaries to deal with this specific problem—that of collocational restriction.[13] However, medium-sized general dictionaries—monolingual as well as bilingual—cannot be depended on to provide coverage of all problematic cases. The challenge for computational research is to extend the coverage, a challenge which the DECIDE team met by attempting to extract collocations both from raw and tagged corpus data and from parts of the microstructure of a standard bilingual dictionary which are not straightforwardly accessible to the ordinary user.

The second of these tasks was tackled in an ingenious way by Thierry Fontenelle (1992, 1994, 1997). Fontenelle had observed that the italicized items used as sense discriminators in the *Robert–Collins dictionnaire français–anglais anglais–français* (Atkins and Duval 1978/1987) often stood in a relationship of subject or direct object to their verb headwords (or of noun to a modifying adjective headword), and that those various syntactic roles were signalled systematically by the presence or absence of square brackets (Fontenelle 1997: 107–8). As the following examples from the English–French part of the dictionary show, those brackets are present when the word in italics is the noun subject of a verb headword, and absent when it is the noun object or a noun modified by an adjective headword:

(9) **trumpet** *vi [elephant]* barrir
     abolish *vt law* abolir, abroger
     addled *adj egg* pourri

Using a version of the machine-readable *Robert–Collins* transformed into a lexical database, Fontenelle was able to retrieve all occurrences of any italicized

---

[13] A revised and updated version of the *BBI Combinatory Dictionary* appeared in 1997. Published in the same year was the *LTP Dictionary of Selected Collocations*, which combined in one volume material from *Selected English Collocations* (1988) and *English Adverbial Collocations* (1991).

word, together with the headword under which that item was found. But by accessing a particular item, say *law*, in all the entries in which it occurred, and treating it as a 'base', he was in fact specifying its entire collocability, or collocational range (thus, *make, break, amend, change*, etc.) (Fontenelle 1997: 109). He was also able to break that collocate list down into grammatical sub-categories (in the examples at (9), Nsubj + Vintr, Vtr + Nobj, Adj + N) as a function of the syntactic link between the base and the collocate.

The specification of such collocabilities, and subcategories, can be performed automatically but the output has the limitations of a standard collocational dictionary: it fails to differentiate between the meanings of the various collocates, say between *decreasing, stable*, and *soaring* as collocates of *price*. This shortcoming was remedied by enriching the collocations with 'lexical functions' (LFs), according to the Meaning-Text Model developed by Igor Mel'čuk (Mel'čuk *et al.* 1984/1988/1992). In the case of a collocation such as *annul the law*, this meant assigning the lexical function 'liqu' ("liquidate", "eradicate"), as this expressed the meaning of the collocate *annul* with respect to the base *law* (1997: 113–20). The system devised by Fontenelle assigned complex as well as simple LFs to the 70,000 collocations extracted from *Robert–Collins* and incorporated them into a lexical-semantic database.

The database thus created has numerous advantages. One is that the user can retrieve all the collocates appropriate to a given base and a selected lexical function. To return to *annul the law*, one can, by specifying the LF 'liqu' as part of a retrieval query, extract all the 'eradication' verbs which can take *law* as direct object (thus, *abolish, do away with, repeal, revoke*, etc.). Another advantage is that the user can select an appropriate range of LFs for a given noun (say, *fox*), and then retrieve the entire range of words (of whatever grammatical class) appropriate to that noun (e.g. *bitch, bark, brush, yelp*).

Information extracted in this way from the *Robert–Collins* database can be of considerable value to compilers of monolingual learners' dictionaries. Considering sets of modifying adjectives, intransitive verbs, and transitive verbs collocating with *price*, Fontenelle points out that this information enables us to answer the questions 'What can prices be like?', 'What can prices do?', and 'What can be done to prices?', and that answering these questions is highly relevant to the dictionary-making process (Fontenelle 1992: 224). Further divisions are possible within each of the grammatical categories mentioned above: one can for instance recognize intransitive verbs referring to a fall or rise in prices, or to their stability. There is also a very interesting range of metaphorical uses, often very informal and usually having to do with steep or sudden price fluctuations: *hit the ceiling, hit the roof, rocket, spiral up*.

Though important, Fontenelle's work on the machine-readable *Robert–Collins* was only part of the DECIDE project. Also significant was the development of tools for the extraction of collocations from tagged and raw text. For work on raw text, the exploitation tools were morphological analysers, part-of-speech taggers, and low-level parsers. These were extended and modified to extract collocations and to mark up English and French text automatically (Grefenstette *et al.* 1996). For the example *correlation coefficients have been determined between the levels*, the following mark-up shows, in the first column, surface forms (with sentence and noun and verb phrase boundaries indicated within angle brackets); in the second, parts of speech; in the third, the lemmas; and in the fourth, low-level syntactic relations (1996: 101):

(10) <s>
      <np>

correlation	NOUN	*correlation*	NN>
coefficients	NOUN	*coefficient*	DOBJ>

      </np>
      <vp>

have	INF	*have*	AUX
been	BE	*been* [sic]	AUX
determined	PPART	*determine*	MAINV

      </vp>
      <np>

between	PREP	*between*	PREP
the	DET	*the*	DET>
levels	NOUN	*level*	<IOBJ

The operation of the parser is of particular interest, and represents a considerable advance on the extraction of collocations from raw text. As can be seen, the parser identifies the semantic object of a verb (here, *coefficient*) even when this precedes the verb as the grammatical subject of a passive construction. It thus overcomes the obstacles to retrieving the members of a collocation created by their syntactic displacement within the same sentence (cf. Cowie and Howarth 1996). By using the parser, frequency lists of collocations can be drawn up which take account of the syntactic relations of a given noun base (say, *effect*) and its collocating transitive verbs (e.g. *have, study, produce, exert*). Such lists would be an invaluable resource for the compiler of a collocational dictionary, since as well as having the virtue of authenticity, they would present the collocations in the syntactic form in which they needed to appear in the dictionary.

4.6.2. Frame Theory, Corpus Data, and Learner Lexicography

As we have just seen, progress in the analysis of corpus data—insofar as it facilitates the systematic retrieval of collocations or grammatical categories—has had to wait on advances in the annotation of computer corpora. A grammatically tagged corpus is, for a variety of reasons, very much more valuable to the lexicographer than raw, unannotated data. It can gather together words of the same grammatical category or sub-category (say, all transitive verbs) to determine, for instance, what their common transformational characteristics are. It can also enable the analyst to retrieve members of the same colligation (any recurrent *combination* of grammatical classes, such as verb transitive + adverbial particle) to determine and record their shared properties.

All the same, this development takes us only so far. It does not, for example, enable the lexicographer to gather together those members of a verb subclass which also happen to be closely related semantically (e.g. verbs of perception such as *feel/touch, smell, taste, hear/listen, see/look at*). For this to be possible, we need to develop a semantic perspective on corpus data. One theory which is already having a significant impact on the way computational linguists approach the analysis of corpora is the 'semantic frame' theory devised by Charles Fillmore and further developed in collaboration with Sue Atkins (Fillmore and Atkins 1992, 1994).

The particular strength of frame theory is that it brings together semantic and syntactic levels of description in a rigorous and systematic way. A 'frame' is a conceptual structure associated with some semantic domain. For a given frame (say 'commercial transactions') we can identify a set of abstract elements and map out ways in which those elements are realized in items and structures which can be built around keywords (in this case, *buy, sell, cost, pay*, etc.) linked to the frame. 'Elements' must be taken to include not only human participants in particular roles—here, buyers and sellers—but conditions and objects relevant to the central concepts of the frame, here, notions of ownership, changes of ownership through time, etc. In the case of the 'risk' frame described by Fillmore and Atkins, and the appropriate set of keywords (i.e. *risk, peril, danger*), the non-human types of element include 'harm' (H) and 'valued object' (VO) (Fillmore and Atkins 1992, 1994).

Recently, corpus linguists and lexicographers working within a semantic frame perspective, and supporting their insights with corpus data, have tackled a number of related tasks, all potentially of some importance to EFL lexicographers. One is to provide a critical perspective on definition practice in currently available dictionaries (Atkins 1994); another is to describe sets of idioms in relation to particular frames (Cowie 1998c); a third is the comparative treatment of parallel sets of verbs, etc., in different European languages (Heid 1996).

One recent study which has focused on the first of these issues is Atkins's analysis of the English verbs of seeing (1994). Examining approaches to defining these verbs in a British and an American mother-tongue dictionary, she notes how the near-synonyms *behold, descry, espy, notice, spot*, and *spy* are defined in terms of each other (resulting, in the case of *notice and spot*, in identical synonym chains). This is just one case of a general failure 'to offer contrastive accounts of word-meaning across sets of semantically related words' (Atkins 1994: 2).

Reference to a large text corpus more often than not provides evidence contradicting the dictionary definitions. But recourse to corpus data alone, rich as it is, does not enable the analyst to identify the tiny shifts of meaning which distinguish one verb from the other. As Atkins puts it: what is needed is 'some formal method of structuring the lexicographical evidence' (1994: 4).

Her approach—in the case of such verbs as *see, behold, catch sight of, spot, spy* —is to recognize a 'perception frame' whose principal elements include a Passive rather than an Active Experiencer (since seeing, unlike looking, does not include an element of volition), a Percept (or object perceived) and a Judgement, which refers to the opinion which the Experiencer forms of the Percept as a result of the visual experience. In the first example at (11), the Judgement being made is comparative, while in the second it is in the nature of an inference:

(11)   He looked to me like a yellow budgerigar. (Judgement-Simile)
       Peter looks relaxed. (Judgement-Inference)

As the examples also show, the relationship between frame elements and grammatical categories or functions is sometimes far from straightforward. In the first example above, the Experiencer is expressed by the prepositional phrase *to me*; while in a sentence such as *Mary saw the duck*, the Experiencer is *Mary*, the grammatical subject of the perception verb *see* (1994: 5).

So as to provide a systematic record of how verbs of seeing are used, at both the syntactic and semantic levels, Atkins has built a database in which about one hundred sentences for each verb are analysed and codified. The analysis names and records the frame elements that are overtly expressed, the grammatical categories that realize them, and the functions of the latter in clauses containing the key verb (1994: 6). The value of the database lies in enabling the analyst to compare the range of data relating to one verb with that relating to its neighbours in the same frame. For example, it reveals that the pattern 'Passive Experiencer + Target Percept' (as in the example *As soon as they sight a predator approaching* . . .) dominates the data for the verb *sight*, and that the most salient difference between *look* and *sight* is that the former allows the expression of the frame element Judgement (as in *Polished tools look better*), while the latter does not. Another significant insight provided by the database is that the circumstances in which people direct their attention to someone or something has an important bearing on the choice of verb. When a speaker selects *sight, see*, or *spy*, for instance, it is because there is something important about the time of the event and the location of the Percept at that time, as for example in: *Jeffries was sighted in Boar Lane on Friday night.*

This meticulous and invaluable work can benefit both mother-tongue and EFL lexicography. Clearly it can help in the design of improved usage notes, both for native and foreign user groups. Atkins is careful to point out that a usage note for any potential user on verbs of seeing should first set aside those verbs not concerned with visual perception and then focus either on those verbs where the Experiencer is active (*look, observe, survey,* etc.) or on those where the Experiencer is passive (*see, sight,* etc., as discussed here). Full information about the semantic type of the Percept (e.g. whether 'of high salience', and therefore impossible to miss, or 'of low salience', and thus hard to catch sight of) would not appear in a college dictionary, but might well be discussed in a foreign learners' dictionary (1994: 14).

4.7. Conclusion

Learners' dictionaries compiled since the mid-1970s have, to a greater or lesser extent, been the offspring of the computer revolution. Central to the radical developments taking place since the early 1980s has been the assembly on computer of a number of large-scale text corpora. From that time also, approaches to the analysis of computer-stored data, especially, though not entirely, for dictionary-making, have been strongly influenced by the theories and analytical procedures associated with the COBUILD project at Birmingham University. (The earliest applications of COBUILD research to dictionary-making will be examined as part of the next chapter.) As we have already seen, however, corpus-based lexicography has developed within a more critical climate in the 1990s, computational linguists involved in dictionary-making in this period are benefiting from more sophisticated data-processing tools than were available a decade earlier, and EFL lexicography continues to profit from ideas drawn from sources far removed from computer studies.

5 The Third Generation of Learners' Dictionaries

5.1. Introduction

The 1980s were a major watershed in learner lexicography. It was clear early in the decade that the next phase in dictionary development would be dominated by the computer, and that it would be affected by the increasing professionalism of lexicography, with its own specialist publications and conferences, and influenced by the growing body of research into dictionary users and dictionary use (Tomaszczyk 1979; Béjoint 1981; Hartmann 1987).[1] Furthermore, the opportunities of an expanding, worldwide market, especially for general-purpose learners' dictionaries, were sharpening competition between the two major publishers already involved (Oxford University Press and Longman), and would lead to the entry of a third (Collins), significantly in collaboration with a research team at the University of Birmingham (Cowie 1989*d*).

The circumstances of production had been tranformed, so that even the titles that would appear in the late 1980s as revisions of existing works—the second edition of the *Longman Dictionary of Contemporary English* (*LDOCE* 2) (1987), and the fourth edition of the *Oxford Advanced Learner's Dictionary* (*ALD* 4) (1989)—could not be expected to base themselves solely, or even primarily, on existing models. The *Collins Cobuild English Language Dictionary* (*Cobuild* 1) (1987) would start completely from scratch. In examining the three dictionaries, then, I shall not only compare them with their predecessors (where they exist) but also consider how far they reflect new developments in linguistic and corpus research. And rather than examine each dictionary more or less independently, I shall consider, side by side, their treatments of the same selected feature. This method is intended not to emphasize the strengths of one treatment to the detriment of another, but to compare and assess different approaches to common problems. Five design features will be examined here: entry structure (5.2), grammatical schemes and codes (5.3), definitions (5.4), style, attitudinal, and register labels (5.5), and sense relations and lexical fields (5.6). These areas include some in which little progress had been made before 1980 (e.g. the treatment of lexical

---

[1] Conferences at which learner lexicography was a major theme were held at Exeter in 1978, 1980, and 1983. A seminar wholly devoted to the MLD was organized at Leeds in 1985.

fields) and others in which new methods were being devised for solving familiar problems (e.g. the design of grammatical systems and codes).

5.2. Microstructure and Macrostructure

In the early and middle years of the learner's dictionary, a tension existed between the need to ensure quick access to specific items of information—an individual sense, a particular idiom—and the no less vital need to develop the learner's sense of semantic and morphological relations within the lexicon (cf. Cowie 1983*b*). This tension surfaced when we discussed the inclusion, in definitions of the verb *design* in *ALD 2*, of references to meanings of the homonymous noun. This device might very well improve the learner's sense of a recurrent type of relationship between words. Equally, it might impede the search for a specific answer to a contingent problem of meaning. Nonetheless, it was unarguable that the advanced learner needed to develop knowledge of the lexicon as a more or less structured whole, and that the dictionary had a part to play in this development.

A similar problem, as we shall now see, arises in connection with the positioning of derivatives and compounds. If they are nested, to highlight connections of meaning, they may be difficult to access. If they are listed as separate entries, they may, though readily accessible, be difficult to link semantically with their roots.

5.2.1. *LDOCE 2*

In *LDOCE 1* (1978) an approach to entry design had been adopted that was in certain key respects a departure from the patterns laid down by *ALD 2* and *3*. The primary aim was to enable users to access individual items quickly and easily. There were four main guiding principles. The first was that, apart from words yielded by highly productive processes of affixation, notably adverbs formed by the addition to adjectives of the *-ly* suffix (cf. *sad, sadly*), derivatives were treated as main entries (and arranged in strict alphabetical order), even when there were evident connections of meaning between derivatives and bases. Consider the series **despot, despotic, despotism**, where each of the two derivatives **despotic** and **despotism** had a single meaning related to that of their base **despot**. The second principle was that so-called 'part-of-speech homonyms'— pairs or sets of words having the same form but membership of different classes, and possibly different meanings—would also be assigned to separate entries. Consider in this respect the two entries for **crown** (noun and verb) and the three for **waste** (noun, verb, and adjective). The third principle was that phrasal verbs, but not other kinds of idioms, would also be assigned to separate main entries. So **ease up** appeared as a separate entry in *LDOCE 1*, but not **ill at ease** or **take one's ease**. The fourth guiding principle was that compounds, whether written open (**manor house**), solid (**southeast**), or with a hyphen (**double-check**) would also appear as main entries. (It is worth noting, incidentally, that the compound **soup spoon**, which is merely institutionalized, is included as a main entry alongside **soup kitchen**, which is lexicalized in addition. There are many parallel cases.) From the standpoint of ease of reference, the advantage of assigning these categories to main entries was clear. Many types of complex items which users might perceive as units were now highlighted by being given their own alphabetical places, where they would be as easy to locate as simple words.[2]

In *LDOCE 2*, there were two important shifts away from these strict principles of separate listing. The first was that phrasal verbs containing a particular verb were now grouped in a special section in the main entry for that verb, as in the following entry for **filter**[2]. This was a concession to the principle of 'linkage' mentioned earlier, but retrieval was still simple because individual phrasal verbs were indented and placed one above the other, as earlier in *ALD 3*.

(1) **filter**[2] *v* 1 [T] to clean, change, etc., by passing through a filter: *You need to filter the drinking water.* | *filtered coffee . . .*
      filter sthg. ↔ **out** *phr v* [T] . . .
      filter through (sthg.) *phr v . . .*[3]

The second shift was that more categories of derivatives than before were assigned to entries for bases. In the first edition it was chiefly adverbs in *-ly* and nouns in *-ness* that were run on—provided they could be understood in terms of the meanings of their bases and their suffixes. Now, provided that the requirement of transparency was met, derivatives such as **despotic** and **despotism** —referred to above as being separately listed in *LDOCE 1*—were run on too, in this case at the entry for **despot**.

However, by a reversal of policy on definitions in certain classes of words, the Longman editors took away, in *LDOCE 2*, the encouragement given in the first edition to make significant connections between entries. Consider the following sequence of entries from *LDOCE 1*:

(2) **gear**[1] . . . *n* . . . **3** . . . any of several arrangements, esp. of toothed wheels in a machine, which allows power to be passed from one part to another . . .
      gear[2] *v.* . . to supply (something) with GEARS
      gearbox . . . *n* a metal case containing the GEARS[1] (3) of a vehicle . . .

---

[2] The approach also reflected American practice, and the fact that some members of the editorial team for *LDOCE 1* had worked alongside the American publisher and editor Laurence Urdang on the *Collins Dictionary of the English Language* (1979) no doubt influenced editorial policy for the learner's dictionary (Quirk 1982: 74).

[3] The word-class label *phr v* is strictly redundant, as the lexical-syntactic shape of the sub-headword indicates the category unmistakably.

Here, the cross-references in capitals not only allowed the user to understand the meanings of *gear* (verb) and *gearbox* in terms of one of the senses of *gear* (noun) —most explicitly referred to in the entry for the compound—but they also linked the entries together in a clear and memorable way.

In the second edition these overt linkages are removed. Even though the noun 'gear' duly appears in the entry for the compound, it is no longer as an explicit cross-reference to the entry for the base:

(3) **gearbox** . . . *n* a metal case containing the gears of a vehicle . . .

Though no impediment to looking up the senses of the compound, such changes were not an encouragement to the user interested in language production, or in vocabulary development fostered by intelligent browsing through adjacent entries.

5.2.2. *Cobuild 1*

In some respects the arrangement of compounds and derivatives in *Cobuild 1* was indistinguishable from that of *LDOCE 1*. Compounds, whether open (*safari park*), hyphenated (*safe-conduct*), or solid (*safeguard*) were listed as main entries, while a large proportion of derivatives were also treated separately (*reminisce, reminiscence, reminiscent* and *segment, segmentation, segmented* all formed part of the macrostructure). Finally, and in line with practice in several dictionaries, including *ALD 3*, regularly formed adverbs such as *peevishly, prematurely* were entered as undefined run-ons in the entries for their bases (Moon 1987).

Yet there were sharp and fundamental differences between the macrostructure and microstructure of *Cobuild 1* and those of its competitors. Perhaps most remarkable was *Cobuild*'s departure from the principle, long observed in lexicographical practice, that at least some homographs (i.e. grammatically and/or semantically distinct words sharing the same written form) were allocated to different entries.[4] Users of the dictionary found, for instance, that not only were **bank** ('an institution where money could be kept') and **bank** ('rising ground at the side of a river') treated in a single entry, but so too were **can** (modal verb) and **can** ('metal container'). This aspect of the organization of the dictionary, which reflected an assumption that the fundamental level of lexical analysis was that of the word-form, not of the lemma or lexeme, in itself caused considerable problems of retrieval. (Note that in the entry for **toast**, which includes verb as well as noun uses, the two sets of inflected forms are conflated, thus: **toasts, toasting, toasted.**)

---

[4] In *ALD 4*, the general editorial rule was that, provided each of the homographs in question (say, *pencil* as noun and verb) had few senses and secondary derivatives, they were combined in one main entry.

What of the organization of related meanings in complex entries? Despite the emphasis generally laid by *Cobuild* editors on frequency of occurrence, the ordering of senses in entries is not based on frequency alone, though this factor is taken into account. More important is whether the sense is simple and 'independent', that is, most likely to suggest itself to a listener if the word is spoken out of context. Such meanings come first. The subsequent development of the entry depends on whether other uses of the same word-class exist, and whether they can be treated within the same framework of explanation (i.e. within a branching explanatory structure of the type illustrated below):

(4) **balloon** . . . 1 A **balloon** is 1.1 a small, thin, rubber bag with a narrow neck that you blow into . . . 1.2 a large, strong balloon filled with gas or hot air . . . 1.3 a rough circle that is drawn near the head of a character in a cartoon . . .

It will be seen from this example that meanings need not be closely related (or related to each other to the same degree) to be treated in such a structure. In fact the possibility of using a particular explanatory pattern (and the possibility of linking two or more of the same type together) may be a more important organizational principle in the microstructure than relatedness of meaning. This is borne out by entries in which there are indeed uses that are close in meaning, but where such closeness is not supported by some kind of hierarchical treatment. The point is illustrated by the following linear arrangement in the entry for **balance**, where senses **12** and **13** are clearly closer to each other than either is to **14**:

(5) **balance** . . .
12 The **balance** of an amount of something, especially money, is the part that remains after some of it has been spent or used. . . .
13 The **balance** in your bank account is the amount of money you have in it.
14 A **balance** is a device for weighing things.

Because of the practice of allocating homonyms to the same entry, *Cobuild* articles tend to be longer than those in *LDOCE* or *ALD*. Moreover, though each sense, or cluster of senses, begins on a separate line, the proliferation of branching structures (as illustrated at **balloon**) make orientation difficult, while the fact that such clusters do not regularly reflect connections of meaning does not encourage vocabulary development.

5.2.3. *ALD 4*

During the planning of *ALD 4*, it was recognized that users of the third edition had difficulty in locating various categories of information, including compounds and idioms, embedded in the microstructure of complex entries. Radical changes to the microstructure were therefore decided on. Access to compounds in *ALD 3* was problematic largely because of their positioning. Unlike derivatives, which were generally clustered at the end of the entry, but like idioms, compounds were located according to the numbered senses to which they were considered to be closest in meaning. In the entry for **joy**, for example, there were two compounds, **joy-ride** and **joy-stick**, which—inexplicably in the case of **joy-stick**— were associated with the sense 'deep pleasure', 'great gladness'.

The policy of dispersing compounds according to meaning could, of course, be challenged not only on the ground that certain items were no longer relatable to any meaning of *joy* alone, but also because it made retrieval difficult and time-consuming. It seemed that the dictionary should either bring compounds together in a block within the entry for the first element, ordering them alphabetically for ease of reference, or (more radically) should treat them as main entries, as in American collegiate dictionaries or (later) in the first edition of *LDOCE*. (Compounds were, in fact, mostly drawn together in blocks in *ALD 4*, and, as a parallel development, idioms were (in all cases) brought together too, with the first (or only) lexical word determining the entry in which they were defined.)

The arrangement of derivatives in *ALD 3* appeared to give rise to fewer problems. They were placed together at the end of the entry and arranged alphabetically—as in the series **suppression** . . . **suppressive** . . . **suppressor**—unless one was a derivative of a derivative of the headword—cf. **ecology, ecological, ecologically**—in which case the words are listed in order of derivation, irrespective of spelling. Some confusion, it is true, could be caused by the use of the tilde (~) as an economizing replacement for the root element in such series as **safe, ~ ly, ~ ness**, and it was dispensed with in the fourth edition.

The more radical of the solutions mentioned earlier was to list compounds (and derivatives, too) as main entries, even where the complex words were clearly related in written form and meaning to their bases, as in the case of *police, policing, police station* (Stein 1979; Cowie 1983*b*). This was the *LDOCE* solution, as we have seen, and it would ensure rapid access to the individual forms.

The solution eventually adopted for the treatment of derivatives and compounds in *ALD 4* was a compromise. It was designed to ensure economy and ease of access, but also intended to reflect the relationship between roots and their complex and compound forms. (The approach owed a great deal to the notion of 'word-family' developed in the lexical research of Palmer, Hornby, and West.) As a consequence, it was decided that unless derivatives and compounds were entirely opaque they should be nested in the entry for the first element, with derivatives placed first. To aid quick retrieval, individual derivatives and compounds were aligned with the edge of the column, each category being introduced by its own identifying symbol. But to indicate the relatedness of those items to idioms—or to further derivatives and compounds—formed from them, the latter were run on (as the idiom **method in one's madness** is at **madness** in the entry for **mad**):

(6) **mad** . . . *adj*
    ▷ **madly** *adv*
    madness *n* [U] 1 state of being insane; insane behaviour: *His madness cannot be cured.* 2 extreme foolishness: *It is madness to climb in such weather.* 3 (idm) **method in one's madness** . . . **midsummer madness** . . .
    □ **'madhouse** *n* . . .
    'madman . . . **'madwoman** *ns*

In practice it was found impossible to apply these policies consistently. There were two obstacles in particular. One was that, though in many cases the derivatives were found to match their roots in all or most of their senses, in many others there was only a partial match—a result of the tendency of derivatives to develop independently of the sources from which they spring. A case in point is *keeper*, which though historically derived from the verb *keep*, now has very few meanings compared with those of the verb. Such partial correspondences made it difficult in many cases to decide whether to assign a base and its derivatives to one entry, or to two or more.

The other obstacle to consistent treatment lay in the complexity of many frequently occurring core items. Consider the verb *carry* and the agentive noun *carrier*. The verb calls for lengthy and complex treatment, having numerous idioms and phrasal verbs and five compounds. The noun, while undoubtedly derived from the verb, is semantically complex, and has two compounds of its own. To embed *carrier* at **carry** would further complicate that entry by calling for additional embedding for the compounds of *carrier*. For these reasons it was decided to treat the verb and noun separately.

Such examples are a reminder that, when allocating compounds and derivatives to one place or another, a balance must be struck between considerations of semantic relatedness, accessibility, and economy of treatment (Cowie 1983*b*, 1990).

5.3. Grammatical Schemes and Codes

Designing grammatical schemes to explain the complementation patterns of verbs, nouns, and adjectives calls for linguistic expertise, but especially perhaps for ingenuity in presentation, and the willingness to modify—or even abandon— an over-complex description or coding scheme in the interests of greater transparency and usability. Other things being equal, a description will succeed which bases itself on an existing and widely-used grammar of English, and codes will be more easily accepted if they include traditional labels and abbreviations (Lemmens and Wekker 1986). Finally, patterns must be fully illustrated by example sentences.

5.3.1. *LDOCE 2*

'The dictionary uses a special system of easy-to-understand grammar codes', runs the first sentence of six pages of notes and examples in *LDOCE 2* explaining the workings of its freshly designed grammatical scheme. The framework is, it is true, far less complex than in *LDOCE 1* and much more clearly set out in the Introduction. The symbols themselves are for the most part transparent. In the interests of user-friendliness, there has been some loss of descriptive fullness and depth—not all the major syntactic differences recognized in the first edition are recorded here (Heath and Herbst 1988). On the whole, though, there is more gain than loss.

As far as verb syntax is concerned, *LDOCE 2* deploys a small and for the most part easily understood set of symbols. It makes do with only one post-verbal clause element—object (*obj*)—and three verb classes—[I] intransitive, [T] transitive, [L] linking. The remaining symbols denote word and clause classes (e.g. *adj* for adjective, '*v-ing*' for verb in the *-ing* form). Drawing on this set of symbols, *LDOCE 2* is able to account for the full set of clause patterns in which the post-verbal element, or elements, are realized by phrases. Among these, we find:

(7) [L + adj] That <u>sounds</u> interesting.
  [L + n] This <u>represents</u> a big improvement.
  [T + obj(i) + obj(d)] I <u>handed</u> her the plate.
  [T + obj + n] They <u>consider</u> this offer a big improvement.

From the purely descriptive standpoint, the scheme has some interesting features. First, it provides for economy of statement. If, for example, there is no '+ adj' or '+ n' after [L], then either an adjective or a noun complement can be selected. If a symbol is included, as in the examples above, choice is restricted to one or the other category. Second, several of the patterns with phrase complementation can be read as combinations of categories *or* functional elements. Consider, for example, the code [T + *to-v*], where *to-v* denotes a *to*-infinitive clause, but also in this case functions as direct object, since a transitive [T] verb is defined as one which 'must have a direct object' (1987: F42). But in the absence of explanation firmly focused on this point, few students will grasp it, and it must be assumed that providing a clearly explained syntactic description on two levels (constituent class and clause elements) was not part of editorial policy. On the other hand, this is not a thorough-going surface-structure scheme either, as patterns such as [T + obj(i) + obj(d)] demonstrate.

In fact, the sentence patterns on which I have concentrated here recall some of the simplifying devices first used by Palmer and Hornby (cf. 3.2.2). In the interests of ease of understanding, element labels would be introduced *only when they are sure to be known*. By this criterion, 'object' would be part of the scheme, but not 'complement' or 'adjunct'. In the same way, a general 'transitive' class of verbs could be recognized, but not a 'di-transitive' one. Finally, and this too harks back to Palmer and Hornby, element labels would only be used at all when the post-verbal constituent was a *phrase*. When it was a subordinate clause, it was referred to by means of a label such as [+ *wh*-], for clauses beginning with a *wh*-element (*I know what I like*), or [+ *that*], for a clause introduced by *that* (*I know that I'm being difficult*).

5.3.2. *Cobuild 1*

The system used in *Cobuild 1* for treating the complementation patterns of verbs in simple sentences—i.e. those in which the complementation consisted of one or two *phrases*—is in several respects highly successful. Because of the larger format and greater overall length of the dictionary, and the decision to place coded information in the centre and to the right of the two-column page, it was possible for *Cobuild* to be more explicit but no less interpretable than either of its two rivals. This is shown by the entry for the verb *christen*, in the first of two numbered senses:

(8) **christen** . . . 1 When a clergyman christens   v + o, or v + o + c:
a baby, he gives the baby a name during the   usu pass
Christian ceremony of baptism, . . .

Here two clause patterns, with function labels made familiar by the grammars of Quirk and his associates, are supported by the indication, based on corpus evidence, that those patterns are usually found in the passive.

The full set of patterns provided in *Cobuild* for clauses with either no complementation at all or with an element or elements realized by phrases (noun, adjective, or prepositional) is as follows:

(9) v
v + o   v + o + o
v + c   v + o + c
v + a   v + o + a

Great economy is achieved here, since only one label is used for verbs of several classes (copular, intransitive, etc.). Furthermore, when direct and indirect objects are realized by phrases, these are always noun phrases, so nothing further need be shown. However, further clarification is needed in the case of complements (c) and adjuncts (a), as the former can be realized by adjective as well as noun phrases and the latter (in post-verbal position) by adverbial particles (*away*, *back*, *down*, etc.) as well as prepositional phrases. There is some inconsistency in recording the nature of complements, or even, in certain cases, in recognizing their presence. The adjectival complementation illustrated by *They painted the wall green* is fully and explicitly conveyed, like this:

(10)　**paint** . . . 3 . . . v + o + c (ADJ COLOUR)

However, the noun-phrase complementation required at **elect**, say, is not similarly represented. Consider:

(11)　**elect** . . . 1 . . . v + o, OR v + o + c

As regards v + c, the pattern with adjectival complement is present at **sound**, but absent from **smell**, despite being twice illustrated there:

(12)　**sound** . . . 7 . . . *He sounded a little discouraged.* . . . v + c (ADJ)
　　　smell . . . 2 . . . *The papers smelt musty and stale.* . . .
　　　Dinner sure smells good.

In the case of clause patterns with predicative adjuncts—the kind illustrated by *Put the vase on the table* and indicated by the pattern v + o + A—the *Cobuild* policy is well conceived and, as far as a random sampling of fifty entries can show, consistently implemented. When the adjunct is prepositional, as in the example just given, and the choice of prepositions is open, only the pattern is given. When the choice of prepositions is limited, the alternatives are spelt out, as here:

(13)　**leave** . . . 5.2 . . . *Leave your phone number with the secretary.* . . . v + o
　　　+ A (*for/with*)

By far the most difficult range of verb-patterns to analyse, and to describe helpfully for the foreign learner, are those in which a post-verbal element is realized by a finite or non-finite clause, as in: *She wanted to finish the course*, or *He liked cooking Italian dishes*. This problem taxed the skill and ingenuity of all three editorial teams, as it had of earlier compilers. As A. S. Hornby had shown in his first two editions, though, it is possible in perhaps a majority of cases to assign post-verbal constituents such as the *to*-infinitive clause or the *-ing* clause confidently to specific functions (cf. Hornby 1937a, b).

At no point do the *Cobuild* editors state explicitly that *to*-infinitive or *-ing* constructions will, where appropriate, be given a functional description. However, there are interesting pointers to editorial intentions, in some verb entries, in the arrangement of certain code symbols. Consider the verb-pattern code in this entry:

(14)　**like** . . . 24 . . . If you **like** something, you enjoy it . . . v + o/-ING/*to*-INF

Here, the *definition* twice commits itself to a verb-object pattern and the two non-finite symbols in the code are linked to 'o' as if sharing its function. Perhaps this is the conclusion the user is intended to draw.

5.3.3. *ALD 4*

ALD 4 had a completely redesigned verb-pattern scheme. This was arguably a more systematic and detailed treatment than either of its rivals, though perhaps not always as transparent or user-friendly. It had been planned with three aims in view. First, it was considered essential to give functional differences between the post-verbal elements greater prominence than before, and to group patterns systematically according to those differences. At the same time, superficial differences of constituent class, though of course recorded, would be made less prominent. The second aim was to ensure that the coherence of the system was reflected in the way verb tables were arranged and above all labelled. The third aim was to design a set of codes that would be both economical and readily understandable.

I began by suggesting that it was important to highlight functional differences and similarities. As Hornby had shown, functional differences are often the basis of meaning differences. In *ALD 4*, the process of identifying those contrasts was taken much farther than before, with transformational possibilities and restrictions being used for diagnostic purposes.[5] The approach can be illustrated by reference to two patterns which were not separated in the earlier editions of *ALD* (Cowie 1992b: 344). These are, first, a transitive clause whose direct object is a non-finite clause with an included noun phrase (here, *Fred*):

(15) I would prefer [DO][Fred to write the invitations].

and, second, a complex-transitive clause with a noun phrase (here, *the porter*) as direct object and a non-finite clause as object complement:

(16) The gang forced [DO](the porter) [C][to hand over the keys].

The contrast between these two patterns (coded respectively [Tnt] and [Cn.t]) could be supported by various formal tests. A pseudo-cleft construction, for instance, shows 'NP + *to*-infinitive' to be a constituent of the main clause in the first example but not in the second. Compare:

(17) What I would prefer is Fred to write the invitations.[6]
      *What the gang forced was the porter to hand over the keys.

---

[5] Transformations such as passivization not only served to differentiate between one 'basic' pattern and another; they were also a part of the encoding information supplied to users of the dictionary.

[6] Note that the variant *I would prefer for Fred to write the invitations* confirms the constituency of *Fred to write the invitations* (as clause object of *for*).

The second aim of the revision was to ensure that underlying similarities and differences were reflected in the verb tables (and in the accompanying codes). In the following example, the final element is the direct object of a mono-transitive verb, and this label is placed above and to the right. But it was also thought important to indicate the grammatical class of the complementation (here a *that*-clause), and this label was inserted below the indication of function:

(18) [Tf]

| subject | transitive verb | direct object: |
		that-clause
Doctors	*had noted*	*that the disease was spreading.*

As well as ensuring, through formal tests, that the syntactic description of each verb-pattern was firmly based, and identifying it clearly in the appropriate table, it was important to adjust the overall ordering of patterns on the basis of functional similarities and differences. Within the new general arrangement, patterns with a particular class of verb, and a particular final element or elements, were grouped together. Ordering within the group was determined by the constituent class of the final element.

Finally, there was the problem of the simplicity and usability of the pattern codes. It was essential that these should be self-explanatory. However, as they had to be short as well as transparent, it was decided not to represent every clause element and category by means of standard labels. As I had argued earlier, every gain in explicitness has to be paid for either by making the dictionary unacceptably large, or by getting rid of other, equally vital, kinds of information (Cowie 1984, 1992*b*).

The problem was to represent the two levels of structure accurately and intelligibly, but to use a simpler notation than had earlier been developed for the second volume of *ODCIE* (1983), and for *Cobuild* (1987), in both of which complement was represented by C, indirect object by IO, adjunct by A, and so on. As a first stage, the capital letters L, I, T, D, and C were chosen to refer to the five verb-classes linking (or copular), intransitive, monotransitive, di- (or double-) transitive, and complex-transitive (Quirk *et al.* 1985: 56). As regards constituent classes such as *that*-clauses, a set of abbreviations was chosen that was as close as possible to standard word or phrase class labels, thus: 'a' (adjective phrase), 'n' (noun phrase), 't' (*to*-infinitive) clause, and so on.[7] These were combined with the verb labels to give, for example: [Ln] 'linking verb + noun phrase', [Tn] 'monotransitive verb + noun phrase'. But the major verb-classes are of course defined syntactically: a monotransitive verb is by definition a verb

---

[7] According to Flor Aarts, 'the choice of the symbols i, t, g and f for the third element . . . is not a felicitous one, since they are not standard abbreviations for the grammatical terms they stand for' (1991: 223).

in construction with a noun phrase or clause functioning as a direct object (Cowie 1992*b*: 345). So by including in a code a particular verb label, we were also indicating the number and function of the post-verbal elements.

Verb-pattern systems and codes are a feature of the learner's dictionary where considerations of economy and informativeness need to be balanced against the user's need for a transparent and usable scheme. One could claim that the new *ALD* system met the first two criteria. It has been argued, though, that even advanced students find it difficult to cope with a scheme which introduces two levels of description and makes use of more than a limited range of familiar abbreviations. As Heath and Herbst have pointed out in support of the much simplified codes introduced in *LDOCE 2*, 'more consistent codes involving such notions as *NP* or *comp* . . . would presuppose more familiarity with linguistic categories than can be expected of many learners' (1988: 316).

5.4. Definitions

In the 1980s, the editors of *LDOCE* and *ALD* persisted with approaches to defining which had been introduced in the 1970s or earlier. While *LDOCE* continued to depend on a controlled vocabulary, its Oxford competitor attempted to achieve simplicity of vocabulary and structure without quantitative constraints. There were strengths as well as weaknesses in both approaches. As a newcomer to the field, *Cobuild* struck out in a new direction. Its original approach to defining allowed for the incorporation of the headword and its lexico-syntactic context in the explanation itself. Though *Cobuild*'s definitions have been criticized for wordiness and imprecision, their pedagogical value has also been recognized. All three of *Cobuild*'s competitors in the 1990s include at least some sentence-length definitions (Herbst 1996).

5.4.1. *LDOCE 2*

The second edition of *LDOCE*, like the first, made use of a controlled defining vocabulary (or CV). However, in *LDOCE 2*, changes were made to the original list of 2,000 words, as can be shown by examining words removed from and added to letter C. Of the thirteen words cut from the 1978 list, six (*camel, Christian, Christianity, Christmas, coconut,* and *crown*) may have been thought too culturally specific to be useful outside a narrow range of definitions, while *cease, coarse, conquer, content* (adjective), may have struck the editors as formal or dated and were, in any case, easily replaced by other words already on the list.

There were sixteen new items, and the reasons for including some may have had to do with a desire to appear more transparent in the use of the CV. As Table 5.1 shows, twelve items were derivatives of existing simple words.

TABLE 5.1. *Additions to the* LDOCE *CV at letter C*

Simple words (roots) in *LDOCE 1*	Added derivatives in *LDOCE 2*
care	careful, careless
centre	central
child	childhood
civilize	civilization
combine	combination
comfort	comfortable
compete	competition, competitor
complain	complaint
confident	confidence
cruel	cruelty

In the first edition, several of these complex items were accounted for by including the relevant suffixes in the controlled vocabulary and leaving the reader to apply the appropriate derivational rules. Now, in the second edition, the list included a selection of the words actually produced by applying those rules. Why was this? Possibly, the editors were anxious to forestall the suggestion that, in allowing too much productivity to the CV, they were leaving themselves free to use many derivatives that were not straightforwardly related to their roots (cf. Stein 1979). Certainly, by listing more of the derivatives that they intended to use, they were in a better position to answer that charge.

By contrast, there was an actual criticism of the use of the CV in the earlier edition about which little seems to have been done. In their computer-based analysis, Jansen, Mergeai, and Vanandroye (1987, and cf. 3.4.3, above) had noted the widespread use in definitions of phrasal verbs composed of items from the CV, thus: *break across*, *break down*, *break into*, etc. The same point was made about the inclusion of such idioms (strictly, restricted collocations) as *break the habit* and *break the law* (1987: 89). It is in fact possible to find in *LDOCE 1* a number of entries with definitions containing word-combinations of a variety of types. In the fifteen-entry series **recommend** to **reconstruct**, for instance, ten phrasal verbs and collocations/idioms (here highlighted by underlining) can be identified:

(19) **recommend** . . . to speak to someone <u>in favour of</u> . . .
    recommend to . . . to <u>give in charge</u> to . . .
    reconcile . . . to <u>make peace</u> between . . .
    recondition . . . to repair and <u>bring back</u> into working order . . .
    reconnoitre . . . <u>in order to</u> <u>find out</u> the enemy's numbers . . .
    reconsider . . . to think again and <u>change one's mind</u> about . . .
    reconstitute . . . to <u>bring back</u> into existence . . .
    reconstruct . . . to <u>build up</u> a complete description . . . (*LDOCE 1*)

Interestingly, while a number of the collocations (*in favour of, give in charge, make peace*) have been dropped from the corresponding entries in *LDOCE 2*, all the phrasal verbs are retained, two (*find out* and *build up*) being idiomatic, while the others are figurative extensions of literal uses. Yet the continuing use of such items is perfectly defensible once it is recognized that, in most cases, they make an essential contribution to the naturalness of the defining language. This is presumably the reason why they are retained. On the other hand, it also has to be recognized that by tacitly acknowledging the importance of definitions which are in the broadest sense idiomatic, one is weakening the case for a narrowly-based defining vocabulary.

5.4.2. *Cobuild 1*

While the editors of *LDOCE 2* and *ALD 4* were largely content to improve on definitions of a conventional type which had appeared in earlier editions, *Cobuild* broke entirely new ground. The classical pattern used by its competitors was one in which the definiendum (the headword) was sharply distinguished from the definiens (the definition), in which the latter was normally an analytical phrase of the same grammatical class as the headword, and in which selection restrictions of the headword, if specified at all, formed part of the definition (Svensén 1993: 120–31). Consider the following example:

(20) **trot** . . . (of horses, etc) go at a pace faster than a walk but not so fast as a gallop. . . . (*ALD 3*)

Definitions in *Cobuild 1* differed from the traditional type with regard to all three of those characteristics. First, the headword formed part of the 'explanation' (a term applied by *Cobuild* lexicographers to the entire explanatory statement, of which the definition, as normally understood, formed only part). Second, explanations were always complete sentences, often, as in the following example, complex sentences:

(21) If something **disturbs** you or **disturbs** your state of mind, it makes you feel upset or worried.

Third, the left-hand part of the explanation (here, a subordinate clause) provided a typical grammatical context for the headword, in which its co-occurrence restrictions with a direct object were also specified. (The object in this case can refer either to a person or to a person's 'state of mind'.) The right-hand part (the main clause), on the other hand, was the definition proper. In fact, suitably adapted, it could serve as a definition in either *LDOCE 2* or *ALD 4*:

(22) **disturb** . . . make (sb) feel upset or worried.

These were important innovations, not only from a theoretical standpoint, but also from the point of view of the learner, who was now confronted by a complete sentence of which the headword formed an integral part, and in which use was indicated and meaning conveyed.

Intransitive as well as transitive verbs could be explained by these methods, as the following example shows:

(23) When a horse **clops**, its hooves make a noise on the ground as it walks or trots.

The entry also illustrates the wider point that specified subjects and objects, depending on the character of the verb, can range from the most general statements of restriction to particular collocates (here, *horse*). According to Aarts (1991: 217), 'the definitions in *Cobuild* are usually so clear and straightforward that the examples are not really necessary.' This may be precisely because the first part often takes on the character of an example. Consider the left-hand part of the following explanation, and compare the supporting example:

(24) If people or things **line** a road, a room, etc, they are present in large numbers along its edges or sides. EG . . . *Crowds lined the processional route.*

As Patrick Hanks has pointed out in his description of the various types of explanation used in *Cobuild*, the pattern of the explanation varies according to the class of word being defined (Hanks 1987). There are in fact several different patterns, and there is a tendency for verbs and adjectives to attract specific types of left-hand element. These are a reflection of the characteristic syntactic patterns in which verbs and adjectives occur (and in terms of which selection restrictions can be stated).

As regards explanations of adjectives, the following pair are interesting, since the first, by the structure of the left-hand part, suggests that the adjective *high*, in the given sense, is used predicatively, while the second, by the pattern of the initial noun phrase, indicates that the adjective is used attributively.

(25) When a river is **high**, it contains much more water than usual.
     A **high** wind blows hard and with great force.

Nouns are particularly difficult to deal with by means of a consistent defining strategy. This is partly because the collocates of nouns do not occur in any regular structural relationship with the noun itself. As a result, noun entries often rely 'on the semantic content of the explanation to distinguish meanings, rather than on a preliminary contextualization in conjunction with the semantic content' (Hanks 1987: 128). This is borne out by the following:

(26) A **cloak** is . . . a wide, loose coat that fastens at the neck and does not have sleeves.

This departs quite radically from the patterns already discussed. Specifically, it lacks a subordinate clause in initial position, so that there is no indication of the possible clause functions of the noun—there would be too many to specify—or of any possible modifiers. (The adjectives 'wide' and 'loose' are of course modifiers of the genus word 'coat', not of the headword **cloak**.) What we in fact have here is something very close to a traditional definition. Though full and precise, it offers nothing over and above what is found in other dictionaries.

Discursive, sentence-length definitions are an important development in learner lexicography. They often resemble the 'folk definitions' which are provided by teachers and parents, and of which they are no doubt a sophisticated outgrowth. Furthermore, they provide, in a great many cases, a syntactic and lexical context for the headword. They are, however, an uneconomical form of definition, and in *Cobuild* often repetitive and imprecise. For the learner, one further disadvantage is that the syntactic complexity of the explanation may make the key elements in the definition ('food' and 'delicious' in the case of the adjective **scrumptious**) difficult to identify (Hausmann and Gorbahn 1989).

5.4.3. *ALD 4*

No attempt was made to set up a limited defining vocabulary for *ALD 4*. The risks to which users of a CV are prone—for instance, of using idiomatic combinations or non-literal meanings of listed words—have already been demonstrated. It can be argued, too, that simplicity is not the only quality that definitions should possess, and that the editor's goal, when drafting definitions, should be to achieve lexical and structural simplicity insofar as this can be reconciled with precision, economy, and naturalness (Cowie 1989*d*).

The entire text of *ALD 3* underwent a fundamental revision, much of which sought to remove, within the overall pattern of the traditional definition, difficulties of vocabulary and structure. Efforts were made, for instance, to replace formal or idiomatic vocabulary that the user might find more unfamiliar than the word being defined. Note, for example, 'settled practice' and 'given up' in the following definition from *ALD 3* and their replacement in *ALD 4* by simpler, more colloquial (though longer) phrases:

(27)   **habit** . . . sb's settled practice, esp something that cannot easily be given up: . . . (*ALD 3*)
　　　　habit . . . thing that a person does often and almost without thinking, esp sth that is hard to stop doing: . . . (*ALD 4*)

Difficulties could also be created for dictionary users by syntactic conventions. One long-established convention in *ALD 3* (inherited from mother-tongue dictionaries) was the practice of coordinating a number of nouns, participles, etc., which were superordinates of the headword, and then attaching a shared adjunct or post-modifier (often a prepositional phrase). Consider this example:

(28) **premature** . . . done, happening, doing sth, before the right or usual time:
   . . . (*ALD 3*)

This is a difficult type of definition to process, since, to make perfect sense, each
of the participles in turn must be linked to the phrase 'before the right or usual
time'. One remedy was to reconstitute the three full structures and make these
the basis of separate definitions, as here, where 'happening' reappears as part of
the first sense and 'done' as part of the second:

(29) **premature** . . . 1 . . . happening before the proper or expected time: . . .
   2 . . . acting or done too soon; hasty: . . . (*ALD 4*)

It was suggested earlier that the restructuring of complex entries in *ALD 4* was
intended to throw into relief the relative closeness or distance of roots and their
derivatives. This had a dual purpose: to help with the quick retrieval of those
words, certainly, but also to provide support for vocabulary development. But
that reorganization went hand in hand with the redrafting of definitions. Consider part of the entry in *ALD 4* for the verb **play**:

(30) **play** . . . 5 (a) . . . take (a particular position) in a team: *Who's playing
   in goal?* ∘ *I've never played (as/at) centre-forward before.* (b) . . . include sb
   in a team: *I think we should play Bill on the wing in the next match.* . . .
   6 (a) . . . (try to) strike, kick, throw, etc (the ball, etc) . . . *In soccer, only
   the goal-keeper may play the ball with his hands.* (b) . . . make (a stroke,
   etc): *play a fast backhand volley.* . . . (*ALD 4*)

The entry illustrates, first, a regular change in the form of the definition. While
definitions in *ALD 3* had often indicated the typical direct objects of a verb in
its various senses ('position' and 'ball' appear in the corresponding entry in
ALD 3) the new edition did so more consistently, and in addition placed the
objects within parentheses. The use of parentheses in definitions has been criticized as a departure from ordinary written English (Hanks 1987: 116). If not
overused, however, 'abbreviatory notations' (Fillmore 1989: 58) play a useful part
in highlighting the semantic role of the object in each case, and providing a clear
visual link with the specific choice of object noun in example sentences (cf.
'position', *centre-forward*; 'stroke', *backhand volley*).
   The entry for **play** also shows that its microstructure is based on the syntactic
relatedness of various senses. As can be seen from 5 (a) and 5 (b), the verb is
sometimes used ergatively (cf. *Who should play on the wing?* and *I think we
should play Bill on the wing.*), and this close relationship can be brought out by
treating the two uses within the same major sense-division of the entry. By contrast, the senses at **6**, though close to each other (in terms of metonymy), are
more remote from those at **5** (the direct objects are animate at **5** and inanimate
at **6**), and it is appropriate that they should form another major division. As has

been suggested, such arrangements are helpful for vocabulary learning, but a branching structure, provided it is meaning-based, can help the user to move systematically through an entry to a specific destination.

5.5. Style, Attitudinal, and Register Labels

Variables such as the currency, regional use, and stylistic level of words and meanings were of interest to the compilers of the first *ALD*. Items such as *fall* (as in *the fall of 1938*), *realtor*, and *sidewalk* were labelled '(U.S.A.)', and informal usage was identified by means of the label 'colloq.', as in the entries for *guts*, *muck up*, and *swipe*. But the labels adopted were unevenly applied, by no means all types of restriction which called for a label were given one (thus, informality was sometimes taken account of but not formality), and, above all, no attempt was made at that stage to organize the various labels into systematic groupings. Lists were set out for the first time in *ALD 3* (1974) and further elaborated in the revised impression of 1980. By that time, *LDOCE 1* had already been giving close attention to style and register labelling. Later, as the new editions of the 1980s were planned and compiled, it became clear that usage labelling was a matter calling for vigilance and sensitivity, especially in the treatment of vocabulary relating to gender and race.

5.5.1. *LDOCE 2*

The compilers of the first edition of *LDOCE* (1978) gave careful thought to the selection and categorization of labels for words or phrases whose use was in some way restricted. The result was a broad and systematic framework. First, the labels took account of a wide spectrum of limitations on use. These were explained and the labels themselves carefully defined and illustrated. The range of categories included the regions or countries to which particular words were restricted; their datedness or rarity; their technical field (e.g. law or medicine); the kinds of occasion on which the words would be used; their social acceptability or propriety; and the attitude of the speaker towards the person or thing denoted. *LDOCE 1* also took account of cases where a word was non-standard or of foreign origin (1978: xxiv–xxv).

Very few changes were made to this framework for the second edition, though there were marked differences in the way the scheme was explained and set out in the front matter. The language was made simpler and the explanations shorter, while the layout became less cramped and better able to support a step-by-step presentation. The major categories of *LDOCE 1* were retained, though now with headings, and care was taken (with the help of white highlighting in shaded example entries) to show whether a label related to the whole of an entry or only part (say to a particular pronunciation or spelling).[8] What the user was being offered, in short, was a more user-friendly presentation of an already sound descriptive scheme.

In the second edition, as in the first, though, there were few labels relating to specific technical or scientific fields (with the exception of such old-established fields as law and medicine) and not even the generic *tech* was applied in all cases where it was called for. The lack of specificity in labels used for fields such as music and architecture in *LDOCE 2* is shown by the absence of labelling from the following list of musical and architectural terms:

(31)   andante (0), coda (0), concerto (0), scherzo (0), sonata (0);
       apse (0), cupola (0), nave (0), pediment (0), pilaster (0).

On the other hand, differences between British and American usage were regularly signalled, and a clear system of labelling was applied both to cases where British speakers would use one word and Americans another and also to instances where one item was used in both varieties while the other was confined to one. The procedure in the latter case was to provide the definition at the entry for the more widely-used word, though with reference to the other, and to give a simple cross-reference in small capitals at the place of the more restricted word:

(32)   **escalator** . . . ‖ also **moving staircase** *BrE*
       moving staircase . . . *n* an ESCALATOR

As regards the labelling of words which can give offence, it was noticeable that whereas *LDOCE 2* marked such words as *prick* and *turd* as *taboo* it added to the entries for *nigger* and *yid* the further qualification 'considered extremely offensive', thus reflecting the greater sensitivity now shown in the use of terms likely to offend on grounds of race, gender, religion, or colour.

5.5.2. *Cobuild 1*

Information about style and register markings in *Cobuild 1* was provided at two points in the front matter. The chief editor's introduction devoted several sections to the problem, focusing chiefly on three aspects of language variety which the dictionary aimed to reflect and describe. These were 'technical terminology', 'social variety', and 'geographical variety'. As regards the first, the discussion had more to say on the difficulty of giving explanations in non-technical language than on the accurate labelling of specific fields. In fact, precise treatment of technical usage did not seem to be a principal aim of *Cobuild*. The texts in

---

[8] Of the labels, *not fml* (not formal) was removed as an intermediate stage beween *fml* and *infml*, while *obs* (obsolete) gave way to *old-fash* (old-fashioned).

the Main and Reserve corpora used for the compilation of the dictionary came
from 'ordinary English', and thus its technical terms occurred chiefly in non-
technical contexts (cf. 4.3.3). Users looking for precise definitions of such terms
were referred to 'the many specialized dictionaries that are compiled by experts
in each field' (1987: xx). This general approach seems to have influenced the
treatment of many particular words. Of the specialist entries listed above at (31),
three were not present at all in *Cobuild*. Of the rest, one carried the non-subject-
specific label *tech*:

(33)   andante (0), coda *tech*, concerto (0), scherzo (no entry), sonata (0);
       apse (no entry), cupola (0), nave (0), pediment (0), pilaster (no entry).

With regard to 'social variety', the introduction identified a number of areas
in which the foreign learner had to take particular care in the choice of words,
and referred to greater tolerance in the use of words concerned with sex or religion. However, it introduced only two labels—*formal* and *informal*—as indica-
tors of variation of a social kind. As for overseas varieties of English, *Cobuild 1*
aimed to exclude words and senses which were distinctive to those varieties and
not familiar to the international community. The aim was to provide a description of 'a form of English which is widely used and usable throughout the
world' (1987: xx).

For more specific guidance on the methods adopted to show that a word was
used 'by a particular group', or 'in a particular social context', and so on, users
were directed to the section headed 'Usage' in the 'Guide to the use of the dictionary' (1987: xi). The guidance offered there was somewhat limited, but the
important point was made that labels were not the only method used in *Cobuild*
to identify specialized words or uses. Among the conventions employed—apart
from a standard phrase containing a label, e.g. '**afters**; an informal use'—were
brief statements of the function or restriction involved, as in:

(34)   **plebeian** . . . 1 . . . a **plebeian** is a member of the lower social classes: used
       showing disapproval.
       friend . . . 7 A **Friend** is a Quaker. This term is preferred by Quakers
       themselves.

Elsewhere, the limitation on use was made part of the definition itself, though
a phrase incorporating a label was sometimes included as well:

(35)   **bathroom** . . . 2 Some people say **bathroom** as a polite way of referring to
       the toilet; used especially in American English.

There was some degree of correspondence between the choice of these conventions and the type of restriction being conveyed (though these underlying
parallels were not, in fact, explained). For example, where there was a need to
show that a lexical unit was a term in some specialist field, was formal or infor-

mal, or belonged to a major regional variety, there was a tendency to prefer those conventions which most resembled labels in other dictionaries:

(36) **coronary thrombosis** . . . a medical term.
    realize . . . **3** If you **realize** a hope, desire, ambition, you succeed in making it happen in reality; a formal use.
    realtor . . . used in American English.

When, on the other hand, the item, in addition to denoting a person or thing, also expressed the speaker's attitude towards them, or when it was concerned more with the expression of feeling than with denotation, there was a greater likelihood of those attitudinal or emotive aspects of meaning being incorporated in the definition, as here:

(37) **damn** . . . **1 Damn, damn you, damn it** and **dammit** are swear words which people sometimes use to express anger or annoyance.

For the treatment of style and register distinctions, *Cobuild 1* provides a range of conventions, including labels, which appear incomplete and are imprecisely defined. (In its handling of words—such as *eraser*—which are normal in American English but have some currency in British English, *Cobuild 1* is far less rigorous than either *LDOCE 2* or *ALD 4*.) The interest, and strength, of *Cobuild's* approach lies rather in its attempt to develop informal means of expressing use restrictions as part of the definition, as demonstrated by entries for words such as *damn* and *bathroom*.

5.5.3. *ALD 4*

On the inside cover of *ALD 3* (1974), a list of labels and abbreviations had appeared denoting 'stylistic values' with a further list referring to 'specialist English registers' (i.e. specialist or technical fields). Terms such as *engineering, geology* and *cricket*, which appeared in the second list, were arguably self-explanatory, but what was the user to make of *formal, euphemistic,* and *laudatory*, which appeared in the first? There was clearly a need to define such terms—even to question their inclusion—all the more so as only a selection were dealt with in an explanatory essay in the introduction.[9]

Apart from the difficulties presented by unfamiliar or ambiguous terms, there was a need to resolve the problem of sets of labels having what appeared to be the same or similar values (compare, on the one hand, *archaic, dated,* and *old,* and, on the other, *facetious, humorous,* and *jocular*). Examining the existing set

---

[9] Almost all the stylistic labels had already been listed, in abbreviated form, in the introduction to *ALD 2,* where they were selectively defined. The following appeared in *ALD 3* for the first time: *dated, facetious, figurative, formal, laudatory, old use, pejorative, rare,* and *taboo.*

of 'stylistic' labels suggested, too, that it could be broken down—helpfully for the learner—into a number of coherent groupings. Labels such as *archaic* and *dated*, for instance, though possibly overlapping in reference and needing careful definition, concerned the datedness (or 'currency') of words. If such variety categories were to be introduced, it would sometimes be necessary to refer a given entry to two or more, as in *dated US infml* (where currency is indicated before region and formality).

Five dimensions of variety according to use were eventually recognized— currency, region, register, technical field, and evaluation—relating respectively to date of use, country or area of use, occasion or setting of use, use in a specialist field, and speaker attitude. As regards currency, it was important to distinguish between the datedness of words and meanings, on the one hand, and the roles, artefacts, and so on to which they referred, on the other. The noun *aerodrome*, for instance, could be referred to as *dated*, as the term had virtually passed out of use. In the case of *battleaxe*, by contrast, it was the weapon that was no longer in use. Its obsoleteness could be shown in the definition, in this way:

(38) 'battleaxe *n* (a) (formerly) heavy axe with a long handle, used as a weapon.

The inclusion in *ALD 4* of words and senses restricted to various parts of the English-speaking world, and their distinctive marking in the dictionary, reflected the growing international character of English. Though South African (*S African*), New Zealand (*NZ*), and Australian (*Austral*) items were all included, chief stress was laid on the major international varieties, United States (*US*) and British (*Brit*) English, and on lexical, semantic, and pronunciation differences between them.

Special conventions of labelling were needed to indicate whether there was a straightforward relationship of equivalence between the American and the British item, or whether the US word (say) was also in British use. In *ALD 4*, an item limited to British English which had a synonym confined to American English was treated in a full entry for the former, with the US equivalent positioned near the beginning. A 'dummy' entry for the US word directed the user back to this full entry. Compare:

(39) 'shop-assistant (*US* salesclerk) *n* person who serves customers in a shop.
'salesclerk *n* (*US*) = SHOP-ASSISTANT (SHOP).

In the case of items associated with technical fields, it was decided to use specific rather than generic labels. Labelling of the musical and architectural terms mentioned earlier, though limited, was fuller than in *LDOCE* or *Cobuild*, and the labels—where they appeared—were more specific:

(40) andante (*music*), coda (*music*), concerto (o), scherzo (o), sonata (o); apse (o), cupola (o), nave (o), pediment (*architecture*), pilaster (o).

Special awareness and sensitivity needed to be shown, as we have already seen, when dealing with words or phrases which imply a disapproving or offensive attitude towards the person or thing denoted. Precise guidance had to be given so that students could avoid giving unnecessary offence through the choice of unsuitable terms. Three categories of words that needed to be labelled with particular care were those designated in *ALD 4* as *derogatory, offensive,* and *sexist.* Derogatory words are those which imply disapproval or scorn of the person or action referred to (e.g. *slob, slug, smarmy, swagger*). When used as terms of address (as *slob* and *slug* can be), they can of course give offence. Particularly offensive, however, are words such as *dago* or *wop*, used to refer to or address people, often with the intention of casting a slur on their religion or ethnic background. These were additionally marked in *ALD 4* with a 'danger' sign, as follows:

(41) **dago** . . . ($\triangle$ *sl offensive*)

The label *sexist* was introduced for the first time in *ALD 4* as a means of encouraging greater awareness of the offence which words such as *bimbo* or *Girl Friday* can cause to women (Whitcut 1984). Its use went hand in hand with the attempt to be more even-handed in referring to women in the dictionary and in portraying women in the full range of occupations and roles which they now fill in advanced societies. This policy met with some success. As a comparative analysis of feminine and masculine nouns and pronouns in examples in parallel sections of *ALD 1* and *ALD 4* has shown, references to females in the fourth edition exceed references to males by a ratio of 7 to 6 (Cowie 1995)[10]—and a similar balance is maintained in the fifth (Herbst 1996).

5.6. Sense Relations and Lexical Fields

We have seen how, during the 1970s, EFL lexicographers absorbed and applied the major grammatical descriptions of English emerging during that period. However, it was not until the late 1970s and early 1980s that they began to draw, to anything like the same extent, on parallel developments in lexical semantics. Its influence was reflected in quite elaborate cross-reference systems in both *LDOCE 1* (1978) and *ODCIE 2* (1983), and was to become even more pronounced in the new general-purpose dictionaries of the late 1980s.

In their work on sense (or semantic) relations, John Lyons (1968, 1977), and Alan Cruse (1986) had refined and extended the limited set of binary semantic relations (chiefly synonymy and antonymy) recognized and sometimes treated

---

[10] The ratio was 2 to 1 in favour of males in the first edition.

by traditional mother-tongue dictionaries.[11] Especially important was Lyons's breaking down of 'antonymy' into three formally distinct categories—complementarity (cf. *married* vs. *single, dead* vs. *alive*), converseness (cf. *mother* vs. *daughter, doctor* vs. *patient*), and antonymy proper (cf. *smooth* vs. *rough, tall* vs. *short*)—and the elaboration of hyponymy (cf. the superordinate *root vegetable* and its co-hyponyms *carrot, swede, parsnip, turnip,* etc.).

As the dictionaries of the 1980s took shape, it was generally recognized that, for the most part, users would not need to understand the fine differences between complementaries and converses, but that it was desirable to deal with 'oppositeness' in general terms, and to draw attention to the synonyms and superordinates of individual entry words. Care would need to be taken with presentation, and the following is an attempt to list the chief requirements (which, as we shall see, were taken account of in varying degrees by the various editorial teams):

- Information needed to be presented prominently, preferably with the help of explicit labels.
- In some cases the labels would need to carry sense-division numbers, reflecting the fact that relations of synonymy, antonymy, and so on, typically hold not between entries (i.e. lemmata or lexemes) as such but between the 'lexical units' of which an entry is made up (Cruse 1986).[12] The noun *man* in one of its senses, 'husband', is the opposite (specifically the converse) of *wife*, but in another, 'ordinary soldier', the opposite (specifically the complementary) of *officer*.
- Ideally, cross-references should be bi-directional (or in cases where more than two entries were involved, multi-directional).
- In the case of synonymy especially, the user should be reminded—preferably through a note in the introduction—that items marked as equivalent did not necessarily have the same stylistic value or syntactic function. In consequence, users would need to be warned that, when referring from A to B, they should note any grammatical (or stylistic) divergences between the two points of reference.

These requirements applied chiefly to pairs of entries or lexical units. But EFL lexicographers were also becoming interested, from the early 1980s onwards, in

---

[11] *Webster's Third New International* (1961) provided in some entries (e.g. **make**) extended comparisons of the meanings and uses of near-synonyms. In the *Dictionnaire du français contemporain*, a remarkable French learners' dictionary of the 1960s, synonyms and antonyms (in the broad sense) were treated, specially labelled, and further categorized, where necessary, as 'familier' (informal) and 'littéraire' (formal) (Cowie 1979).

[12] Note that 'lexical unit' refers not only to the numbered senses of a main entry, whether simple word (**pot**), derivative (**potty**), or compound (**pothole**), but also to the senses of derivatives and compounds which happen to be located within main entries, as is the case in ALD 4 (Cowie 1995).

semantic groupings of words, like the set of vegetable names shown above. These complexities made their own demands, and in particular editors would have to decide whether the groupings could best be presented verbally—in special 'usage notes'—or in tables and charts.

5.6.1. *LDOCE 2*

How fully were binary relations of synonymy and oppositeness treated in *LDOCE 2*? A list of twenty-four lexical units (i.e. words and senses) based initially on a succession of *LDOCE* entries containing cross-references, and then adjusted to account for cross-referenced units in *Cobuild 1* and *ALD 4* that were not in *LDOCE*, shows that *LDOCE* provided cross-references to synonyms or antonyms in almost half the cases (9), and that it generally included a 'return' cross-reference in entries for synonyms or antonyms.[13] *LDOCE* also employed a greater *variety* of devices to connect entries that were related in sense than either *Cobuild 1* or *ALD 4*, though it is worth noting that some simply linked equivalents that were closely related in *form* as well as meaning. In the following entry, for instance, *pot* is simply a 'clipped' form of *potbelly*.

(42) **potbelly** . . . also **pot**

The same conventions ('also' introducing another form in bold print) are used to link a neutral word with a more formal or technical equivalent:

(43) **postmortem** . . . also . . . *fml*, **autopsy**

In fact, the devices linking *commonplace* words in *LDOCE* that are not formally connected (e.g. *posture* vis-à-vis *stance*) account for only nine of the twenty-four listed units. Nonetheless, all the conventions denote important types of equivalence, and all are useful to the foreign learner.

As regards commonplace words, synonymy is indicated by placing the synonym in capitals immediately after the analytical definition:

(44) **posture**[1] . . . **2** [C] a particular bodily position: POSE . . .

Opposites (not represented in this sequence) also appear after the definition of the lexical unit to which they belong, with the label 'opposite':

(45) **offensive**[1] . . . **1** causing offence; . . .— opposite **inoffensive** . . .

---

[13] The list was made up of the following: **postmortem, postnatal, postpone, postponement, postulate** *n*, **posture** *n* 2 'pose', 3 'stance', **posture** *v*, **postwar, posy, pot** *n* 2 'potful', 4 'potty', 5 'pots', 6 'kitty', 8 'marijuana', 9 'potbelly', 10 'potshot', **potato, potato beetle, potato crisp, potbelly, potency, potent** 2 'convincing', 3 'powerful'.

There is also the label 'compare', which can signal different kinds of sense relations. It is used in the entries **postnatal** and **postwar**, where the relationship is one of opposition (specifically complementarity):

(46) **postwar** . . .— compare PREWAR . . .

In some cases (though not in this sequence of entries), the label is helpfully used to indicate co-hyponyms, and here we move beyond the purely binary relations so far discussed:

(47) **macaroni** . . . Italian PASTA . . .— compare SPAGHETTI, TAGLIATELLE, VERMICELLI . . .

Also helpful for developing awareness of groups of related words is the label 'see also', which may introduce a number of compounds incorporating the head-word, as in this item from the listed items:

(48) **potato** . . .—see also HOT POTATO, SWEET POTATO . . .

Of much greater usefulness, though, for making users aware of semantic groupings of words, or 'lexical fields', are the so-called Usage Notes. The value of such notes is that they contain explanations and examples clarifying differences—grammatical and stylistic as well as semantic—between words of roughly similar meaning. An example appears below the entry **refuse**, where the verbs *refuse, decline, reject,* and *turn down* are first shown to be similar in having shared opposites (*agree to* and *accept*) and are then distinguished in terms of their differing collocability with nouns, like this:

(49) You can **refuse** or **decline** an invitation; **refuse** permission; **decline, reject** or **turn down** a suggestion; **refuse, decline, reject** or **turn down** an offer; **reject** or **turn down** a plan or proposal.

This is valuable guidance, since it warns the user against forming collocations (e.g. *decline permission, *refuse a suggestion) that may seem plausible to foreign learners but are unacceptable to native speakers.

5.6.2. *Cobuild 1*

Cobuild's approach to the treatment of sense relations was innovative in several important respects. First, it used the so-called 'extra column' (a broad column at the centre and to the right of the page) to indicate those relations. That in itself made for clarity of presentation. Second, it introduced three more or less self-explanatory symbols to indicate cross-references to synonyms (=), antonyms (≠)—again the term covered a number of more specific types of binary opposition—and superordinates (⇑) (Sinclair *et al.* 1987: xi). And partly because it was the first EFL dictionary to refer systematically to the superordinates of entries, *Cobuild 1* indicated the sense relations of more lexical units than either of its rivals. This is clear from the entries for the listed items, where in a spread of 21 out of a possible 24 lexical units, *Cobuild 1* has 18 cross-references to synonyms or superordinates and makes up for the non-inclusion of entries for *potato beetle* and *potato crisp* by being the one dictionary of the three to include cross-references for the following entries:

(50)   **postponement** . . . ⇑ *delay*
                          = *referral*
       postulate . . . = *assumption,*
                          hypothesis
       potato . . . ⇑ *tuber*

This is above all helpful information for language production or vocabulary building, but the inclusion of contrastive synonyms alongside neighbouring definitions is also helpful in establishing meaning differences. Consider:

(51)   **pot 1.4** a container . . .   = flowerpot . . .
       1.5 a deep bowl, used as a toilet . . . = chamber pot, potty

However, the clarity and depth of detail visible in these entries is offset by flaws in the overall organization of the cross-reference system. In the sequence of 21 *Cobuild* entries, none of the cross-references directing the user to a complex (polysemous) entry has a sense-division number (even though they may *originate* in an entry with numbered senses), and indeed this is true of the dictionary generally. As a result, the user must search through the destination entry for the appropriate meaning and any distinctive grammatical or stylistic features. The chief weakness, though, is a lack of consistency in ensuring that, whenever reference is made from entry A to entry B, reference is also made back from B to A. Consider the following imperfect matches, where not only are the 'return' B to A cross-references to **postulate** missing, but other items are introduced (e.g. *theory*) which are clearly not synonyms of *postulate*:

(52)   A   ⇒   B   B   ⇒   A
       postulate = assumption,   **assumption** = notion, idea
                    hypothesis   **hypothesis** = theory

This is not an isolated case. Reference to **pot** in the gaming sense throws up 'kitty' and 'pool' as synonyms. Reference to **kitty** (in the appropriate sense) yields 'pool' but not 'pot', and a new superordinate in 'money'. One is led to assume that the connection between *postulate* and *assumption* (say) was suggested by the limited substitutability of *assumption* in contexts gathered for the entry for *postulate* and not on the basis of a close comparison of contexts and definitions for both items.

5.6.3. *ALD 4*

A number of new conventions were introduced in *ALD 4* to convey meaning relations (though there was no separate label to distinguish opposites from other kinds of non-synonymous items). Coverage of lexical units in which a label of some kind was called for was, however, uneven and though the 24 listed units were all included in the dictionary, there were only 14 entries with cross-references, of which 11 were to synonyms or antonyms.

Where one form was produced from another by clipping, the clipped forms were regularly included (in brackets and in bold print) in the entries for the compound words from which they were derived, and for which they often served as informal synonyms:

(53) 'pot-belly . . . (also **pot**)
      'pot-shot . . . (also **pot**)

At the entries for the clipped forms, there would be cross-references to the full forms, with the sense letter or number of the latter included as appropriate:

(54) **pot**¹ . . . 5 [C] = POT-BELLY a. . . . 8 [C] = POT-SHOT.

Opposites of various kinds were inserted in capitals at the end of sense-divisions, as in the following entry for **postpone**. Care was taken to ensure that where a meaning of one complex entry (A) was related to a sense of another (B), the cross-reference at A should include the sense-division number of B—and, where necessary, its homonym number—to indicate unambiguously the point to which the user was being directed. (The arrangements at B should of course parallel those at A.) Compare:

(55) **postpone** . . . 1 . . . arrange sth at a later time; . . . Cf ADVANCE 6 . . .
      advance . . . 6 . . . bring (an event) to an earlier date . . . Cf POSTPONE 1 . . .

With synonyms, especially, users needed to know that, when they referred to the other entry, items which were cognitively equivalent might differ in grammar and/or style. The noun *afters*, for example, which was given as a synonym of *pudding* (sense 1) in *ALD 4*, was more informal. (And, unlike *dessert*, both are confined to British English.) It was important then to warn dictionary users to beware of substituting a word referred to as a synonym without first checking the entry for the synonym, and an appropriate warning appeared in the introduction to *ALD 4* (Cowie 1989c: 1575).

The most ambitious part of the treatment of word relationships was the description of complex semantic groupings: ranks (e.g. *lieutenant, captain, major*), scales (e.g. *cold, cool, warm, hot*), cycles (e.g. *Monday, Tuesday, Wednesday*, etc.), and lexical fields (e.g. *drip, seep, ooze, run*). Some of this information had been presented in earlier learners' dictionaries in the form of tables and charts (Ilson

1987). For instance, the second, third, and fourth editions of *ALD* and the first of *LDOCE* had included tables comparing ranks in the various armed services—information now likely to be of dwindling interest to overseas students. *LDOCE 1* had also included a diagrammatic presentation of kinship terms. However, the most significant addition to this range was the 'lexical field', included in *ALD 4* as a 'note on usage'.

The description of lexical fields in *ALD 4* arose directly out of a programme of lexical research, funded by OUP, and conducted at the University of Leeds in the early 1980s (Cowie 1989*d*). The project had as its particular aim the analysis of lexical fields, reflecting the strong interest being shown in hierarchical word-fields by such linguists as Nida (1975), Lyons (1977), and Lehrer (1974). Since the research focused chiefly on verbs, in their various senses, verbs played a large part in the notes on usage eventually compiled for the dictionary.

Members of one field which later formed the basis of a usage note in *ALD 4*—it comprised verbs of cutting—were verbs with the same syntactic function, and with two semantic features in common ('removal' and 'with a sharp instrument'). Most of the verbs had a superordinate term in *cut* or *cut off*. Central to the general definition of the field was the notion that either the body being made smaller, or the parts being removed, could be realized as the grammatical direct object. Compare *Have you finished clipping the hedge?*—where the 'body' is object—and *I want to clip that picture from the magazine*—where the 'part' is object. These details were incorporated as follows in the note:

(56) NOTE ON USAGE: Compare **clip**, **pare**, **prune**, **trim** and **shave**. The verbs refer to cutting off an unwanted part to make an object smaller, tidier, etc. Note that with all except **pare** the direct object can be either (**a**) the main body that is made smaller, smoother etc or (**b**) the part that is cut off. . . . **Clip** can relate to cutting off an unwanted part or to removing a part in order to keep it: (**a**) *Have you finished clipping the hedge?* (**b**) *I want to clip that picture from the magazine.* We **prune** plants to make them stronger: (**a**) *The roses need pruning.* (**b**) *I've pruned all the dead branches off the tree.*

5.7. Conclusion

During the late 1980s, EFL lexicographers kept in balance the two long-established functions of the learner's dictionary—its role as a storehouse of meanings and its role as an activator of language use and vocabulary development. The refinement of the *LDOCE* controlled defining vocabulary and the emergence of a new definition style from COBUILD largely favoured decoding. But the encoding function was also strengthened during this period. Devoting additional space to related pairs or groupings of words, as distinct from defining words in isolation, was significant in this respect. As well as reflecting a growing interest amongst editors in presenting in one place semantic *relationships*, it narrowed the gap between the learner's dictionary and the learner's thesaurus, as represented by Tom McArthur's *Longman Lexicon* (1981). How far this equilibrium could be sustained in the face of growing evidence of how foreign learners actually use their dictionaries will be a major theme of the next chapter.

6 Focus on the Dictionary User

6.1. Introduction

In the early history of the monolingual learner's dictionary, three design features in particular came to dominate the plans conceived by lexicographers—though in fact no dictionary published at the time incorporated them all. These were: definitions based on a controlled defining vocabulary that the foreign student could be expected to understand; detailed information about function words, 'heavy-duty' lexical words, and verb-patterns (the latter in a specially 'coded' form); and coverage of a great number and variety of word-combinations (idioms, collocations, and formulae). If they had been brought together in a single work, those features would have ensured that the decoding and encoding needs of the learner were equally fulfilled, since while the first favours the user wishing to understand the foreign language and the second—grammatical information—is designed to meet the needs of the learner wishing to write in the L2, the third supports activity of both kinds. However, there can be little doubt that both philosophically and in practice Palmer and Hornby favoured the encoding function. At the practical level, as we saw earlier, Palmer's *GEW* overwhelmingly, and Hornby's *ISED* to a considerable extent, laid stress on support for the writer and translator. The many years of research devoted to core vocabulary items, and their patterns and uses, were eventually to bear fruit in dictionary information for encoding rather than decoding (Cowie 1983*b*, 1984). Significantly, too, the early bilingual dictionary which Hornby produced was intended not so much to help with comprehension at the lower-intermediate level as to serve as an introduction to grammatical terms and syntactic patterns (Hornby 1938: 23).

At the theoretical level, commitment to the encoding function was virtually total. How can this be explained? We know that at the time—the mid- to late 1930s—there was little discussion of the linguistic or study needs of EFL dictionary users, as perceived by the users themselves. There is certainly no evidence of contemporary research into such needs. The explanation is that Palmer and Hornby in particular realized that the learner's linguistic and communicative needs encompassed more than the requirement to understand, and thus more than the traditional mother-tongue dictionary could provide. Departing from the widely-held view of the dictionary as a repository of information about the meanings of words, a resource which was turned to occasionally for answers to specific decoding problems (Marello 1989; Cowie 1990; Béjoint 1994), Palmer and

Hornby developed highly innovative designs which were strong in those areas of content where the traditional mother-tongue dictionary was weak; which would bridge the gap between the teaching grammar and the teaching lexicon; which would encourage the learner to break free from the mother tongue; and which would serve as learning and teaching handbooks rather than as crutches to lean on in moments of linguistic crisis (Palmer 1934c: 2, 1938a: vi; Stein 1989a: 38).

The *Idiomatic and Syntactic English Dictionary*, it is true, dealt with much more than structural and heavy-duty words—it marked the beginning of the *general-purpose* learner's dictionary—and from the second edition of *ALD* (1963: v–vi), and increasingly in the third (1974), A. S. Hornby laid stress on the inclusion of technical and scientific vocabulary in common use.[1] The prominence later given by the compilers of the first *LDOCE* (1978) to a limited defining vocabulary, based on the pioneering work of Michael West, was a further decisive step towards the balanced decoding-encoding design that the second generation of EFL lexicographers—those of the 1970s—bequeathed to the third.

This equilibrium, however, has been increasingly challenged since the early 1980s, and, side by side with a general increase in 'user-friendliness', the 1990s have witnessed a shift in favour of designs which prioritize decoding. This is reflected particularly in the inclusion—in *CIDE* (1995) and *LDOCE 3* (1995)—of introductory keywords intended to facilitate access to the sense-divisions of complex words; in the universal adoption of limited defining vocabularies; in the tendency, especially through the removal of information on syntactic functions and transformations, to lessen the encoding power of grammatical systems; and in the wider use of sentence-type definitions of a kind first introduced in *Cobuild 1* (1987).

Contributing to all these changes has been the rapid development since the early 1980s of a new field of dictionary-related research, one which focuses not on the linguistic content and structure of dictionaries but on their users and uses. Briefly, by citing evidence that foreign learners use their dictionaries— bilingual as well as monolingual—overwhelmingly for purposes of decoding, and so in ways not far removed from those of the traditional native user, some researchers have urged that EFL lexicographers should devote much more attention to facilitating *understanding* of the L2 than to providing the 'kinds of information for which the vast majority of users have no need and [which they] would not miss if they were not included in dictionaries' (Jackson 1988: 198–9).

It is this body of research which I now wish to survey, chiefly to bring to light the purposes for which students refer to their EFL dictionaries, the levels of reference skill which they display, and the implications of those findings for the future of learner lexicography. I also wish to determine how far a number

---

[1] The early 1970s witnessed a rapid growth in the publication of ELT course materials, which also influenced the choice and treatment of vocabulary in *ALD 3* (Christina Ruse, personal communication).

of specific developments in learner lexicography are justified by this evidence.

6.2. Types of User-Related Research

Our starting point is the late 1970s, when a conference organized at Exeter by Reinhard Hartmann—and aptly entitled *Dictionaries and their Users*—inaugurated a period of intense interest in user-centred dictionary studies, especially with reference to foreign learners of English (Hartmann 1979). Since then, investigations into the users and uses of learners' dictionaries—bilingual as well as monolingual—have been conducted in several countries, at several proficiency levels, and against a variety of first-language backgrounds.

Almost a decade after helping to set this movement in train, Hartmann published a valuable critical survey of the research that had appeared up to that point (Hartmann 1987: 12). He distinguished four points of focus, around which subsequent studies (e.g. Battenburg 1991; Béjoint 1994) have tended to cluster:

(*a*) Identifying the specific categories of linguistic information (e.g. meaning, spelling, pronunciation, grammar) perceived as important by particular groups of dictionary users.

(*b*) Seeking to throw light on the users themselves, and on their assumptions and expectations in turning to the dictionary.

(*c*) Investigating the study or occupational activities (e.g. writing in the L2, translating into the L1) in the course of which and in support of which a dictionary is used (sometimes called the 'reference needs' of users (Béjoint 1981; Cowie 1983*b*)).

(*d*) Investigating the reference skills which users have developed, or need to develop, to use their dictionaries more effectively, and evaluating teaching programmes or aids designed to enhance such skills.

To these can be added two further types of enquiry which have developed as a result of research within the above fields and which to some extent cut across them:

(*e*) Assessment of the special merits, compared with the standard monolingual learner's dictionary, of the so-called 'bilingualized' dictionary (usually an adaptation of an existing monolingual EFL work with glosses in the user's L1).

(*f*) Consideration of which types of dictionary—monolingual EFL, bilingual or bilingualized—need to be used at various stages of the learning process and for what purposes.[2]

---

[2] For learners of European languages other than English and French the choice until recently was—and for most languages still is—a choice between a bilingual dictionary and a monolingual dictionary of the L2 designed for its native speakers (Marello 1989).

These various fields of enquiry will be explored and their findings evaluated in this chapter. Some aspects of user-centred research have attracted criticism. Teachers and lexicographers have asked, for instance, whether the views of dictionary users, especially when gathered by means of questionnaires, provide an adequate basis for major decisions concerning the content and structure of EFL dictionaries.[3] It is easy to identify the linguistic and communicative needs of students with their expressed desires and preferences, and not all EFL lexicographers have drawn appropriately balanced conclusions from user-related research. This survey will attempt to provide an even-handed critical perspective on the field.

6.3. Categories of Information and their Importance to Dictionary Users

As a general rule, dictionaries are turned to as sources of information about meaning, and to a lesser extent spelling. This has long been the case and, as far as English dictionaries are concerned, is a generalization that applies as much to foreign as to native users. It was borne out by the earliest user-related study, which focused on mother-tongue dictionaries and invited teachers in 99 American colleges to rank six categories of information commonly found in collegiate dictionaries according to their importance to freshmen students (Barnhart 1962). The study revealed that the most sought-after information was meaning, though spellings were looked up almost as often. Pronunciation was third, with synonyms, usage, and etymology the least important. (It is important to note, however, that this study was concerned with what teachers *assumed* their students' priorities to be.)

In a later investigation by Randolph Quirk into dictionary use by native speakers of English (220 British students—half in the humanities, half in the sciences—at University College London), meaning also figured prominently, and 'parts of speech' hardly at all (only 20 humanities and 7 science students referred to their dictionaries for information on word class) (Quirk 1974). However, perhaps the most striking feature of Quirk's study, which employed a 30-item questionnaire, was that it brought into play a variety of user- or use-related categories, such as field of study or average frequency of consultation, which made possible a detailed cross-classification of findings. One discovery that was to be echoed in later work with EFL dictionary users was the close relationship

---

[3] Users of questionnaires unsupported by any other investigative technique should take note of Hatherall's much-quoted probing of their effectiveness: 'Are subjects saying . . . what they do, or what they think they do, or what they think they ought to do, or indeed a mixture of all three?' (Hatherall 1984: 184).

existing between reported difficulty with the metalanguage of definitions and 'the unfamiliarity that proceeds from infrequent dictionary use' (1974: 159).

The first study of any scope and complexity to be devoted to the foreign user of dictionaries was that of Jerzy Tomaszczyk (1979). His investigation was bold and enterprising, partly because it examined dictionary use by two major groups —university students, on the one hand, and instructors and translators, on the other, the latter also being at a higher stage of proficiency—but also because it was the first study to compare the use of bilingual and monolingual dictionaries. Tomaszczyk's work sometimes falls victim to its own complexity, as when users of MLDs—who must in this study be learners of English—are compared with users of bilingual dictionaries—who may be learners of any one of sixteen languages. Nonetheless, the cross-classification of results is often most revealing. When asked to say which dictionaries they consulted for information of a given type, a higher proportion of subjects who owned bilingual dictionaries (whether L2–L1 or L1–L2) referred to them for meaning (95.3 per cent and 97.7 per cent respectively) than did owners of monolingual (including EFL) dictionaries (85.4 per cent). However, the highest level of satisfaction with the information provided was registered by the monolingual dictionary owners (Tomaszczyk 1979: 111).

There are some parallels between Tomaszczyk's study and a later investigation by Henri Béjoint (1981). Studying dictionary use among French students of English at the University of Lyon, and using a questionnaire that was based partly on Tomaszczyk's, Béjoint focused his attention on monolingual dictionaries—for the most part MLDs. He took his sample of 122 informants from the second, third, and fourth years of study. Though answers to the question 'Which types of information do you look for most often . . . ?' are not correlated with the year of study, the global percentage for meaning is strikingly high at 87 per cent, putting this category well in front of syntax (53 per cent) and synonyms (52 per cent) (Béjoint 1981: 215). Carla Marello, too, when she put a similar question to 58 Italian university students of English, found that 98 per cent chose meaning as the kind of information they looked for in their bilingual dictionaries, followed by 70 per cent who chose spelling.[4] When the same question was put to users of MLDs, meaning scored 51 per cent, synonyms 49 per cent, and grammar 36 per cent—the latter two categories, note, being chiefly useful for encoding (Marello 1989: 107).

Marello, like Béjoint, made no distinction as to year of study when asking this question. As Tomaszczyk had already shown, though, the most sought-after categories of information may very well vary according to such variables as the level of proficiency in the L2 and the types of dictionary available, and for a

[4] As in several of the studies reported here, Marello's subjects are free to tick more than one information category, thus often producing percentages which add up to more than 100 per cent.

precise account of student preferences such variables need to be considered.[5] In a study of dictionary use by Italian students of English at the University of Turin, Carla Bareggi produced findings which, though based on a smaller sample than Béjoint's (70 students in all—50 from the first year and 20 from the third), were more finely differentiated (Bareggi 1989). Among first-year students using an MLD, the most sought-after type of information—surprisingly enough—was pronunciation, and the least in demand morphology, syntax, and style. This does not of course mean that Bareggi's freshmen did not need guidance on grammar, rather that typically they were unable to retrieve the relevant information from their monolingual learners' dictionaries (1989: 167). Significantly, her first-year students seldom turned to MLDs for help with meaning, referring mainly to bilinguals for this category of information. (By the third year, this would be the chief reason for referring to MLDs.) Worth noting, too, is the fact that Bareggi's students at all levels were concerned with *collocation*. In this respect, her findings differ from the studies by Tomaszczyk and Béjoint and may reflect the growing emphasis given to the teaching of collocation and 'usage' in the 1980s.

A more recent and much more ambitious undertaking has been the study carried out by Hashan Al-Ajmi among Arabic-speaking undergraduates at the University of Kuwait (Al Ajmi 1992). As well as surveying a much larger group (320 students) and taking account of the bilingual/monolingual distinction, Al Ajmi took note of differences—at two levels within the degree programme— between students specializing in English (240) and science majors using English as an essential medium of instruction (80). (There is a parallel here with Quirk's investigation.) With regard to the type of linguistic information most often sought, he observed that when a bilingual dictionary (L2 to L1) was used, there was very little difference between the English specialists and the scientists: both groups use their bilingual dictionaries overwhelmingly for meaning (English 97.4 per cent, Science 98.7 per cent), followed at some distance by spelling. A detail that interestingly reinforces Bareggi's conclusions is that meaning was also the type of information predominantly sought by MLD users, and more so by upper- than lower-level students.

This indicates—as did Tomaszczyk's study—that while bilingual dictionaries are used at all levels for decoding, the monolingual learner's dictionary comes into its own as a source of meanings at the more advanced level, where the students' proficiency in the L2 has improved. As Marello puts it: 'arrivati ad una maggior padronanza in genere preferiscono usare per tale scopo il monolingue di L2' (i.e. 'having achieved a better command [of the L2] they generally prefer to use the monolingual L2 [learner's] dictionary for this purpose') (1989: 109).

---

[5] Also to be considered is the possible effect within an informant group of linguistic and cultural differences. One study in which the L1s of participants were noted reported no corresponding differences in dictionary use (Battenburg 1991).

At the same time, there is also evidence that advanced-level users of the MLD show a greater degree of interest in its guidance on grammar, spelling, and collocation, all of which are associated with the productive use of the language (e.g. Al Ajmi 1992: 157). This is interestingly borne out by Atkins and Varantola in their recent large-scale experiment in recording dictionary use for translation purposes. Focusing at one point on the type of dictionary (bilingual or L2 monolingual) chosen for specific L1 to L2 translation tasks by users *with advanced skills in the foreign language*, they show that 'when looking for primary information (an unknown translation) people tend to go to the bilingual dictionary', but add that 'the monolingual dictionary comes into play as their need for secondary information grows' (Atkins and Varantola 1997: 33). By 'secondary' here is meant information on the grammar and collocations of words in the L2. This view of the growing usefulness of the MLD as proficiency develops is one which Marello's findings also support. When her group of university students were asked which of a number of standard aids to study were most useful in learning a language, over a period from middle school to university, it appeared that while the perceived importance over that period of the grammar and the bilingual dictionary declined, that of the MLD greatly increased (1989: 112).

There is a final body of evidence, from several sources, which further reinforces our sense of the dictionary user's overwhelming preoccupation with meaning. This has to do with the grammatical and semantic categories of words and multi-word units which users of bilingual and monolingual dictionaries typically look up. According to Marello, the parts of speech most often consulted by her students are—in order—verbs, nouns and adjectives. These are of course full or open-class categories, to be contrasted with the empty or closed-class categories—prepositions, conjunctions, articles—which users seldom consult. Fully in line with those informants' preference for lexical rather than grammatical words, is their ranking of other lexical categories. While over half of Marello's sample often looked up sayings and proverbs and one third consulted culture-specific items, only 13 per cent showed an interest in 'common' words (Marello 1989: 109). Or consider Béjoint's data. Here too there is evidence of a dominant interest in semantically and culturally rich items and a corresponding neglect of 'heavy-duty' words and function words. Thus, 68 per cent of his respondents very often looked up idioms; 55 per cent sometimes referred to encyclopaedic words; 53 per cent sometimes consulted entries for culture-specific words. Conversely, 66 per cent never looked up 'common' words and 47 per cent never looked up structural words (Béjoint 1981: 217).

What this data indicates, without doubt, is a complete reversal of the priorities —as regards favoured lexical categories and preferred study activities— recognized by Palmer and Hornby. Whereas Hornby, like Sweet before him, laid stress on those common-core words which typically have many senses and present difficulties of collocation and syntax—thus posing problems for the encoder

—the students whose responses are surveyed here turn for the most part to entries for relatively infrequent, open-class words, often with a rich cultural content (cf. Cowie 1983*b*). They are concerned, in other words, with aspects of semantic and cultural content in regard to medium- and low-frequency words, chiefly though not exclusively for purposes of decoding. That this is a limited and unbalanced view of the student's lexical needs, and one unlikely to promote his or her full linguistic development, is confirmed by a number of the research-ers referred to in this chapter. It arises from and is sustained by powerfully entrenched views of the dictionary's status and function. The situation is well captured by Marello when she states that 'lo studente continua ad avere una vi-sione poco strumentale del dizionario, perfino di quello bilingue, e lo considera un magazzino di parole, più che un mezzo per svolgere attività' (i.e. 'students still have a perception of the dictionary, even of the bilingual dictionary, which is far from "instrumental". They regard it as a storehouse of meanings rather than as a resource for developing [language] activities') (1989: 110).

6.4. Students and the EFL Dictionary: Their Attitudes, Expectations, and Criticisms

Any reader of the growing body of research into the attitudes of learners or teachers of English towards the dictionaries they use is immediately struck by a paradox. On the one hand, there is the high value that users customarily place on their dictionaries—especially monolingual learners' dictionaries—and on the other the quite widespread ignorance of their structure, content, and possible functions, to which reference has just been made. Among lower-level learners especially there is often a wide discrepancy between the strong approval with which they speak of their EFL dictionaries and the unreasonable expectations which they entertain of them as practical users.

Jerzy Tomaszczyk (1979) was the first to study evaluations of monolingual and bilingual dictionaries by foreign users—in his case, as we have seen, university students, teachers, and translators. One revealing observation was that *ALD* 3, the only MLD available to his subjects, and used by 69 out of 90 students of English, was rated more highly by those students than were general monolingual dictionaries, or bilingual dictionaries, by their respective user groups (1979: 107). Yet despite this high level of approval, seven students reported that they found the definitions in *ALD* hard to understand, while only 23 out of 69 made use of the grammatical information provided for encoding in the L2 (1979: 112).

Further evidence of the contradictory nature of student evaluations of diction-aries is provided by Béjoint. Of those questioned by him, 77 per cent expressed satisfaction with their learners' dictionaries and 36 per cent were more satisfied with their monolingual than with their bilingual dictionaries (1981: 217). Béjoint's findings were confirmed by Marello (1989: 111), who found that 67 per cent of her group expressed satisfaction with monolingual learners' dictionaries—as compared with only 29 per cent taking the same view of bilingual works—and by Bareggi, 67 per cent of whose sample declared themselves more satisfied with monolingual learners' than with bilingual dictionaries, considering the former sounder and more up to date, and more useful for production (1989: 169). On the other hand, of Béjoint's 122 informants more than half (55 per cent) stated that they did not use the codes indicating the syntactic functions of words, being 'unable—or unwilling—to master the codes used' (1981: 217). It is worth noting in this connection that only 11 per cent of Béjoint's subjects and 23 per cent of Bareggi's had read the introduction to their learners' dictionaries with the degree of attention needed to guarantee confident use of such codes.

Evidence is gathering, too, of students' reactions to recent innovations designed to facilitate understanding or help with language production. I am thinking particularly of the 'full-sentence' definitions introduced in *Cobuild* (1987) as compared with the 'phrasal' definitions based on a controlled vocabulary introduced earlier in *LDOCE 1* (1978). Both types are of course aimed at facilitating access to meaning, but how do students react to them? One experiment has provided answers that give food for thought (Cumming, Cropp, and Sussex 1994). It attempted to compare the effectiveness, for both encoding and decoding tasks, of the sentence and phrasal definitions, presenting instances of each type with or without supporting examples. But the study also asked subjects to say how helpful they considered each of the four experimental conditions to be. Here there were pronounced differences. For almost three-quarters of the group (71 per cent), the first choice was '*sentence* type + example', while for 27 per cent it was '*phrasal* type + example' (my emphasis). Only 1 per cent chose 'phrasal type – example', while no one chose 'sentence type – example'.[6] Those were the students' evaluations. In marked contrast, there were no significant differences corresponding to the experimental conditions chosen, between the levels of performance actually achieved by the subjects, whether in comprehension or in production.

I referred earlier to reports of the dictionary enjoying an emblematic status, comparable to that of the Bible, especially among lower-proficiency foreign students. (That they are repositories of truth as well as information is a belief widely held of their own monolingual dictionaries by native speakers (Quirk 1974; Cowie 1990).) Giuseppina Coviello, who conducted an investigation of dictionary use among students of French at the University of Turin, discovered (1987: 114) that, among her first-year students, the dictionary enjoyed an almost

---

[6] Interestingly, the 'sizeable minority' who nominated phrasal type + example as their first choice mentioned 'the brevity of the definition, and the simplicity of its language' (1994: 373).

mythical status, being regarded as the fountain of all human knowledge (cf. Galisson 1983: 84). However, such views often co-exist with the conviction that what, after all, are only medium-sized general-purpose dictionaries should provide exhaustive lexical coverage. Carla Marello, working with student and teacher users of French–Italian and English–Italian dictionaries, met with the belief that dictionaries should contain everything and last a lifetime—a view also expressed by Mary Snell-Hornby's German-speaking students (1987). Tomaszczyk, too, found that while beginners and intermediate students generally 'do not know their dictionaries well enough' they often make 'unreasonable and contradictory demands' of them (1979: 116). Alongside these somewhat unfocused criticisms and demands, we also encounter complaints of specific deficiencies in dictionaries, of students being unable to locate a particular lexical category (say, idioms or phrasal verbs), or of the lack of a specific type of information (for example, collocations or levels of usage) (Sora 1984; Coviello 1987).

How can we explain the strongly approving attitudes which are often expressed by students towards their MLDs at a stage when they are not able to use them, let alone evaluate them? Note, for instance, that while Bareggi showed 50 per cent of a sample of first-year students to be owners of MLDs, no less than half of the 50 per cent used those dictionaries seldom or not at all (Bareggi 1989: 166). Part of the answer, surely, is to be found in the circumstances in which students first acquire their MLDs. The fact is that students do not depend on their own perceptions of present or future need when buying dictionaries, but rely overwhelmingly on the advice of their teachers—whose positive views they understandably echo. In Béjoint's study, which was confined to monolin gual (chiefly EFL) dictionaries, 85 per cent of respondents gave 'tutor's recommendation' as their reason for choosing one title rather than another (Béjoint 1981: 214). In Bareggi's study, 79 per cent of the students questioned chose their dictionary on the advice of a teacher—at school or university in about equal proportions (Bareggi 1989: 165). Of the student participants in the Research Project into Dictionary Use organized under the auspices of Euralex/AILA, just over half (50.8 per cent) had followed similar advice (Atkins and Knowles 1990: 385). It does not follow, of course, that teachers always had detailed knowledge of the works they were recommending or that they provided advice on how they should be used—only 25 per cent of Bareggi's subjects had received such guidance. And a recommendation to buy one dictionary may also discourage the acquisition or use of others: 73 per cent of those questioned in her study were unaware of the existence of other monolingual dictionaries.

If there is evidence that, when a MLD is first acquired, a wide gap often exists between a student's perception of the dictionary's value and its actual usefulness as an aid to learning, there is also evidence from several sources that this gap closes as proficiency in the foreign language develops and the range of study activities is extended. The growing perception and exploitation of the MLD's special strengths is one of the themes of the next section.

6.5. Study Activities and Dictionary Use

As well as being the first widely-known investigation of user attitudes and expectations, Tomaszczyk's study was the first to consider the study activities in the course of which, and in support of which, dictionaries were normally used by the foreign learner.[7] Asked which types of activity they most often used their dictionaries for, bilingual and/or monolingual, his students replied that they used them especially for reading comprehension and written composition, and rather less for translation, listening comprehension, and speaking. His students thus prioritized activities in the written over those in the spoken medium—as did those of Béjoint, whose results, in descending order of choice, were: translation from the L2 ('version'), written (i.e. 'reading') comprehension, written composition/translation into the L2 ('thème'), oral (i.e. listening) comprehension, and oral composition (Béjoint 1981: 216).

If we now add to those rankings the replies obtained by Marello (1989) to her question 'For what activity do you chiefly use a bilingual dictionary?' and plot on a table (see Table 6.1) the types of dictionary used in the three studies against (*a*) decoding vs. encoding activity in the written or spoken medium and (*b*) the ordering of specific activities (e.g. translation from the L2, oral composition in the L2), we find that, regardless of the dictionaries used, students give the highest priority in using them to the written medium and the lowest to the spoken (oral encoding in all three cases being placed below aural decoding).

Reading comprehension is the dominant single activity, but there is variation in the ranking of other written medium activities, reflecting in the case of translation the differences of emphasis laid on this activity in particular study programmes. It is worth noting, for instance, that in Hartmann's investigation of dictionary use—though in this case by English learners of German—translation from and into the L2 is the leading activity, being practised regularly by 90 per cent of Hartmann's respondents and reflecting the continuing dominance of translation in many secondary-school language programmes (Hartmann 1983*a*).

Again, there may be shifts in the purposes for which the learner's dictionary is used according to stages in an undergraduate degree programme, as Bareggi helpfully indicates. Whereas for her students there is an overall predominance of written activities, she shows that in the first year the MLD is used essentially for 'decoding' activities (written comprehension and translation from English

---

[7] We should bear in mind, however, that Tomaszczyk was not simply concerned with foreign learners of *English*.

TABLE 6.1. *Order of selection of written and spoken media and of specific study activities in relation to dictionaries used (Tomaszczyk 1979; Béjoint 1981; Marello 1989)*

(a) Orientation to L2 and medium	(b) Study activity	Tomaszczyk: bilingual and monolingual	Béjoint: mono-lingual LD	Marello: bilingual
Decoding:	Translation from L2	3=	1	3
written medium	L2 Reading comprehension	1	2	1
Encoding:	Translation into L2	3=	3=	2
written medium	L2 Written composition	2	3=	4
Decoding:	L2 Listening comprehension	5	5	5
spoken medium				
Encoding:	L2 Oral composition	6	6	6
spoken medium				

Note: Activities marked '3=' were equally rated in third place by the students concerned.

into Italian), while in the third year, 'encoding' (writing in, and translating into, English) assumes an importance equal with decoding (Bareggi 1989: 168).

As is the case with information categories, bilingual as well as monolingual dictionaries can be brought into play when the focus is on study activities. The choice of dictionary (or combination of choices) will depend on several factors, including the level of study and whether L1⇒L2 as well as L2⇒L1 bilinguals are available. In their report of the AILA/Euralex project, Atkins and Knowles (1990) plotted choice of monolingual or bilingual dictionary against post-school use and each of three study activities. One of their findings interestingly underpins the conclusion reached by Tomaszczyk, Marello, Bareggi, and Al Ajmi concerning the value of the MLD as a dependable source of meanings (section 6.2, above). This is that 70 per cent of higher-level students would choose a monolingual dictionary for understanding an unfamiliar L2 expression. However, 63.6 per cent prefer a bilingual dictionary when translating from the L1 into the L2, and rather more students would turn to a bilingual (51.1 per cent) than to a mono-lingual dictionary (43.1 per cent) for information on the usage of a known L2 item (Atkins and Knowles 1990: 386).

In Al Ajmi's study the distinction is drawn between the use of Arabic–English and English–Arabic dictionaries, and between both of these and MLDs, so that in plotting their use in relation to various study activities a complex classifica-tion is possible. With regard to English–Arabic dictionaries (for Kuwaiti students, L2 ⇒ L1), it is evident that students turn to them chiefly for help with translation into the L1, but the interesting finding was that a small number of students use this type when writing in the L2, possibly in conjunction with the other types.[8] MLDs were found to be used by most students for written composition (68.8 per cent of English students as against 47.1 per cent of science students), while half the students of English and considerably more of the science students used their MLDs for translation from English. The first half of this statement is especially interesting, as it suggests that the English specialists are able to make fruitful use of the encoding information in the MLD to cope with the exacting demands of composition in the L2. It also invites comparison with Marello's comments (6.2, above) on the greater perceived value of the MLD as a learning resource at advanced level.

As was shown by Hartmann's 1983 study, an important category of dictionary use is translation, and here we may expect highly specific patterns of dictionary selection and use. Moulin (1987) is concerned with translation as an advanced exercise at university level and shows how, in the course of rendering French texts into English, the skilled translator may make use of several dictionaries— and other reference works—ranging from the MLD, or the English–French part of a bilingual dictionary, for checking on the appropriateness of an L2 equivalent, to handbooks of style for dealing with the niceties of business correspondence (Moulin 1987). Moulin's study is a helpful reminder that, among the most sophisticated language users, constant movement from one reference resource to another is the rule rather than the exception (cf. Stein 1989*a*; Atkins and Varantola 1997).

6.6. The Reference Skills of Dictionary Users

We have already seen how imperfect a user's understanding can be of the information categories which a monolingual learner's dictionary contains. We have found much evidence, too, that the user's perception of the range of activities that the MLD in particular can support is often depressingly limited. It might therefore be thought that any attempt to determine the reference skills of a student dictionary user must be foredoomed to failure. There seems little point in trying to assess the ability of students to retrieve information of whose existence they are hardly aware or to judge their performance of activities which they have seldom tackled.

Yet, despite these reservations, the study of reference skills should not be dismissed as valueless. At the very least we can observe students attempting to access types of information that they already believe to be important (especially meaning). More positively, we can set up programmes of training in dictionary

---

[8] It is worth noting that 72 per cent of Marello's sample claim that, when translating into the L2, they check in the L2 $\Rightarrow$ L1 half of their bilingual dictionaries the equivalents suggested in the L1 $\Rightarrow$ L2 half (Marello 1989: 110).

use and measure their success in improving consultation (Nuccorini 1995). Perhaps the most important reason, though, for encouraging research into reference skills is the positive effect it can have—and is already having—on the investigative methods employed. The study of reference skills must include the observation of dictionary users as they apply them, and it is noteworthy that several of the investigations reported here have introduced fresh and resourceful approaches to overcoming the problems that such observation presents (see especially Atkins and Varantola 1997).

Discussion has long centred on the question whether failure to use dictionaries effectively results from inadequacies on the part of users or deficiencies in the dictionaries themselves. Until quite recently commentators have tended to attribute shortcomings to dictionary-makers rather than dictionary users. Certainly, much more effort, throughout the 1980s and early 1990s, went into improving learners' dictionaries than into improving learners' capacity to profit from them (Tickoo 1989*a*).

However, the fault has never lain entirely with the lexicographers. Almost twenty years ago, Tomaszczyk showed that, especially at the elementary and intermediate levels, students had a very limited understanding of dictionaries and consequently used them badly (Tomaszczyk 1979). Certainly the view is now widespread that successful use of a dictionary calls for a special 'competence', which for want of appropriate training, many students do not possess (Herbst and Stein 1987: 115).[9]

How is evidence of a poor standard of reference skill obtained, and how can we be sure that performance errors are due to inadequate skills, rather than deficiencies in the dictionaries used? In the early 1980s, Yukio Tono mounted an ingenious experiment in dictionary look-up which involved control of two key variables. He contrived, by using invented words, to ensure that no subject could have prior knowledge of the entries involved; and he chose a look-up process— in this case, accessing meanings—that he was sure his informants already had experience of (Tono 1984). Tono asked 402 Japanese university students (63 of whom were English specialists) to translate a number of English texts into Japanese. The texts contained a number of invented words which also appeared, with definitions, in specially prepared bilingual dictionaries. However, the students were divided into groups, and not all groups received the same dictionary entries for specific made-up words. Some, for instance, had to take account of syntactic information in order to access the appropriate meaning. Tono showed that of the various Japanese equivalents available for each invented word, the students

---

[9] The fairly recent appearance on the market of EFL courses providing exercises on dictionary use is partly traceable to the distribution of dictionary sales in the 1970s and later. In the 1970s, the great bulk of sales were in English as a Second Language areas (such as the Commonwealth), and this may have diverted publishers from providing support for the dictionary user in the English as a Foreign Language areas where it was particularly needed (Christina Ruse, personal communication).

tended to choose the first listed. They would only proceed to the next if the first was patently unsuitable. They were not, moreover, guided by the syntactic and other clues provided: such information was only used if the equivalent could not be adapted to the context.

Tono provides clear evidence of poor standards of retrieval being wholly or largely attributable to low levels of skill. His findings, though, were not unique. Bareggi too was struck by the inability of students to use contextual clues to locate the appropriate sense in polysemous entries—and a consequent tendency to fall back on the first listed sense (1989: 172). Similar findings were also reported by Nuccorini (1994), whose approach was to examine students' errors in written translation tests (English into Italian) against the microstructure of the dictionaries they used. She noted that though the majority of her sample used dictionaries dating from the 1960s, in which the organization of the microstructure undoubtedly hampered retrieval, nevertheless most errors were due to the students' inadequate look-up skills, to the extent that there was no significant difference between their using dictionaries in the way they did and not being allowed to use them at all. Nuccorini observed that idioms were usually translated correctly, suggesting that students consulted their dictionaries carefully when faced with supposedly opaque items. When dealing with polysemous entries, however, they exhibited the failing noted by Tono of not venturing beyond the first listed sense.

Faulty retrieval strategies of a different kind were investigated by Nesi and Meara (1994). They were aware that a group of English-speaking schoolchildren studied by E. Mitchell (1983) had tended, when asked to look up words in a dictionary and complete sentences in which the target word appeared, to focus not on the genus word, but on a part of the definition they could easily understand. Thus, they were extracting information from a part of the definition where the meaning of the word was *elaborated* rather than *defined*. In a later independently designed experiment by Miller and Gildea (1987), using 10–11-year-old native speakers, similar results were obtained. The commonest source of error was found to be the application of a look-up technique the investigators called KIDRULE, which involved (*a*) reading the definition, (*b*) selecting a short familiar segment, (*c*) composing a sentence using the segment, and (*d*) substituting the target word for the segment. Application of kidrule resulted in such bizarre sentences as *The news was very tenet*, where the subject had substituted *tenet* for the segment 'true' (the last word in the definition):

(1) **tenet** . . . opinion, belief, principle, or doctrine held as true

Does the kidrule strategy also account for the errors that adult non-native speakers make when looking up meanings in dictionaries? Nesi and Meara found that it accounts for a considerable proportion. Using 52 subjects, who were asked to make up sentences using a common and a less familiar word in each case, and who had the option of consulting a definition of the harder word on screen, they found that 402 (56.5 per cent) of all sentences written after consulting a dictionary were unacceptable to native assessors (1994: 7). Moreover, of the errors, about half were a product of the kidrule strategy. Its influence was easiest to detect where the subject chose a non-synonymous segment from the dictionary entry, as in the sentence *I will begin a new job that is version,* where the student substituted *version* for 'different' (or 'slightly different') in this definition:

(2) **version** . . . 1 a slightly different form, copy or style of an article

How are lexicographers to react to such evidence? They must surely be led to reflect not so much on their own professional competence as on how effectively EFL teachers are trained to teach dictionary use.

What levels of skill do users display in retrieving information other than definitions or translation equivalents? The levels vary considerably, with both the information category involved and the language proficiency of the subjects. In Bareggi's study, for instance, a large proportion of the whole group were able to distinguish British and American pronunciations and to identify primary stress on entry words. Ability to understand grammatical abbreviations (e.g. [C] for 'countable'), on the other hand, varied between 50 per cent in the first year and almost 100 per cent in the third (1989: 170), and this helps to explain the almost total neglect by freshmen (reported at 6.3, above) of syntax and morphology.

Despite the often ingenious methods used in these studies and their value in laying bare weaknesses of understanding and skill, they were typically small in scale. On the grand scale and with the promise of further extension and exploitation, was the project mounted by Sue Atkins and her colleagues under the joint auspices of Euralex and AILA (Atkins *et al.* 1987; Atkins and Knowles 1990). This study has sought to address several of the issues raised in this chapter, including the efficacy of dictionaries in helping foreign learners of English to perform various study tasks (including comprehension of the L2, and translation into and out of the L2); the relative effectiveness of bilingual and monolingual dictionaries in meeting specific needs; and instruction in the use of dictionaries. (The goals of the project thus cut across the section boundaries of this chapter.)

This ambitious project (1,600 sets of papers—400 in French, German, Italian and Spanish, respectively—were distributed to organizers and over 1,100 student responses eventually gathered in) is noteworthy for its methodology and for the informativeness of its early results (published in Atkins and Knowles 1990). First, it adopted investigative procedures (a questionnaire and two tests) that were well suited to the goals of the research. Second, it administered a 'placement', or language proficiency test, allowing cross-comparison with the 'dictionary research' test (and possible confirmation of the view that sophisticated dictionary use depends crucially on competence in the L2). Third, the research test itself aimed to 'replicate as far as possible the natural use of the learners' dictionary' (Atkins and Knowles 1990: 383). It was also multifaceted, calling for (*a*) knowledge of grammatical terms and dictionary metalanguage; (*b*) skill in retrieving various types of lexical item, including multi-word items; and (*c*) the application of such understanding and skill in comprehending and translating texts.

Only a small selection of the results published in 1990 can be set out here, my choice being governed by the possibility of comparison with the findings of other researchers and by my own perception of central issues. Among the most revealing discoveries is that, of the larger set of 1,140 respondents, 60.4 per cent had never received any instruction in dictionary use, while only 12.9 per cent had been given 'precise and systematic instruction' in reference skills.

There are marked discrepancies in the levels of reference skill displayed. These seem to be related to the type of task set rather than the level of language ability of the subject. For instance, when asked to identify the part of speech of a given word the exceptionally high percentage of 85 per cent responded correctly. Similarly, almost 100 per cent of all students were able to interpret grammatical labels. When however one considers ability to locate such compounds as *lame duck*, 55.7 per cent of the most able students expected to find it under *duck* despite the fact that all monolingual learners' dictionaries order compounds—whether as main entries or sub-entries—according to their initial element. Though no explanation is offered by the researchers, it may be that—as argued by Béjoint (1981)—the more advanced students correctly perceived that in adjective-noun compounds the noun was the head and assumed that structural factors, rather than linear order, determined dictionary placement. The least able might be expected to have no such perceptions, which may explain why a large percentage (47 per cent) would search for the compound under *lame* (Atkins and Knowles 1990: 388).

There is evidence that, for some study activities, the dictionary does little to improve performance, despite—or perhaps because of—the language proficiency of students. As studies by Marsha Bensoussan *et al.* (1984), Della Summers (1988), and Nesi and Meara (1994) have shown, the use of dictionaries has little contribution to make to improved reading comprehension. This is an interesting and complex question. There is some student resistance to using dictionaries in any case, as it interferes with the reading process. Moreover, effective use of a dictionary (especially a learner's dictionary) already calls for a high level of reading comprehension. Thus, as Bensoussan *et al.* point out, low-level students lack the competence to profit from dictionaries, while advanced level students know enough of the L2 to be able to do without them!

On a more positive note, there is a growing understanding—in France, Germany, Italy, and elsewhere—of how we should set about teaching the effective use of dictionaries. Clearly, students need to be made aware of the variety of reference works which exist—including encyclopaedic dictionaries and thesauruses—and of how they can help with specific language problems and study activities (Prat Zagrebelsky 1989). Then, learners need to know that the successful use of a dictionary as specialized in its design and functions as the MLD requires a specific 'dictionary-using competence' (Herbst and Stein 1987). This in turn requires the integration of the teaching of dictionary reference skills within the foreign language programme: dictionary use cannot simply be another item on the language syllabus (Moulin 1987; Nuccorini 1995). Such integration implies that teaching puts the emphasis on language rather than the dictionary. As Béjoint puts it: 'students should be shown how to use dictionaries, rather than how dictionaries are made' (1981: 211).

Efforts are already being made to increase awareness of the full range of dictionaries as study resources (Prat Zagrebelsky 1989); to foster study skills through raising teacher awareness (Nuccorini 1993a, b); and to develop student skill through exercises in ELT coursebooks and special workbooks—though these vary widely in quality (Stark 1990). In countries where the school system has failed to provide training in dictionary use, courses need to be made part of language degree programmes in universities, especially where, as in Germany, Italy, and France, university language departments are chiefly concerned with training the next generation of school teachers (Bareggi 1989). But not all lexicographers are fully alert to these issues either, and the practical workshops on dictionary use organized under the auspices of Euralex (see especially Atkins and Varantola 1997), should be imitated, and their implications for the production of teaching materials carefully weighed.

6.7. The 'Bilingualized' Learner's Dictionary

Though the chief focus of this chapter has been on the monolingual learner's dictionary, several of the studies referred to have shown that in the language-learning process the bilingual dictionary (as the term is generally understood) is normally the first to come into play and that, even at the advanced level, it may continue to be preferred to the MLD for a number of study purposes. The so-called 'bilingualized' dictionary is a separate development and, in the case of titles derived from monolingual learners' dictionaries, more recent. For various reasons, including the economies achieved by basing a new dictionary on an existing, often largely unmodified, MLD, bilingualized dictionaries for learners of English have been in circulation since the 1960s.[10] The current interest in bilingualized dictionaries, on the part of dictionary researchers as well as publishers, has to do with the claim that it is a more effective resource than the MLD for some study activities.[11]

---

[10] The earliest title I have been able to trace is an English–Chinese bilingualization of *ALD 2* (Hornby *et al.* 1966).

[11] Some doubt must be cast on the results of a recently reported experiment (Laufer and Melamed 1994) in which subjects were asked to perform tests in the comprehension and use of isolated words, using either an MLD, a bilingual (Hebrew–English) dictionary, or a bilingualized dictionary, since (a) the MLD (*LDOCE*) was an advanced-level work and the bilingualized work (*OSDHS*) an intermediate text, and (b) *OSDHS*, as we shall see, has a feature not common to all bilingualized dictionaries: it retains the original English definitions alongside the L1 (in this case, Hebrew) glosses.

The following critical survey will examine three aspects of the question. First, it will provide a brief description of the bilingualized dictionary and indicate the range of types that can be subsumed under this heading. Second, it will address theoretical issues raised by the use of bilingualized dictionaries by foreign learners of English. Finally, it will attempt to assess the value of the bilingualized dictionary as a reference tool for foreign learners, principally in comparison with the standard MLD. (For a critical survey of a number of bilingualized dictionaries based on MLDs compiled by A. S. Hornby, see Marello 1998.)

The standard bilingual dictionary to which constant reference has been made throughout this chapter is bidirectional; that is to say, it consists of two alphabetical listings, in each of which words (in their various senses) in one language are explained in terms of the other (Landau 1984; Marello 1989; Cowie 1990). Ideally, a bilingual dictionary should meet the encoding and decoding needs of speakers of both languages, but it is not uncommon to find dictionaries which fulfil both functions but are designed for speakers of only one of the languages represented (e.g. Skey 1977). A bilingualized dictionary by contrast, consists of a *single* alphabetical listing, in a language foreign to its intended users, and is based, as I have suggested, on an existing dictionary of that language. In the examples to be considered here this language is English. As the following extract from the *Oxford Engelsk–Norsk Ordbok* (*OENO*) (1983) shows, translations in the mother tongue of the users (here Norwegian) are introduced into the single alphabetical list, actually replacing the original definitions of the monolingual *Oxford Student's Dictionary of Current English* (*OSDCE*) (1978), on which the bilingualization is based.

(3) (*OENO*)

> **worry** . . . 1 irritere, plage: *The noise of the traffic worried her. What's ~ing you? He'll ~ himself to death.*
> 2 være bekymret/engstelig; engste/uroe seg: *You have no cause to ~. What's the use of ~ing?*

(*OSDCE*)

> **worry** . . . 1 trouble; give (a person, oneself) no peace of mind; cause anxiety or discomfort to: *The noise of the traffic worried her. What's ~ing you? He'll ~ himself to death.*
> 2 be anxious, uneasy, troubled: *You have no cause to ~. What's the use of ~ing?*

Worth noting here is the use of one-word equivalents ('irritere', 'plage') in the first *OENO* sub-entry, as compared with the analytic, idiomatic defining style of the original. Yet the nature of translations in bilingualized dictionaries, and their range in terms of features of the original microstructure, can vary quite considerably, according to the estimated needs of their users (Cowie 1990; Hartmann 1994*b*; Marello 1998). In *OENO*, only headwords in their various senses and subheadwords (idioms, compounds and derivatives) are translated. In the much smaller *Oxford English–Spanish Reader's Dictionary* (Hornby, Parnwell, and Norro 1979), examples are translated as well, reflecting the lower proficiency level of the intended readership.

Some editors of bilingualized works, while wishing to introduce glosses in the L1 to aid quick comprehension of the L2, nevertheless wish the basic mono-lingual character of the original work to be preserved. This is the approach followed by Joseph Reif in the *Oxford Student's Dictionary for Hebrew Speakers* (1985), which, like *OENO*, is an adaptation of the *Oxford Student's Dictionary of Current English* (1978). As the following extract shows, Reif's dictionary, though providing translations for headwords in their various meanings, as well as for derivatives and compounds—though not for examples—also preserves the original definitions. This balance between L1 and L2 information reflects Reif's clearly stated pedagogical aim, which was not to produce 'a bilingual dictionary which the student could use for translating English texts into Hebrew', but rather 'to encourage him to understand English by providing limited help in the mother tongue' (Reif 1987: 153). The notion of 'limited help'—specifically 'help with understanding'—is one to be kept in mind when considering more recent discussion of the bilingualized dictionary.

Clearly a number of theoretical issues need to be addressed if the role of the bilingualized dictionary in foreign language learning is to be fully understood. Some of these have been taken up in recent articles by Reinhard Hartmann (1992, 1994*a*, *b*). Hartmann is quite right to claim that the bilingualized model has been largely overlooked in theoretical discussions of the learner's dictionary, though it is not strictly true to say that this is a 'relatively new category' (1992: 66, 1994*a*: 171). As I have indicated, bilingualized English dictionaries for foreign learners have been in circulation for over thirty years. As for their structure, it is somewhat misleading to situate them 'halfway between the unilingual and the interlingual' (1992: 63) and to describe them as a sub-type of the interlingual. As the existence of bilingualized Japanese and Chinese versions of *ALD* would suggest, and as I have already shown, dictionaries of the type are adaptations—partial and often limited—of existing monolingual learners' dictionaries. The source may be a general advanced-level dictionary, but equally it may be an *abridgement* of a major work such as *ALD*—as Hartmann demonstrates (1994*b*:

> **flash²** *vi,vt* **1** send, give out, a sudden bright light: *Lightning flashed across the sky.* לְהַבְזִיק
> **2** come suddenly (into view, into the mind): *The idea flashed into/through his mind.* לְהַבְזִיק
> **3** send instantly: *flash news across the world* (by radio or TV). לְהַבְזִיק
> **4** send or reflect like a flash: *Her eyes flashed de-fiance.* לְנַצְנֵץ/לְהִתְנוֹצֵץ בְּ–

FIG. 6.1. Excerpt from *Oxford Student's Dictionary for Hebrew Speakers* (Hornby and Reif 1985)

210). Of seven bilingualized dictionaries to which I have ready access, one is based on *ALD 2*, one on *ALD 3*, two on *OSDCE* (an intermediate title), two on *An English-Reader's Dictionary* (pre-intermediate), and one on *The Progressive English Dictionary* (elementary).

If progress is to be made towards a precise categorization of bilingualized dictionaries, it is essential to recognize the sources from which they come, as well as the modifications made to the parent works and the purposes these are intended to serve. Hartmann's observation that the bilingualized dictionary is 'clearly better suited for passive decoding' (1992: 66) is correct, and we should note that in cases where—as in Reif's adaptation of *OSDCE*—the gloss is intended simply as a prompt or reminder to the reader, the needs of understanding are being served, not of precise translation into the mother tongue.

As Hartmann shows (1994*b*: 208), the typical bilingualized dictionary is of very limited usefulness for writing in, or translating into, the *foreign* language, since the dictionary normally provides no alphabetical means of access to the glosses in the user's mother tongue. An ingenious attempt to get around this difficulty is the inclusion of an index of French words in the end-matter of Dubois Charlier's *Dictionnaire de l'anglais contemporain* (1980), a small-scale reader's dictionary of contemporary English with French glosses.

In summary, any assessment of the bilingualized dictionary must be based on an understanding of its source, and should recognize that while the type is best suited to decoding, the precise nature of the help it provides will depend on the adaptations made to the original dictionary—which may extend to full or partial translations of illustrative examples (Marello 1998). The bilingualized dictionary cannot supplant the monolingual learner's dictionary, but the fact that it is almost certainly based on one—usually an earlier edition of an MLD currently in use—suggests that a work with L2 glosses, and other features carefully designed to suit a particular mother-tongue and learner population, can serve as a bridge between a standard bilingual and a fully-fledged monolingual work. The notion of a progression within a given language-teaching programme from one dictionary type to another, and the place in that progression of the bilingualized dictionary, is taken up more fully in the next section.

6.8. Bilingual and Monolingual Learners' Dictionaries in the Language-Teaching Process

As we have seen at several points in this chapter, the precise relationship between the use of bilingual and monolingual learners' dictionaries in a given language programme or study situation will vary according to several factors, including the year of study, the level of linguistic proficiency of the users, and the nature of the study activity. The number of variables and their precise interaction in specific cases makes it impossible to lay down rigid guidelines governing the introduction or sequencing of MLDs and bilingual dictionaries in teaching programmes.[12] We can, however, gain a useful perspective on the relationship between the types, first by ignoring parallel use and assuming a gradual transition from one type to the other; second by taking account of the relative linguistic demands which (say) an advanced-level MLD and a 'desk-size' bilingual make of their users; and third by considering the transition from one dictionary type to the other in the course of a European secondary school or university English programme.

Gabriele Stein has argued convincingly that the transition is from bilingual to monolingual use when one takes account of differences of sophistication in the dictionary types and of the growing proficiency of students in the situations I have just outlined (Stein 1990). Each dictionary type, she contends, corresponds to a specific level of competence in English. So the bilingual dictionary, while meeting the need for quick decoding of scientific and technical terms, falls short of providing the fine semantic, grammatical, and stylistic specifications, and the wider range of illustrative examples, which are noteworthy strengths of the monolingual learner's dictionary (cf. the Preface to Hornby *et al.* 1981). Then, too, students need to be weaned away from the belief—fostered by over-dependence on the bilingual dictionary—that a foreign language is simply another means of labelling the conceptual system of the mother tongue. The MLD, by contrast, encourages students to realize that each language 'has its own view of the world which they are gradually penetrating' (Stein 1989*a*: 43).

But the particular strengths of the MLD are the very source of the problems— of accessibility and intelligibility—of which students and teachers constantly complain. There is therefore a good case, as Stein goes on to argue, for introducing a special type of bilingual resource to help in the transition from the bilingual to the monolingual phase. Two questions then arise. How far does the bilingual guide resemble the bilingualized model as it already exists? According to Stein's plan, they correspond in various key respects, including the provision of translations in the mother tongue and the recognition—in line with Reif's— that 'the goal is not translation but the internalization of word meanings' (Stein 1990: 405). However, Stein's model goes well beyond existing bilingualized dictionaries in certain key respects, including reduction of the nomenclature to 2,000—the size of the defining vocabulary of the MLD—the introduction of explanatory notes and, most interestingly, the inclusion of simplified grammat-

---

[12] Part of the wider problem may be that learners of various L1 backgrounds are lacking in bilingual dictionaries designed to meet their specific needs. With German-speaking learners of English chiefly in mind, Mary Snell-Hornby is one of the few to address the relevant design problems. She also introduces a strategy showing when and how bilingual (and monolingual) dictionaries should be introduced into the teaching process (Snell-Hornby 1987).

ical labels in the mother tongue. (There are echoes here of the aims and design features of Hornby's first bilingual dictionary.)

It will be noted that none of these recommendations implicitly or explicitly challenge the central design features of the MLD itself—say, the coded syntactic information or the close attention given to core vocabulary items. On the contrary, the MLD is the major goal (major but intermediate—the end-point in the European high-school or university context often being the native-speaker monolingual dictionary) to which the newly conceived model serves as a bridge.

6.9. User-Related Research and the Design of Monolingual Learners' Dictionaries

The body of research surveyed in this chapter not only throws a good deal of light on the particular strengths of MLDs, as perceived or demonstrated by their users; it also supports an approach to dictionary design which, while favouring decoding information, does not neglect the MLD's long-established encoding function. The survey also makes clear that certain areas of user research—especially research into reference skills—are severely under-developed, and that the views of dictionary users do not in themselves provide an adequate critical platform for launching major changes in the design of MLDs. The expressed desires and preferences of lower-level student users—in particular—should not be identified with their present and future linguistic and communicative needs, many of which they are not capable of perceiving, let alone formulating. With those reservations in mind, let us pinpoint by way of conclusion a number of findings which enable us to grasp more fully the particular strengths of the MLD as a learning and teaching resource; to identify the stages of the language-learning process at which it is most fully and profitably used; and to understand the nature of its interaction, actual and potential, with the bilingual dictionary.

- Studies of all types of dictionary users have demonstrated that they are overwhelmingly concerned with meaning, and with those categories of lexical items which present semantic or cultural, rather than syntactic or functional, difficulties. There are, however, clear indications from studies made against a variety of first language backgrounds that the MLD is often preferred to the bilingual dictionary as a source of meanings at the advanced level, where its definitions are valued for their fullness and precision. (Section 6.3)
- When a monolingual learner's dictionary is first acquired, usually on the advice of a teacher, a wide gap often exists between a student's positive perception of the dictionary and his or her capacity to make full and proper use of it. However, there is also clear evidence that the gap between perception and practical exploitation narrows as proficiency in the L2 develops and the range of learning activities widens. (Section 6.4)

- At various levels of proficiency in the L2, and regardless of the types of dictionary used, students give the highest priority in using them to the written language (especially comprehension of texts in the L2) and the lowest to the spoken language. There is some evidence from the more detailed studies, however, that equal weight tends to be given to encoding and decoding in the written medium at advanced levels, and also that students are able, at that stage, to make fruitful use of the information for encoding in the MLD in order to cope with written composition in the L2. (Section 6.5)
- As studies based on various user groups have shown, levels of dictionary reference skill are in general still extremely low, and following the major improvements made to MLDs in the 1980s, many researchers are inclined to attribute these poor levels primarily to a lack of systematic training in dictionary use. More positively, teachers are becoming more aware of how the teaching of reference skills needs to be tackled, though it has to be acknowledged that many are still unaware of what an MLD contains. There is some recognition that effective use of the MLD calls for a special 'competence', and that this needs to be systematically taught. Teaching should be supported by materials designed to instil dictionary awareness and develop reference skills. (Section 6.6)
- It has recently been argued that the 'bilingualized' dictionary should be given a more prominent role in learning and teaching alongside—or in place of—the standard monolingual model. Before deciding if, or at what point, such dictionaries should be introduced into a teaching programme, however, teachers should recognize that a bilingualized dictionary is usually an adaptation of an existing monolingual EFL work, and that in a given language-learning situation the available bilingualized dictionary may be based on an abridged, intermediate-level title. Such a dictionary cannot replace (or be properly compared with) an MLD for advanced learners, though some studies have suggested that a well-designed volume with glosses and explanations in the mother tongue could serve as a bridge between an introductory bilingual dictionary and the advanced monolingual work. (Sections 6.7, 6.8)

Postscript

The centenary, in 1998, of A. S. Hornby's birth, coinciding happily with the fiftieth anniversary of the first worldwide edition of his classic work and, more recently, the fiftieth anniversary of the death of Harold Palmer, provide a fitting vantage-point from which to survey and summarize the achievements, over the past sixty years, of ELT dictionary-makers.

There has been much to record and celebrate. In the 1930s and 1940s, Michael West, Harold Palmer, and A. S. Hornby added to the familiar conventions of the native speaker dictionary a number of features expressly designed to meet the needs of foreign students of English. These remarkable innovations, which were grounded in over a decade of research into vocabulary control, construction-patterns, and phraseology, in time acquired the status of conventions as the monolingual learners' dictionary developed into a distinct genre (Rundell 1998). Despite the fundamental changes brought about by recent developments in corpus and computational research, the elements of structure and content be-queathed by the founding fathers of the MLD remain central defining features of the type in the late 1990s.

Though those core features—and the pedagogical assumptions which underlie them—have changed relatively little over the past sixty years, there have none-theless been marked improvements in the information upon which description is based and in the ways in which it is presented to the dictionary user. We have seen, for instance, what changes were brought about, in the 1980s, by develop-ments in structural semantics and (increasingly) in corpus linguistics. Advances in corpus gathering and data processing have pushed lexicographical innovation forward at an ever accelerating pace in the 1990s.

The speed of current change, though, should not cause EFL dictionary-making to lose the quality of judicious balance for which, in the past, it has often been remarkable. It was A. S. Hornby who, by providing for a broad reading vocabulary in *ISED*, first ensured that the learner's dictionary would cater even-handedly for readers as well as writers. More recent research into the uses made of their MLDs by advanced learners, especially, confirms the wisdom of Hornby's balanced stance.

After the sometimes exaggerated claims and predictions of the 1980s, a sense of equilibrium now also characterizes the view which lexicographers take of the benefits and limitations of corpus data. In the best dictionary work of the 1990s, the analysis of collocations, for instance, is guided by recent advances in the field of phraseological research (Howarth 1996; Fontenelle 1997; Cowie 1998*b*; Moon 1998*b*), while there is a growing alliance between corpus and computational linguists, on the one hand, and practising lexicographers, on the other (Atkins 1992–3).

Current developments give good grounds for confidence in the monolingual work itself, as the model *par excellence* for advanced foreign learners. Bilingual and bilingualized works have their places, in many learning contexts, in the progression towards advanced proficiency. There is no risk, however, of their threatening, much less supplanting, the monolingual learner's dictionary.

References

1. Dictionaries, Grammars, and Other Reference Works

Atkins, B. T. S., and Duval, A. (1978), *Robert–Collins dictionnaire français–anglais, anglais–français* (First edition) (Paris: Le Robert and Glasgow: Collins).

Benson, M., Benson, E., and Ilson, R. (1986), *The BBI Combinatory Dictionary of English: A Guide to Word Combinations* (First edition) (Amsterdam and Philadelphia: John Benjamins). (*BBI 1*)

——— ——— ——— (1997), *The BBI Dictionary of English Word Combinations* (Second edition of Benson, Benson, and Ilson 1986) (Amsterdam and Philadelphia: John Benjamins). (*BBI 2*)

Cowie, A. P. (ed.) (1989*c*), *Oxford Advanced Learner's Dictionary of Current English* (Fourth edition) (Oxford: Oxford University Press). (*ALD 4*)

—— and Mackin, R. (1975), *Oxford Dictionary of Current Idiomatic English*, Volume 1. *Verbs with Prepositions and Particles* (London: Oxford University Press). (*ODCIE 1*)

—— —— (1993), *Oxford Dictionary of Phrasal Verbs* (Second edition of Cowie and Mackin 1975) (Oxford: Oxford University Press).

—— —— and McCaig, I. R. (1983), *Oxford Dictionary of Current Idiomatic English*, Volume 2. *Sentence, Clause and Phrase Idioms* (Retitled *Oxford Dictionary of English Idioms*, 1993) (Oxford: Oxford University Press). (*ODCIE 2*)

Crowther, J. (ed.) (1995), *Oxford Advanced Learner's Dictionary of Current English* (Fifth edition) (Oxford: Oxford University Press).

Dubois, J. (1966), *Dictionnaire du français contemporain* (First edition) (Paris: Larousse).

Dubois Charlier, F. (1980), *Dictionnaire de l'anglais contemporain* (Paris: Larousse).

Fowler, H. W., and Fowler, F. G. (eds.) (1911), *The Concise Oxford Dictionary of Current English* (First edition) (Oxford: Clarendon Press). (*COD 1*)

—— and Le Mesurier, H. G. (eds.) (1934), *The Concise Oxford Dictionary of Current English* (Third edition) (Oxford: Clarendon Press). (*COD 3*)

Friederich, W., and Canavan, J. (1979), *Dictionary of English Words in Context* (Dortmund: Verlag Lambert Lensing).

Greenbaum, S., and Quirk, R. (1990), *A Student's Grammar of the English Language* (London: Longman).

Hanks, P. (ed.) (1979), *Collins Dictionary of the English Language* (First edition) (London and Glasgow: Collins).

Hill, J., and Lewis, M. (1997), *LTP Dictionary of Selected Collocations* (Hove: Language Teaching Publications).

Hornby, A. S. (1954), *A Guide to Patterns and Usage in English* (First edition) (London: Oxford University Press).

—— with Cowie, A. P., and Windsor Lewis, J. (1974), *Oxford Advanced Learner's Dictionary of Current English* (Third edition) (London: Oxford University Press). (*ALD 3*)

—— —— and Gimson, A. C. (1980), *Oxford Advanced Learner's Dictionary of Current English* (Third edition; revised and reset impression) (Oxford: Oxford University Press).

—— Gatenby, E. V., and Wakefield, H. (1942), *Idiomatic and Syntactic English Dictionary* (Photographically reprinted and published as *A Learner's Dictionary of Current English* by Oxford University Press, 1948; subsequently, in 1952, retitled *The Advanced Learner's Dictionary of Current English*) (Tokyo: Kaitakusha). (*ISED/ALD 1*)

—— —— —— (1963), *The Advanced Learner's Dictionary of Current English* (Second edition) (London: Oxford University Press). (*ALD 2*)

—— —— —— (1966), *The Advanced Learner's Dictionary of Current English, English–Chinese* (Taipei: Tung-Hua Shu Chu).

—— —— —— (1981), *Kaitakusha's Contemporary English–Japanese Dictionary* (Tokyo: Kaitakusha). (*KCEJD*)

—— and Ishikawa, R. (1940), *A Beginners' English–Japanese Dictionary* (Tokyo: Kaitakusha).

—— and Parnwell, E. C. (1952a), *The Progressive English Dictionary* (London: Oxford University Press). (*PED*)

—— —— (1952b), *An English-Reader's Dictionary* (London: Oxford University Press). (*ERD*)

—— —— and Norro, L. (1979), *Oxford English–Spanish Reader's Dictionary* (Oxford: Oxford University Press and Lago Mayor: Cultural Mexicana).

—— and Reif, J. (1985), *Oxford Student's Dictionary for Hebrew Speakers* (Tel Aviv: Kernerman Publishing). (*OSDHS*)

—— and Ruse, C. (1978), *Oxford Student's Dictionary of Current English* (First edition) (Oxford: Oxford University Press). (*OSDCE*)

—— and Svenkerud, H. (1983), *Oxford Engelsk–Norsk Ordbok* (Oslo: J. W. Cappelens Forlag). (*OENO*)

Jones, D. (1940), *An English Pronouncing Dictionary* (Fifth edition) (London: Dent).

—— (1950), *An English Pronouncing Dictionary* (Tenth edition) (London: Dent).

—— (1969), *Everyman's English Pronouncing Dictionary* (Thirteenth edition revised by A. C. Gimson) (London: Dent). (*EPD 13*)

—— (1977), *Everyman's English Pronouncing Dictionary* (Fourteenth edition revised by A. C. Gimson; revision and supplement by S. Ramsaran) (London: Dent). (*EPD 14*)

Kozłowska, C. (1991), *English Adverbial Collocations* (Warsaw: Państwowe Wydawnictwo Naukowe).

—— and Dzierżanowska, H. (1988), *Selected English Collocations* (Second edition) (Warsaw: Państwowe Wydawnictwo Naukowe). (*SEC*)

Little, W., Fowler, H. W., and Coulson, J. (1933), *The Shorter Oxford English Dictionary* (First edition, revised and completed by C. T. Onions) (Oxford: Clarendon Press).

Long, T. H., and Summers, D. (eds.) (1979), *Longman Dictionary of English Idioms* (London: Longman). (*LDEI*)

McArthur, T. (1981), *Longman Lexicon of Contemporary English* (London: Longman).

Neilson, W. A. (ed.) (1934), *Webster's New International Dictionary* (Second edition) (Springfield, Mass.: G. & C. Merriam Co.).

Palmer, H. E. (1938a), *A Grammar of English Words* (London: Longmans, Green). (*GEW*)
—— (1938b), *The New Method Grammar* (London: Longmans, Green).
—— (1943–4), *English–French Phraseological Dictionary* (London: Evans).
Procter, P. (ed.) (1978), *Longman Dictionary of Contemporary English* (First edition) (London: Longman). (*LDOCE 1*)
—— (ed.) (1995), *Cambridge International Dictionary of English* (Cambridge: Cambridge University Press). (*CIDE*)
Quirk, R., and Greenbaum, S. (1973), *A University Grammar of English* (London: Longman). (*UGE*)
—— —— Leech, G., and Svartvik, J. (1972), *A Grammar of Contemporary English* (London: Longman). (*GCE*)
—— —— —— —— (1985), *A Comprehensive Grammar of the English Language* (London: Longman). (*CGEL*)
Saito, H. (1915), *Idiomological English–Japanese Dictionary* (Second edition, 1936) (Tokyo: SEG Press).
—— (1932), *Monograph on Prepositions* (Tokyo: SEG Press).
—— (1933), *Studies in Radical English Verbs* (Tokyo: SEG Press).
Sinclair, J. M., Hanks, P., Fox, G., Moon, R., and Stock, P. (eds.) (1987), *Collins Cobuild English Language Dictionary* (First edition) (London and Glasgow: Collins). (*Cobuild 1*)
Skey, M. (1977), *Dizionario inglese–italiano italiano–inglese* (Turin: Società Editrice Internazionale).
Summers, D. (ed.) (1995), *Longman Dictionary of Contemporary English* (Third edition) (London: Longman). (*LDOCE 3*)
—— and Rundell, M. (eds.) (1987), *Longman Dictionary of Contemporary English* (Second edition) (London: Longman). (*LDOCE 2*)
Thorndike, E. L. (1921), *The Teacher's Word Book.* (New York: Columbia University Teacher's College).
West, M. P. (1953), *A General Service List of English Words* (London: Longmans, Green).
—— (1965), *An International Reader's Dictionary* (London: Longman).
—— and Endicott, J. G. (1935), *The New Method English Dictionary* (London: Longmans, Green).
Windsor Lewis, J. (1972), *A Concise Pronouncing Dictionary of British and American English* (London: Oxford University Press). (*CPD*)

2. Other Literature

Aarts, F. (1991), 'OALD, LDOCE and COBUILD. Three learner's dictionaries of English compared', in S. Granger (ed.), 211–26.
Aarts, J., de Haan, P., and Oostdijk, N. (eds.) (1993), *English Language Corpora: Design, Analysis and Exploitation* (Amsterdam and Atlanta: Rodopi).
Aisenstadt, E. (1979), 'Collocability restrictions in dictionaries', in R. R. K. Hartmann (ed.), 71–4.
Akkerman, E. (1989), 'An independent analysis of LDOCE grammar coding system', in B. Boguraev and T. Briscoe (eds.), *Computational Lexicography for Natural Language Processing* (London: Longman), 65–83.

Al Ajmi, H. (1992), 'The use of monolingual English and bilingual Arabic–English dictionaries in Kuwait: an experimental investigation into the dictionaries used and reference skills deployed by university students of arts and science', Ph.D. thesis (University of Leeds).

Anderson, D. (1969), 'Harold E. Palmer: a biographical essay', in H. E. Palmer and H. V. Redman, *This Language-Learning Business* (Language and Language Learning 22) (London: Oxford University Press).

Arnaud, P. J. L., and Béjoint, H. (eds.) (1992), *Vocabulary and Applied Linguistics* (London: Macmillan).

Atkins, B. T. S. (1992–3), 'Tools for computer-aided corpus lexicography: the Hector Project', *Acta Linguistica Hungarica*, 41: 5–71.

—— (1994), 'Analyzing the verbs of seeing: a frame semantics approach to corpus lexicography', in S. Gahl, C. Johnson, and A. Dolbey (eds.), *Proceedings of the Twentieth Annual Meeting of the Berkeley Linguistics Society, 1994* (Berkeley: University of California at Berkeley), 1–17.

—— and Knowles, F. E. (1990), 'Interim report on the EURALEX/AILA research report into dictionary use', in T. Magay and J. Zigány (eds.), 381–92.

—— Lewis, H., Summers, D., and Whitcut, J. (1987), 'A research project into the use of learners' dictionaries', in A. P. Cowie (ed.) (1987b), 29–43.

—— and Varantola, K. (1997), 'Monitoring dictionary use', *International Journal of Lexicography*, 10.1: 1–45.

Bahns, J. (1996), *Kollokationen als lexikographisches Problem. Eine Analyse allgemeiner und spezieller Lernerwörterbücher des Englischen*. (Lexicographica, Series maior 74) (Tübingen: Max Niemeyer).

Bailey, R. W. (1986), 'Dictionaries of the next century', in R. Ilson (ed.), *Lexicography: An Emerging International Profession* (Manchester: Manchester University Press), 123–37.

Bareggi, C. (1989), 'Gi studenti e il dizionario: un'inchiesta presso gli studenti di inglese del corso di laurea in lingue e letterature straniere moderne della facoltà di lettere di Torino', in M. T. Prat Zagrebelsky (ed.), 155–79.

Barnhart, C. L. (1962), 'Problems in editing commercial monolingual dictionaries', in F. Householder and S. Saporta (eds.), *Problems in Lexicography* (Bloomington: Indiana University and The Hague: Mouton), 161–81.

—— (1973), 'Plan for a central archive for lexicography in English', in R. I. McDavid and A. R. Duckert (eds.), 302–6.

Battenburg, J. D. (1991), *English Monolingual Dictionaries. A User-Oriented Study* (Lexicographica, Series maior 39) (Tübingen: Max Niemeyer).

—— (1994), 'Pioneer in English lexicography for language learners: Michael Philip West', *Dictionaries*, 15: 132–48.

Béjoint, H. (1981), 'The foreign student's use of monolingual English dictionaries. A study of language needs and reference skills', *Applied Linguistics*, 2.3: 207–22.

—— (1994), *Tradition and Innovation in Modern English Dictionaries* (Oxford Studies in Lexicology and Lexicography) (Oxford: Clarendon Press).

Benson, M. (1985), 'Collocations and idioms', in R. Ilson (ed.), 61–8.

—— (1989), 'The structure of the collocational dictionary', *International Journal of Lexicography*, 2.1: 1–14.

Bensoussan, M. *et al.* (1984), 'The effect of dictionary usage on EFL test performance compared with student and teacher attitudes and expectations', *Reading in a Foreign Language*, 2.2: 262–76.

Bolinger, D. (1985), 'Defining the undefinable', in R. Ilson (ed.), 69–73.

Bongers, H. (1947), *The History and Principles of Vocabulary Control*, Parts 1 and 2 (Woerden: Wocopi).

Brown, J. (1978), 'Foreword', in P. Strevens (ed.) (1978*b*), vii–xi.

Burnage, G., and Dunlop, D. (1993), 'Encoding the British National Corpus', in J. Aarts *et al.* (eds.), 79–95.

Burnard, L. (1992), 'Tools and techniques for computer-assisted text processing', in C. S. Butler (ed.), 1–28.

Butler, C. S. (1990), 'Language and computation', in N. E. Collinge (ed.), 611–67.

—— (ed.) (1992), *Computers and Written Texts* (Oxford: Blackwell).

Calzolari, N., Picchi, E., and Zampolli, A. (1987), 'The use of computers in lexicography and lexicology', in A. P. Cowie (ed.) (1987*b*), 55–77.

Carter, R., and McCarthy, M. J. (eds.) (1988), *Vocabulary and Language Teaching* (Applied Linguistics and Language Study) (London: Longman).

Clear, J. (1987), 'Computing: overview of the role of computing in Cobuild', in J. M. Sinclair (ed.) (1987*d*), 41–61.

—— Fox, G., Francis, G., Krishnamurthy, R., and Moon, R. (1996), 'COBUILD: the state of the art', *International Journal of Corpus Linguistics*, 1.2: 303–14.

Collier, P., Neale, D., and Quirk, R. (1978), 'The Hornby Educational Trust: the first ten years', in P. Strevens (ed.) (1978*b*), 3–7.

Collinge, N. E. (ed.) (1990), *An Encyclopaedia of Language* (London: Routledge).

Cop, M. (1990), 'The function of collocations in dictionaries', in T. Magay and J. Zigány (eds.), 35–46.

Coviello, G. (1987), 'Il dizionario oggi. Due gruppi di studenti messi a confronto su un "oggetto" molto discusso', *Rassegna italiana di linguistica applicata*, 11.1: 109–29.

Cowie, A. P. (1975), 'General introduction', in A. P. Cowie and R. Mackin, vi–lxxxi.

—— (1978*a*), 'Problems of syntax and the design of a pedagogic dictionary', *Rassegna italiana di linguistica applicata*, 2.1: 255–64.

—— (1978*b*), 'The place of illustrative material and collocations in the design of a learner's dictionary', in P. Strevens (ed.) (1978*b*), 127–39.

—— (1979), 'The treatment of polysemy in a learner's dictionary', in R. R. K. Hartmann (ed.), 81–8.

—— (1981), 'The treatment of collocations and idioms in learners' dictionaries', *Applied Linguistics*, 2.3: 223–35.

—— (1983*a*), 'On specifying grammatical form and function', in R. R. K. Hartmann (ed.) (1983*b*), 99–107.

—— (1983*b*), 'English dictionaries for the foreign learner', in R. R. K. Hartmann (ed.) (1983*b*), 135–44.

—— (1983*c*), 'General introduction', in A. P. Cowie, R. Mackin, and I. R. McCaig, x–lxiii.

—— (1984), 'EFL dictionaries: past achievements and present needs', in R. R. K. Hartmann (ed.), 155–64.

Cowie, A. P. (cont.) (1986), 'Collocational dictionaries—a comparative view', in M. J. Murphy (ed.), *Proceedings of the Fourth Anglo-Soviet English Studies Seminar* (London: British Council), 61–9.

—— (1987*a*), 'Syntax, the dictionary and the learner's communicative needs', in A. P. Cowie (ed.) (1987*b*), 183–92.

—— (ed.) (1987*b*), *The Dictionary and the Language Learner* (Lexicographica, Series maior 17) (Tübingen: Max Niemeyer).

—— (1988), 'Stable and creative aspects of vocabulary use', in R. Carter and M. J. McCarthy (eds.), 126–37.

—— (1989*a*), 'The language of examples in English learners' dictionaries', in G. James (ed.), *Lexicographers and their Works* (Exeter Linguistic Studies 14) (Exeter: University of Exeter), 55–65.

—— (1989*b*), 'Information on syntactic constructions in the general monolingual dictionary', in F. J. Hausmann *et al.* (eds.), 588–92.

—— (1989*d*), 'Pedagogical descriptions of language: lexis', *Annual Review of Applied Linguistics*, 10: 196–209.

—— (1990), 'Language as words: lexicography', in N. E. Collinge (ed.), 671–700.

—— (1991), 'Multiword units in newspaper language', in S. Granger (ed.), 101–16.

—— (1992*a*), 'Multiword lexical units and communicative language teaching', in P. Arnaud and H. Béjoint (eds.), 1–12.

—— (1992*b*), 'Verb syntax in the revised *Oxford Advanced Learner's Dictionary*: descriptive and pedagogical considerations', in M. A. Ezquerra (ed.), 341–7.

—— (1993), 'Getting to grips with phrasal verbs', *English Today*, 9.4: 38–41.

—— (1994), 'Phraseology', in R. E. Asher and J. Simpson (eds.), *The Encyclopedia of Language and Linguistics* (Oxford: Pergamon Press), 3168–71.

—— (1995), 'The learner's dictionary in a changing cultural perspective', in B. B. Kachru and H. Kahane (eds.), *Cultures, Ideologies and the Dictionary: Studies in Honor of Ladislav Zgusta* (Lexicographica, Series maior 64) (Tübingen: Max Niemeyer), 283–95.

—— (1996), 'The "dizionario scolastico": a learner's dictionary for native speakers', *International Journal of Lexicography*, 9.2: 118–31.

—— (1998*a*), 'Phraseological dictionaries—some East–West comparisons', in A. P. Cowie (ed.) (1998*b*), 209–28.

—— (ed.) (1998*b*), *Phraseology: Theory, Analysis and Applications* (Oxford Studies in Lexicography and Lexicology) (Oxford: Clarendon Press).

—— (1998*c*), 'Semantic frame theory and the analysis of phraseology', *Moscow State University Bulletin*, 19. 1: 40–50.

—— and Howarth, P. (1996), 'Phraseological competence and written proficiency', in G. M. Blue and R. Mitchell (eds.), *Language and Education* (British Studies in Applied Linguistics 11) (Clevedon: Multilingual Matters), 80–93.

Cruse, D. A. (1986), *Lexical Semantics* (Cambridge: Cambridge University Press).

Cumming, G., Cropp, S., and Sussex, R. (1994), 'On-line lexical resources for language learners: assessment of some approaches to word definition', *System*, 22.3: 369–77.

Drysdale, P. (1987), 'The role of examples in a learner's dictionary', in A. P. Cowie (ed.) (1987*b*), 213–23.

Dubois, J. (1962), 'Recherches lexicographiques: esquisse d'un dictionnaire structural', *Études de linguistique appliquée*, 1: 43–8.

—— (1981), 'Models of the dictionary: evolution in dictionary design', *Applied Linguistics*, 2.3: 236–49.

Eyes, E., and Leech, G. (1993), 'Progress in UCREL research: improving corpus annotation practices', in J. Aarts *et al.* (eds.), 123–43.

Ezquerra, M. A. (ed.) (1992), *EURALEX '90: Proceedings IV International Congress* (Barcelona: Biblograf).

Faucett, L., Palmer, H. E., Thorndike, E. L., and West, M. P. (1936), *Interim Report on Vocabulary Selection for the Teaching of English as a Foreign Language* (London: P. S. King & Son).

Fillmore, C. J. (1989), 'Two dictionaries', *International Journal of Lexicography*, 2.1: 57–83.

—— and Atkins, B. T. S. (1992), 'Towards a frame-based lexicon: the semantics of RISK and its neighbours', in A. Lehrer and E. Kittay (eds.), *Frames, Fields and Contrasts* (Hillsdale, NJ: Lawrence Erlbaum Associates), 75–102.

—— —— (1994), 'Starting where the dictionaries stop: the challenge of corpus lexicography', in B. T. Atkins and A. Zampolli (eds.), *Computational Approaches to the Lexicon* (Oxford: Oxford University Press), 349–93.

Firth, J. R. (1951), 'Modes of meaning', *Essays and Studies*, 4: 118–49 (reprinted in *Papers in Linguistics: 1934–1951*, London: Oxford University Press, 1957).

Fontenelle, T. (1992), 'Collocation acquisition from a corpus or from a dictionary: a comparison', in H. Tommola *et al.* (eds.), 221–8.

—— (1994), 'Towards the construction of a collocational database for translation students', *META* 39.1: 47–56.

—— (1997), *Turning a Bilingual Dictionary into a Lexical-Semantic Database* (Lexicographica, Series maior 79) (Tübingen: Max Niemeyer).

Fraser, B. (1970), 'Idioms within a transformational grammar', *Foundations of Language*, 6: 22–42.

Fries, C. C., and Traver, A. A. (1960), *English Word Lists. A Study of their Adaptability for Instruction* (Ann Arbor: George Wahr).

Galisson, R. (1983), 'Image et usage du dictionnaire chez les étudiants en langue de niveau avancé', *Études de linguistique appliquée*, 49: 5–88.

Gatenby, E. V. (1947), 'English language studies in Turkey', *English Language Teaching* 2.1: 8–15.

Gellerstam, M. *et al.* (eds.) (1996), *Euralex '96 Proceedings* (Göteborg: Göteborg University).

Gimson, A. C. (1980), 'Preface to the phonetic information', in A. S. Hornby *et al.*, vii.

—— (1981), 'Pronunciation in EFL dictionaries', *Applied Linguistics*, 2.3: 250–62.

Gläser, R. (1986), *Phraseologie der englischen Sprache* (Leipzig: VEB Verlag Enzyklopädie).

Granger, S. (ed.) (1991), *Perspectives on the English Lexicon: A Tribute to Jacques van Roey* (Louvain-la-Neuve: Cahiers de l'Institut de Linguistique de Louvain).

Grefenstette, G. *et al.* (1996), 'The DECIDE project: multilingual collocation extraction', in M. Gellerstam *et al.* (eds.), 93–107.

Hanks, P. (1987), 'Definitions and explanations', in J. M. Sinclair (ed.) (1987*d*), 116–36.

Hartmann, R. R. K. (ed.) (1979), *Dictionaries and their Users* (Exeter Linguistic Studies 4) (Exeter: University of Exeter).

—— (1983*a*), 'The bilingual learner's dictionary and its user', *Multilingua*, 2.4: 195–201.

—— (ed.) (1983*b*), *Lexicography: Principles and Practice* (Applied Language Studies 5) (London: Academic Press).

Hartmann, R. R. K. (cont.) (ed.) (1984), *LEXeter '83 Proceedings* (Lexicographica, Series maior 1) (Tübingen: Max Niemeyer).

—— (1987), 'Four perspectives on dictionary use: a critical review of research methods', in A. P. Cowie (ed.) (1987*b*), 11–28.

—— (1992), 'Learner's references: from the monolingual to the bilingual dictionary', in H. Tommola *et al.* (eds.), 63–70.

—— (1994*a*), 'The bilingualised learner's dictionary: a transcontinental trialogue on a relatively new genre', in G. James (ed.), *Meeting Points in Language Studies* (Hong Kong: University of Science and Technology), 171–83.

—— (1994*b*), 'Bilingualised versions of learners' dictionaries', *Fremdsprachen Lehrer und Lernen*, 23: 206–19.

Hatherall, G. (1984), 'Studying dictionary use: some findings and proposals', in R. R. K. Hartmann (ed.), 183–9.

Hausmann, F. J. (1979), 'Un dictionnaire des collocations est-il possible?', *Travaux de linguistique et de littérature*, 17: 187–95.

—— (1985), 'Kollokationen im deutschen Wörterbuch. Ein Beitrag zur Theorie des lexikographischen Beispiels', in H. Bergenholtz and J. Mugdan (eds.), *Lexikographie und Grammatik* (Lexicographica, Series maior 3) (Tübingen: Max Niemeyer), 118–29.

—— (1989), 'Le dictionnaire de collocations', in F. J. Hausmann *et al.* (eds.), 1010–19.

—— and Gorbahn, A. (1989), 'COBUILD and LDOCE II. A comparative review', *International Review of Applied Linguistics*, 2.1: 44–56.

—— Reichmann, O., Wiegand, H. E., and Zgusta, L. (eds.) (1989), *Wörterbücher/Dictionaries/Dictionnaires*, Volume 1 (Berlin and New York: Walter de Gruyter).

Heath, D. (1982), 'The treatment of grammar and syntax in monolingual English dictionaries for advanced learners', *Linguistik und Didaktik*, 49/50: 95–107.

—— and Herbst, T. (1988), 'Review of *Longman Dictionary of Contemporary English*', *ELT Journal*, 42.4: 315–17.

Heid, U. (1996), 'Creating a multilingual data collection for bilingual lexicography from parallel monolingual lexicons', in M. Gellerstam *et al.* (eds.), 573–90.

Henrichsen, L. E. (1989), *Diffusion of Innovations in English Language Teaching: The ELEC Effort in Japan, 1956–1968* (Westport, Conn.: Greenwood Press).

Herbst, T. (1984), 'Adjective complementation: a valency approach to making EFL dictionaries', *Applied Linguistics*, 5.1: 1–11.

—— (1986*a*), 'Drei einsprachige englische Wörterbücher des Jahres 1983', *Die Neueren Sprachen*, 6: 669–86.

—— (1986*b*), 'Defining with a controlled defining vocabulary in foreign learners' dictionaries', *Lexicographica*, 2: 101–19.

—— (1996), 'On the way to the perfect learner's dictionary: a first comparison of OALD5, LDOCE3, COBUILD2 and CIDE', *International Journal of Lexicography*, 9.4: 321–57.

—— and Stein, G. (1987), 'Dictionary-using skills: a plea for a new orientation in language teaching', in A. P. Cowie (ed.) (1987*b*), 115–27.

Hornby, A. S. (1931), 'Some grammatical implications of doubt and negation', *IRET Bulletin*, 79: 3–4.

—— (1932), 'Further notes on "some" and "any" ', *IRET Bulletin*, 81: 2–3.

—— (1937*a*), 'Editorial: a complex task', *IRET Bulletin*, 135: 1–6.

—— (1937*b*), 'Report on research activities, 1936–37', *IRET Bulletin*, 139: 5–14.

—— (1938), 'Report on the year's work: dictionary problems', *IRET Bulletin*, 148: 20–8; 36.

—— (1939*a*), 'Editorial: objects and objections', *IRET Bulletin*, 155: 147–57.

—— (1939*b*), 'Editorial: problems of terminology and classification', *IRET Bulletin*, 159: 259–64.

—— (1946), 'Linguistic pedagogy: I. The doctrines of de Saussure', *English Language Teaching*, 1.1: 6–11.

—— (1947*a*), 'Editorial: vocabulary control and vocabulary layout', *English Language Teaching*, 1: 89–90.

—— (1947*b*), 'Linguistic pedagogy: IV. The contextual procedure—word families', *English Language Teaching*, 1.4: 91–5.

—— (1950), 'H. E. Palmer', *English Language Teaching*, 4.4: 87–90.

—— (1954–6), *Oxford Progressive English for Adult Learners* (Three volumes) (London: Oxford University Press).

—— (1959–66), *The Teaching of Structural Words and Sentence Patterns* (Four volumes, stages 1–4) (London: Oxford University Press).

—— (1965), 'Some problems of lexicography', *English Language Teaching*, 19.3: 104–10.

—— (1966), 'Looking back', *English Language Teaching*, 21.1: 3–6.

—— and Mackin, R. (1964), *Oxford Progressive English for Adult Learners, Alternative Edition* (Four volumes) (London: Oxford University Press).

—— and Ruse, C. (1974), *Hornby on Hornby and the Advanced Learner's Dictionary* (Tokyo: Oxford University Press).

Howarth, P. A. (1996), *Phraseology in English Academic Writing. Some Implications for Language Learning and Dictionary Making* (Lexicographica, Series maior 75) (Tübingen: Max Niemeyer).

Howatt, A. P. R. (1984), *A History of English Language Teaching* (Oxford: Oxford University Press).

Ilson, R. (ed.) (1985), *Dictionaries, Lexicography and Language Learning* (ELT Documents 120) (Oxford: Pergamon).

—— (1987), 'Illustrations in dictionaries', in A. P. Cowie (ed.) (1987*b*), 193–212.

Imura, M. (1997), *Palmer to Nihon no Eigokyouiku* (*Harold E. Palmer and Teaching English in Japan*) (Tokyo: Taishukan).

Institute for Research in English Teaching (1934), *A Commemorative Volume* (issued by the Institute for Research in English Teaching on the occasion of the Tenth Annual Conference of English Teachers held under its auspices) (Tokyo: IRET).

Jackson, H. (1988), *Words and their Meaning* (London: Longman).

James, G. (ed.) (1989), *Lexicographers and their Works* (Exeter Linguistic Studies 14) (Exeter: University of Exeter).

Jansen, J., Mergeai, J. P., and Vanandroye, J. (1987), 'Controlling LDOCE's controlled vocabulary', in A. P. Cowie (ed.) (1987*b*), 78–94.

Jespersen, O. (1914), *A Modern English Grammar on Historical Principles* (Heidelberg: Carl Winter).

—— (1933), *Essentials of English Grammar* (London: George Allen and Unwin).

—— (1938), *Analytic Syntax* (London: George Allen and Unwin).

Klappenbach, R. (1968), 'Probleme der Phraseologie', *Wissenschaftliche Zeitschrift der Karl-Marx-Universität*, 17.5: 221–7.

Knowles, F. (1983), 'Towards the machine dictionary', in R. R. K. Hartmann (ed.) (1983*b*), 181–92.

—— (1984), 'Dictionaries and computers', in R. R. K. Hartmann (ed.), 301-14.

Landau, S. I. (1984), *Dictionaries: The Art and Craft of Lexicography* (New York: Scribner).

Laufer, B. (1992), 'Corpus-based versus lexicographer's examples in comprehension and production of new words', in H. Tommola *et al.* (eds.), 71–6.

—— and Melamed, L. (1994), 'Monolingual, bilingual and "bilingualised" dictionaries: which are more effective, for what and for whom?', in W. Martin *et al.* (eds.), 565–76.

Leech, G. (1991), 'The state of the art in corpus linguistics', in K. Aijmer and B. Altenberg (eds.), *English Corpus Linguistics. Studies in Honour of Jan Svartvik* (London and New York: Longman), 8–29.

—— and Fligelstone, S. (1992), 'Computers and corpus analysis', in C. S. Butler (ed.), 115–40.

Lehrer, A. (1974), *Lexical Fields and Semantic Structure* (Amsterdam and London: North Holland and New York: American Elsevier).

Lemmens, M., and Wekker, H. Ch. (1986), *Grammar in English Learners' Dictionaries* (Lexicographica, Series maior 16) (Tübingen: Max Niemeyer).

Lipka, L. (1974), 'Probleme der Analyse englischer Idioms aus struktureller und generativer Sicht', *Linguistik und Didaktik*, 20: 274–85.

Lyons, J. (1968), *Introduction to Theoretical Linguistics* (London and New York: Cambridge University Press).

—— (1977), *Semantics* (Two volumes) (Cambridge: Cambridge University Press).

McArthur, T. (1978), 'The vocabulary-control movement in the English language', *Indian Journal of Applied Linguistics*, 4.1: 47–68.

McDavid, R. I., and Duckert, A. R. (eds.) (1973), *Lexicography in English* (New York: Annals of the New York Academy of Sciences).

MacFarquhar, P. D., and Richards, J. C. (1983), 'On dictionaries and definitions', *RELC Journal*, 14.1: 111–24.

Mackin, R. (1978), 'On collocations: "words shall be known by the company they keep" ', in P. Strevens (ed.) (1978*b*), 149–65.

—— (1983), 'Foreword', in A. P. Cowie, R. Mackin, and I. R. McCaig, vi–ix.

Magay, T., and Zigány, J. (eds.) (1990), *BudaLEX '88 Proceedings: Papers from the EURALEX Third International Congress* (Budapest: Académiai Kiadó).

Maingay, S., and Rundell, M. (1990), 'What makes a good dictionary example?', Paper presented at the 24th IATEFL Conference, Exeter.

Marello, C. (1989), *Dizionari bilingui* (Bologna: Zanichelli).

—— (1998), 'Hornby's bilingualized dictionaries', *International Journal of Lexicography*, 11.4: 292–314.

Martin, W. *et al.* (eds.) (1994), *Euralex '94 Proceedings* (Amsterdam: Euralex).

Meijs, W. (1992), 'Computers and dictionaries', in C. S. Butler (ed.), 141–65.

Mel'čuk, I. *et al.* (1984/1988/1992), *Dictionnaire explicatif et combinatoire du français contemporain: Recherches lexico-sémantiques I, II, III* (Montréal: Presses de l'Université de Montréal).

Michiels, A. (1982), 'Exploiting a large dictionary database', Ph.D. thesis (Université de Liège).

Miller, G., and Gildea, P. (1987), 'How children use words', *Scientific American*, 86–91.

Mitchell, E. (1983), *Search-Do Reading: Difficulties in Using a Dictionary* (Formative Assessment of Reading, Working Paper 2) (Aberdeen: College of Education).

Mitchell, T. F. (1958), 'Syntagmatic relations in linguistic analysis', *Transactions of the Philological Society*, 101–18.

——— (1966), 'Some English phrasal types', in C. E. Bazell, J. C. Catford, M. A. K. Halliday, and R. H. Robins (eds.), *In Memory of J. R. Firth* (London: Longman), 335–58.

——— (1971), 'Linguistic "goings-on": collocations and other matters arising on the syntagmatic record', *Archivum linguisticum*, 2: 35–69.

Moon, R. (1987), 'The analysis of meaning', in J. M. Sinclair (ed.) (1987*d*), 86–103.

——— (1988), '"Time" and idioms', in M. Snell-Hornby (ed.), 107–15.

——— (1998*a*), 'Frequencies and forms of phrasal lexemes in English', in A. P. Cowie (ed.) (1998*b*), 79–100.

——— (1998*b*), *Fixed Expressions and Idioms in English* (Oxford Studies in Lexicography and Lexicology) (Oxford: Clarendon Press).

Moulin, A. (1987), 'The place of the dictionary in an EFL programme. Part II: The dictionary and encoding tasks', in A. P. Cowie (ed.) (1987*b*), 105–14.

Naganuma, K. (1978), 'The history of the *Advanced Learner's Dictionary*: A. S. Hornby, *ISED*, and Kaitakusha, Tokyo', in P. Strevens (ed.) (1978*b*), 11–13.

Nattinger, J. (1988), 'Some current trends in vocabulary teaching', in R. Carter and M. J. McCarthy (eds.), 62–80.

——— and DeCarrico, J. (1992), *Lexical Phrases and Language Teaching* (Oxford: Oxford University Press).

Nesi, H., and Meara, P. (1994), 'Patterns of misinterpretation in the productive use of EFL dictionary definitions', *System*, 22: 1–15.

Newmeyer, F. J. (1974), 'The regularity of idiom behaviour', *Lingua*, 34: 327–42.

Nida, E. (1975), *Componential Analysis of Meaning* (The Hague: Mouton).

Nuccorini, S. (1993*a*), 'Dizionari: contenuti, tipologia, caratteristiche', in S. Nuccorini (ed.) (1993*c*), 3–162.

——— (1993*b*), 'Approccio teorico e pratico all'uso del dizionario', in S. Nuccorini (ed.) (1993*c*), 165–76.

——— (ed.) (1993*c*), *La parola che non so. Saggio sui dizionari pedagogici* (Firenze: La Nuova Italia).

——— (1994), 'On dictionary misuse', in W. Martin *et al.* (eds.), 586–97.

——— (1995), 'Dictionary reference skills', *Annali della Facoltà di Scienze Politiche a.a. 1991–92*, 28: 73–89.

Ogawa, Y. (1978), 'Hornby osei: a tribute from Japan', in P. Strevens (ed.) (1978*b*), 8–10.

Ooi, V. B. Y. (1998), *Computer Corpus Lexicography* (Edinburgh Textbooks in Empirical Linguistics) (Edinburgh: Edinburgh University Press).

Palmer, F. R. (1965), *A Linguistic Study of the English Verb* (Second edition, entitled *The English Verb* 1974) (London: Longman).

Palmer, H. E. (1907), *Méthode Palmer: Esperanto à l'usage des Français* (Bruges: A.-J. Witterijck-Deplace).

——— (1917), *The Scientific Study and Teaching of Languages* (London: Harrap).

——— (1921), *The Principles of Language-Study* (London: Harrap).

——— (1924), *A Grammar of Spoken English* (First edition) (Cambridge: Heffer).

——— (1925), *Systematic Exercises in Sentence Building* (Two volumes) (Tokyo: IRET).

Palmer, H. E. (cont.) (1926*a*), *The Noun Complex* (Supplement to *IRET Bulletin* 26) (Tokyo: IRET).

—— (1926*b*) *The Theory of the 24 Anomalous Finites* (Supplement to *IRET Bulletin* 28) (Tokyo: IRET).

—— (1927), *The Reformed English Teaching in the Middle-Grade Schools* (Supplement to *IRET Bulletin* 32) (Tokyo: IRET).

—— (1929*a*), 'What shall we call a "word"?', *IRET Bulletin*, 54: 1–2.

—— (1929*b*), 'Lexicological research', *IRET Bulletin*, 55: 1.

—— (1929*c*), 'Editorial: what is an idiom?', *IRET Bulletin*, 56: 1–2.

—— (1930*a*), 'Editorial: two sorts of units', *IRET Bulletin*, 61: 1–2.

—— (1930*b*), 'Editorial: a standard English vocabulary', *IRET Bulletin*, 64: 1–2.

—— (1930*c*), 'Editorial: word counts and word selection', *IRET Bulletin*, 67: 1–2.

—— (1930*d*), *First Interim Report on Vocabulary Selection* (Tokyo: Kaitakusha).

—— (1931*a*), 'Editorial: progress of our statistical lexicology', *IRET Bulletin*, 72: 1–2.

—— (1931*b*), 'Some aspects of lexicology', *IRET Bulletin*, 72: 6–8.

—— (1931*c*), *Second Interim Report on Vocabulary Selection* (Tokyo: Kaitakusha).

—— (1932*a*), 'Our research on vocabulary limitation, its origin and development', *IRET Bulletin*, 87: 1–4.

—— (1932*b*), *Some Notes on Construction-Patterns* (Institute Leaflet 38) (Tokyo: IRET).

—— (1933*a*), 'Editorial: sentences worth memorizing', *IRET Bulletin*, 91: 1–2.

—— (1933*b*), 'Editorial: our research on collocations', *IRET Bulletin*, 95: 1–2.

—— (1933*c*), *Second Interim Report on English Collocations* (Fourth impression 1966) (Tokyo: Kaitakusha).

—— (1934*a*), *Specimens of English Construction Patterns* (Based on the General Synoptic Chart Showing the Syntax of the English Sentence) (Tokyo: IRET).

—— (1934*b*), *The 24 'Anomalous Finites' (Otherwise the 24 Finite Forms of the 12 Anomalous Verbs)* (Supplement to *IRET Bulletin*, 105) (Tokyo: IRET).

—— (1934*c*), *An Essay in Lexicology in the Form of Specimen Entries in Some Possible New-Type Dictionary* (Tokyo: Kaitakusha).

—— (1934*d*), 'Director's report for the year 1933–34', *IRET Bulletin*, 108: 16–24.

—— (1935), 'When is an adjective not an adjective?', *IRET Bulletin*, 114: 1–10.

—— (1936*a*), 'The history and present state of the movement towards vocabulary control', *IRET Bulletin*, 120: 14–17; 121: 19–23.

—— (1936*b*), 'The art of vocabulary lay-out', *IRET Bulletin*, 121: 1–8; 14–19.

—— (1938*c*), 'Denbun wa, Jikken ni shikazu', *IRET Bulletin*, 147: 7–10.

—— (1942), 'Category two of English linguistic symbols; nature and extent of an enquiry now proposed' (Unpublished MS).

—— and Hornby, A. S. (1937), *Thousand-Word English* (London: George Harrap).

—— and Redman, H. V. (1932), *This Language-Learning Business* (Reissued in a new edition in the series Language and Language Learning, London: Oxford University Press, 1969) (London: Harrap).

—— Martin, J. V., Downs, D., and Stier, W. R. F. (1923), 'History of the Institute for Research in English Teaching', *IRET Bulletin*, 1.1: 2–3.

Pawley, A., and Syder, F. H. (1983), 'Two puzzles for linguistic theory: nativelike selection and nativelike fluency', in J. C. Richards and R. W. Schmidt (eds.), *Language and Communication* (London: Longman), 191–226.

Peters, A. (1983), *The Units of Language Acquisition* (Cambridge: Cambridge University Press).

Prat Zagrebelsky, M. T. (ed.) (1989), *Dal dizionario ai dizionari. Orientamento e guida all'uso per studenti di lingua inglese* (Torino: Tirrenia Stampatori).

Quirk, R. (1973), 'The social impact of dictionaries in the U.K.', in R. I. McDavid and A. R. Duckert (eds.), 76–88.

—— (1974), 'The image of the dictionary', in R. Quirk (ed.), *The Linguist and the English Language* (Revised version of Quirk (1973)) (London: Edward Arnold), 148–63.

—— (1982), 'Dictionaries', in R. Quirk, *Style and Communication in the English Language* (London: Edward Arnold), 73–8.

Redman, H. V. (1966), 'Foreign teachers in Japan: Harold Palmer's impact on Japan. Part 1', *Isahi Evening News*, 7 Apr. 1966.

—— (1967), 'Harold E. Palmer—pioneer teacher of modern languages', *English Language Teaching*, 22.1: 10–16.

Reif, J. A. (1987), 'The development of a dictionary concept: an English learner's dictionary and an exotic alphabet', in A. P. Cowie (ed.) (1987*b*), 146–58.

Renouf, A. (1987), 'Corpus development', in J. M. Sinclair (ed.) (1987*d*), 1–40.

Rey, A. (1977), *Le Lexique: Images et modèles: du dictionnaire à la lexicologie* (Paris: Armand Colin).

Rundell, M. (1998), 'Recent trends in English pedagogical lexicography', *International Journal of Lexicography*, 11.4: 315–42.

Saussure, F. de (1916), *Cours de linguistique générale* (edited by C. Bally and A. Sèchehaye, with the assistance of A. Riedlinger) (Paris: Payot).

Sawayanagi, M. (1924), 'Dr Sawayanagi's Preface to "Memorandum" translated from the Japanese text', *IRET Bulletin*, 5: 3–5.

Sèchehaye, A. (1934), 'A personal tribute to Mr H. E. Palmer', in IRET, *Commemorative Volume* (Tokyo: IRET), 10–14.

Sinclair, J. M. (1985*a*), 'Lexicographic evidence', in R. Ilson (ed.), 81–94.

—— (1985*b*), 'Selected issues', in R. Quirk and H. G. Widdowson (eds.), *English in the World: Teaching and Learning the Language and the Literatures* (Cambridge: Cambridge University Press in association with the British Council), 248–54.

—— (1987*a*), 'Introduction', in J. M. Sinclair *et al.* (eds.), xv–xxi.

—— (1987*b*), 'The nature of the evidence', in J. M. Sinclair (ed.) (1987*d*), 150–9.

—— (1987*c*), 'Collocation: a progress report', in R. Steele and T. Threadgold (eds.), *Language Topics: Essays in Honour of Michael Halliday*, Volume 2 (Amsterdam: John Benjamins), 319–31.

—— (ed.) (1987*d*), *Looking Up. An Account of the COBUILD Project in Lexical Computing* (London and Glasgow: Collins).

—— (1991), *Corpus, Concordance and Collocation* (Oxford: Oxford University Press).

—— and Renouf, A. (1988), 'A lexical syllabus for language learning', in R. Carter and M. J. McCarthy (eds.), 140–58.

Smith, R. C. (1998*a*), 'The Palmer–Hornby contribution to English teaching in Japan', *International Journal of Lexicography*, 11.4: 269–91.

—— (1998*b*), 'Harold E. Palmer's formative years (1877–1901)', *Area and Cultural Studies (Tokyo Gaikokugo Daigaku Ronshu)*, 57: 1–37.

Snell-Hornby, M. (1987), 'Towards a learner's bilingual dictionary', in A. P. Cowie (ed.) (1987*b*), 159–70.

—— (ed.) (1988), *ZüriLEX '86 Proceedings* (Tübingen: Francke).

Sora, F. (1984), 'A study of the use of bilingual and monolingual dictionaries by Italian students of English', *Papers on Work in Progress*, 12: 40–6.

Souter, C., and Atwell, E. (eds.) (1993), *Corpus-Based Computational Linguistics* (Amsterdam and Atlanta: Rodopi).

Stark, M. P. (1990), *Dictionary Workbooks. A Critical Evaluation of Dictionary Workbooks for the Foreign Language Learner* (Exeter Linguistic Studies 16) (Exeter: University of Exeter).

Stavropoulos, D. N. (1978), 'English language teaching in Greece and A. S. Hornby's influence upon it', in P. Strevens (ed.) (1978*b*), 14–20.

Stein, G. (1979), 'The best of British and American lexicography', *Dictionaries*, 1: 1–23.

—— (1989*a*), 'EFL dictionaries, the teacher and the student', *JALT Journal*, 11.1: 36–45.

—— (1989*b*), 'Recent developments in EFL dictionaries', in M. L. Tickoo (ed.) (1989*b*), 10–41.

—— (1990), 'From the bilingual to the monolingual dictionary', in T. Magay and J. Zigány (eds.), 401–7.

Strevens, P. (1978*a*), 'The English language made plain for the teacher of English: the descriptivist and the linguistic traditions', in P. Strevens (ed.) (1978*b*), 103–16.

—— (ed.) (1978*b*), *In Honour of A. S. Hornby* (Oxford: Oxford University Press).

Summers, D. (1988), 'The role of dictionaries in language learning', in R. Carter and M. J. McCarthy (eds.), 111–25.

—— (1993), 'Longman/Lancaster English Language Corpus—criteria and design', *International Journal of Lexicography*, 6.3: 181–208.

Svensén, B. (1993), *Practical Lexicography: Principles and Methods of Dictionary-Making* (Translated from the Swedish by John Sykes and Kerstin Schofield) (Oxford: Oxford University Press).

Sweet, H. (1899), *The Practical Study of Languages* (Reissued in a new edition in the series Language and Language Learning, London: Oxford University Press, 1964) (London: Dent).

Ter-Minasova, S. (1992), 'The freedom of word-combinations and the compilation of learners' combinatory dictionaries', in H. Tommola *et al.* (eds.), 533–9.

Tickoo, M. L. (1988), 'Michael West in India: a centenary salute', *ELT Journal*, 42.4: 294–300.

—— (1989*a*), 'Introduction', in M. L. Tickoo (ed.) (1989*b*), v–xvi.

—— (ed.) (1989*b*), *Learners' Dictionaries: State of the Art* (Anthology Series 23) (Singapore: SEAMEO Regional Language Centre).

Tomaszczyk, J. (1979), 'Dictionaries: users and uses', *Glottodidactica*, 12: 103–19.

Tommola, H. *et al.* (eds.) (1992), *Euralex '92 Proceedings* (Series translatologica, Series A, Volume 2) (Tampere: University of Tampere).

Tono, Y. (1984), 'On the dictionary user's reference skills', B.Ed. dissertation (Tokyo: Gakugei University).

Urdang, L. (1973), 'Technological potentials', in R. I. McDavid and A. R. Duckert (eds.), 282–6.

Weiner, E. S. C. (1987), 'The *New Oxford English Dictionary*: progress and prospects', in R. W. Bailey (ed.), *Dictionaries of English: Prospects for the Record of our Language* (Ann Arbor: University of Michigan Press), 30–48.

Weinreich, U. (1969), 'Problems in the analysis of idioms', in J. Puhvel (ed.), *Substance and Structure of Language* (Berkeley: University of California Press), 23–81.

West, M. P. (1914), *Education and Psychology* (London: Longmans, Green).

—— (1926), *Bilingualism (with Special Reference to Bengal)* (Calcutta: Bureau of Education).

—— (1929), *Language in Education* (Calcutta: Longmans, Green).

—— (1935), *Definition Vocabulary* (Bulletin no. 4 of the Department of Educational Research) (Toronto: University of Toronto Press).

—— (1960), *Teaching English in Difficult Circumstances* (London: Longmans, Green).

Whitcut, J. (1984), 'Sexism in dictionaries', in R. R. K. Hartmann (ed.), 141–4.

Wilkins, D. (1976), *Notional Syllabuses* (Oxford: Oxford University Press).

Windsor Lewis, J. (1965), 'Review of *The Advanced Learner's Dictionary of Current English* (Oxford University Press, 2nd edition, 1963)', *Le Maître Phonétique*, 3.123: 14–15.

—— (1978), 'New directions in pronunciation transcription', in P. Strevens (ed.) (1978*b*), 183–9.

Zgusta, L. (1971), *Manual of Lexicography* (Janua linguarum, Series maior 39) (The Hague: Mouton).

Index

Note: Page references in *italics* indicate tables and figures.

DATE DUE
